NINE PATHS

Nine Paths

A Year in the Life of an Indian Village

LEXI STADLEN

Chatto & Windus
LONDON

1 3 5 7 9 10 8 6 4 2

Chatto & Windus, an imprint of Vintage, is part of the
Penguin Random House group of companies whose addresses
can be found at global.penguinrandomhouse.com

First published by Chatto & Windus in 2022

penguin.co.uk/vintage

A CIP catalogue record for this book is available from the British Library

ISBN 9781784744106

Typeset in 10.5/16pt Haarlemmer MT Std by Jouve (UK), Milton Keynes
Printed and bound in Great Britain by Clays Ltd, Elcograf S.p.A.

The authorised representative in the EEA is Penguin Random House Ireland,
Morrison Chambers, 32 Nassau Street, Dublin D02 YH68

Penguin Random House is committed to a
sustainable future for our business, our readers
and our planet. This book is made from Forest
Stewardship Council® certified paper.

For the women

Contents

Characters

Kalima, a widow, mother of six, two of whom (Riyaz and Asad) live
in the village

Roshini, married to Riyaz, mother of Shahara, Sumaya and Said

Nusrat, soon to be married to Kalima's son, Asad

Maryam, a widow and matriarch of the Lohani family, mother to
Ali Tariq and his brother; mother-in-law to Bashira and Tabina,
grandmother to Rubina and Rani

Tabina, married to Ali Tariq's brother, daughter-in-law of Maryam,
sister-in-law to Bashira and aunt of Rani

Bashira, married to Ali Tariq, daughter-in-law of Maryam, sister-
in-law to Tabina and mother of four children, including Rubina
and Rani

Mira, Rani's sister-in-law, the wife of Bashira and Ali Tariq's only
son

Rubina, Rani's older sister, Bashira and Ali Tariq's second daughter

Rani, Bashira and Ali Tariq's third and youngest daughter, niece of
Tabina and granddaughter of Maryam

Sara, married to Khan, mother to a son and a daughter, Nadia, mother-in-law to Parveen and grandmother of Aryan

Nura, married to Mahir, mother of three boys, Hafaz, Yusuf and Ibrahim, and a daughter, Radhia

Nani Ashima, one of the oldest women in the village and Aliya's mother-in-law

Aliya, mother to six children, including her daughter Amal

FAMILY TREES

LOHANI FAMILY

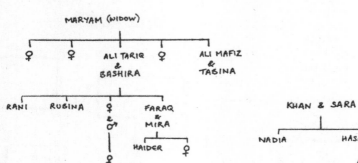

MARYAM (WIDOW)

♀ ♀ ALI TARIQ & BASHIRA ♀ ALI HAFIZ & TASINA

RANI RUBINA ♀ & ♂ FARAQ & MIRA

♀ HAIDER ♀

KHAN & SARA

NADIA HASAN & PARVEEN

ARYAN

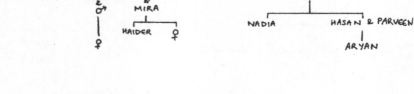

NURA & MAHIR

RADHIA IBRAHIM YUSUF HAFAZ

KALIMA (WIDOW)

ASAD & NUSRAT ♀ & ♂ RIYAZ & ROSHINI ♀ RUPA & ♂

WAHID ♀ ♂

IFFAT

SAID SUMAYA SAHARA

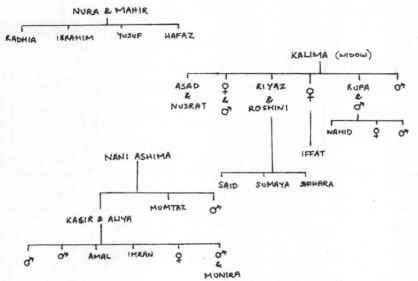

NANI ASHIMA

KABIR & ALIYA MOMTAZ ♂

♂ ♂ AMAL IMRAN ♀ ♂ & MUNIRA

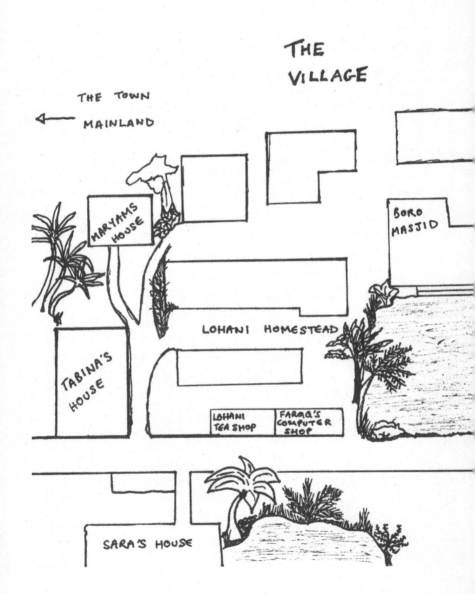

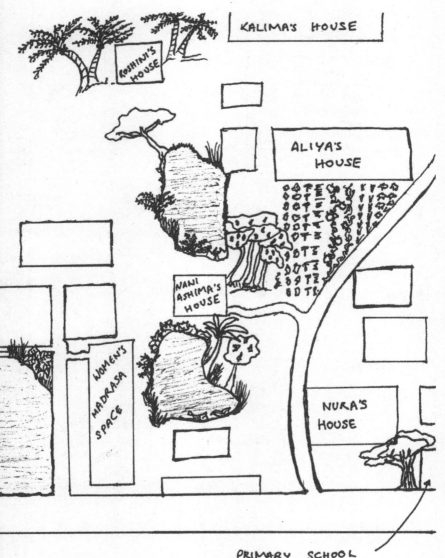

KALIMA'S HOUSE

ROSHINI'S HOUSE

ALIYA'S HOUSE

NANI ASHIMA'S HOUSE

WOMEN'S MADRASA SPACE

NURA'S HOUSE

PRIMARY SCHOOL

GRAVE YARD ➤
SUNDARBANS

CALENDAR

CODA
1. HINDU FESTIVALS
2. BENGALI SEASONS
3. BENGALI SEASONS
4. MONTHS IN VILLAGE
5. CLIMATE
6. ISLAMIC FESTIVALS
7. KEY DATES 2015 - 2016

19th-23rd DURGA PUJO 10th KALI PUJO

1.

2. গ্রীষ্ম   বর্ষা   শরৎ   হেমন্ত

3. SUMMER   RAINY   EARLY AUTUMN   AUTUMN

4. APR" MAY" JUNE" JULY" AUG" SEPT" OCT" NOV"

5. HOT & DRY MONSOON COOL &

6.
5th SHAB-E BARAT   18th ← RAMZAN → 17th   2nd BOI MELA   23rd EID-AL ADHA

EID-AL FITR

7. 15th BENGALI NEW YEAR

5th SARASWATI PUJO 24th HOLI

শীত বসন্ত গ্রীষ্ম বর্ষা
WINTER SPRING SUMMER RAINY

DEC" JAN" FEB" MAR" APR" MAY" JUNE" JULY"

RY HOT & DRY MONSOON

11th AILAD UN-NABI

22nd SHAB-E BARAT ← 6th RAMZAN → 5th

EID-AL FITR

1st NEW YEAR 14th BENGALI NEW YEAR 5th ELECTION

Author's Note

Anthropologists are caretakers of stories. The narratives are those belonging to others, those who over time and through considerable effort we come to know intimately, and who in turn trust us with the details of their lives. This trust is a privilege, as well as a responsibility.

This book contains the stories of nine women. They live in a village, on an island, at India's eastern edge. They are Muslim, part of the beleaguered minority about which so little is known and yet who number more than 200 million. Their mother tongue is Bangla, a handful also speak Hindi or Urdu, and some have scraps of Arabic, gleaned from an early madrasa school education. Once upon a time, one of them knew English. What follows charts the sixteen months I spent in their village and represents the culmination of eight years devoted to the wider study of their lives, resulting in a master's degree, a master's in research, a PhD and, ultimately, this book.

There is a further story that is ever-present, whilst also totally absent from these pages, and that is my own. Everything that occurs here has been witnessed or recorded by me and does not come from some hallowed place, lacking subjectivity. Whilst I have taken the greatest pains to construct these narratives as the women would tell them, their stories will inevitably bear the imprint of the vessel that has contained them.

My preparations for our encounters were substantial. A doctorate requires rigorous grounding, and I spent three and a half years learning all that I could about Muslim lives, both in India and more widely. I learned Bangla, first in Streatham in South London, then in Santiniketan, a university town in Bengal's hinterland, and then in Kolkata. I carried on learning every day I spent in the village, where the women delighted in encouraging me and laughing at my faltering pronunciation.

I began my time on the island slowly. Living initially in Kolkata, several times a week I would rise before dawn, travelling the long, lurchingly potholed road to and from the city. As I grew more comfortable in my surroundings, after five months I moved down to the island, renting a room in the small town ten minutes away from the village.

Over the course of my time there I visited more than one hundred households. I spent time with the imams of the mosques, at the tea stalls, the doctor's studio, the tailor's, the boys' madrasa school and at a nearby healer's chambers. Gradually I was drawn into the lives of nine women in particular and, as the days passed, I grew ever more entangled in their worlds. I conducted extended interviews, recorded oral histories, made complex genealogical maps and organised focus groups, which they all, along with some other women, attended. More significantly, I observed them; I watched, I followed, I listened. I accompanied them to madrasa meetings, to micro-finance groups, to the bazaar, to the tea shop, to *Durga pujo pandals*, to one another's houses, to several matchmakings, to a wedding and to a funeral. More often than not, I spent time as they almost always did, whiling away the long mornings and still afternoons whilst they undertook their seemingly endless domestic and caring responsibilities.

Every night I wrote. Aside from fieldwork, any time I had alone was spent making notes, by hand and in detail, about the events of the days before. I recorded the smells, the weather, the sounds, what people wore, what people did, what people said and how they said it. I made pencil drawings to enshrine in my memory an event or a particular scene, sketching figures to capture how someone had appeared, how they held their body. I drew a map of the village – an exact geography to cement the location of every house, stall and shop. I made more than one hundred hours of audio recordings. These enabled me to transcribe key conversations, to hear the lilt and flow of the voices, the pauses, the hesitations.

Anthropologists often collaborate with the people whose stories they gather, but sometimes this is not possible. Working with women who are largely illiterate, who do not speak English and who lacked the time, technology and inclination to be involved in the production of a book meant that opportunities for working together were scant. My plans to return to the village to share with them drafts of my work have been curtailed at every juncture. Instead, whilst writing I have kept in mind a single mantra that was repeated to me by all of them, on many different occasions: tell our stories.

Where possible, I have used direction quotation. I have kept many words in Bangla and have used transliteration, as opposed to direct translation, to more accurately mirror their speech. I witnessed many of the events that follow. For those that I did not, I relied on the women's own recollections and revisited the same topics on multiple occasions, corroborating their memories wherever possible with those of others around them.

This book is not a conventional work of anthropology. It is not theoretical, it uses no technical terminology and it makes no greater argument beyond the lives depicted on its pages. I have never understood why ethnography must be an argument as opposed to just being; an artefact, a product of a deep and sustained encounter, a reminder of how alike we are to people we will never meet. I have listened to my doubts, refusing to portray these women's lives in theoretical terms, which they themselves would not recognise or relate to. I have listened to what they have asked of me.

I have anonymised all names and refrained from identifying the island or village, thereby upholding the ethical commitment to privacy that I made to myself, but also to the nine women themselves, who so generously and without hesitation invited me into their lives.

This book is dedicated to them.

The Island

The women will only be glimpsed from the roadside. To find them, one takes the paths, the winding dirt furrows that snake away from the tarmac, into the green. Nestled amongst the trees are earthen houses, their backs turned to outsiders, their sun-baked walls and sloping roofs deflecting any unwanted gaze. The women will be seated in the courtyards slicing vegetables, sweating over pans of darkening spices, sweeping floors, sewing saris, sieving palmfuls of rice for the stones and the husks. They will be crouched along the edge of the ponds, toes deep in cool mud, washing children, washing clothes, scouring the scraps from plates and pots, their splashes and the crackle of cooking fires drifting on the breeze.

The women live on an island, one of the last splutters of land before it finally gives way to the vast, deep blue of the Bay of Bengal. It belongs to the Sundarbans, a conjunction of the Bengali words for 'beautiful' and 'forest'. These islands are part of a sprawling coastal mangrove jungle, the largest in the world, whose immense 10,000-square-kilometre girth comfortably straddles the border between

India and Bangladesh. Composed of shape-altering landmasses and ever-changing currents, this riverine landscape is always on the move. This geographical flux defies the strictures of cartography and has long posed challenges for those who seek to enforce boundaries, across which at these southern verges people, goods and histories have long slipped with ease.

'Beautiful' may be an exaggeration. These are strange, untameable spaces where, as the mainland peels back, the balance between the earth and the water tilts alarmingly towards the latter. Encircling the islands, salty rivers run grey, merging imperceptibly into banks of mud the colour of clay or an elephant's skin, from which gnarled tree roots and thick grasses have dragged themselves upright. On the islands that remain uninhabited there are dense forests, tangles of vines, wooded clearings receding into grassy-floored depths through which faint paths mark the tracks of those brave or greedy enough to venture in. On the inhabited islands the forests have been hacked away and settlements have blossomed. Houses crouch low to the earth alongside sunken paddy fields, clutches of scattered shops and food stands, an occasional school or medical facility. Some harbour the luxury of a bazaar that pulses in the cool of the morning and the early evening, as eager patrons weave a well-rehearsed dance between the stalls.

As the women will proudly tell you, their island is distinct. It has recently been linked to the mainland by a bridge, painted in the cheery blue-and-white candy-stripe beloved by a current politician. Such connection has brought commerce, and the bustling town at the foot of the bridge boasts colourful brick buildings squatting along the steep grey river banks, trailing back to congested streets that hum with a newfound purpose. A tarmac road now crosses the middle of the island, forking halfway along its meandering journey to the other side. There is now electricity, although its sporadic efficiency decreases the further away from the bridge, and the road, one travels. There is now a mobile-phone signal, though the kind permitting only scratchy, muffled conversation. The tigers that were once believed to rule these lands are seldom encountered on the island these days, although their hunger occasionally drives them this far north.

In their village, found at the centre of this island, the women know hunger of a different kind. It is a Muslim village, home to some 4,000 people. The oldest of the women – those married so young that they have outlived their husbands by a decade or more – remember well what it was like in the past: a contradictory kind of place. There were no roads, no amenities, just a handful of homesteads. 'Life was hard!' they say, laughing. But surrounding them were clear ponds teeming with fish, generous forests and fertile fields rich with things to be eaten. It was a frontier, a boundary between the two worlds of the remoter islands further south and the mainland to the north; the kind of place where those looking to escape from either one, or from the violence flaring across the border to the east, were able to find a home.

Slowly the land has grown tired of its burden. The once-clear ponds are murky now with too many clothes, too many utensils, too many bodies dependent on them for cleanliness, and fish are scarce. One generation has quickly followed another, and the ample space of the past has been greedily eaten up by growing families. Overcrowded homes jostle for position alongside coconut palms, banana trees, ponds, patches of jungle and the swaying fields of wheat and rice that many people struggle to cultivate, in an increasingly volatile climate. The once predictable seasons have warped and shifted, the summers longer, hotter, the rains always late then lingering beyond expectations. Most have come to realise that the land and the weather can no longer be relied upon, though they remain trapped, wrestling an existence from nature's inconsistencies.

The Hindu families who once lived in the village have now moved to the town, or to other Hindu villages on the island. The reasons are practical: proximity to their community, to temples, to the superior comforts offered by other places; an aversion to the consumption of meat, which those they once lived alongside indulge in, whenever they can afford to. There are no grievances, although their paths rarely cross with those of the village any more. For years a home to Hindus and Muslims, even Christians, the island now witnesses stirrings, bitter murmurs of division. All are aware of the hardening of religious boundaries occurring across the country, the old wounds, the differences that cause rancour, needlessly threatening once again to split apart this hastily sewn-together nation.

The Sundarbans have a history as a cradle for enchantment of a sort that ignores such partitions. It is a place where Bonbibi has been worshipped as the protector of the forests, a Muslim goddess venerated by those of all faiths. Born in Mecca, Bonbibi was called upon by Allah to the lands of the eighteen tides in order to protect those venturing into the jungles from the lurking brutality of the demon tiger-king Dokkhin Rai – he who rules the uninhabited islands. Then there are the *jinni*, beings who have roamed these lands far longer than humankind. They too come from Islam, believed to have been made by Allah from a smokeless fire, leading lives that are longer and more fantastical than those made of flesh and bone. The women say that, long ago, the *jinni* were congenial neighbours, with whom food and celebrations might be shared. Now it is as though the *jinni* too are growing restless, catching the unprepared in their grasp.

4

The Island

The women know all about the *jinni* – just one of the many threats that stalk their days as they grapple for survival. Along the paths in the village, you will hear the rumble of their hunger: hunger for inclusion, hunger for security, hunger for change. Theirs are houses that don't like to keep secrets. The open verandahs and the absence of windowpanes mean that one person's triumphs, conflicts and intimacies become everybody's business.

PART ONE

Restless Summer, Endless Rains

Chapter One

A Time of Accidents

The accidents always happened after dark. More often than not, it was only the victims who were present when misfortune stole upon them. That something had happened was not in question; the broken bones, or the damage to property proved beyond doubt that an incident had taken place. Rather, it was whether the events had unfolded as was stated that was under consideration. All of the nine women knew that, when it came to truthful observation, it was only Allah who could be trusted.

The night of the storm had been a restless one for Kalima. This was no ordinary thunderstorm, but one of the *kaalboishaakhi* – those that arrived with the steaming April days and were notorious on the islands for their remarkable, somewhat ostentatious cruelty. Their violence was acknowledged in whispers behind the wizened palms of women like Kalima. She had passed enough summers on this earth to believe that the storms were a necessary, if ruthless, cleansing, ridding the land of the accumulated dirt and grime of the past twelve months in preparation for the beginning of the Bengali New Year.

Ominous charcoal clouds scudded across the skies in a masquerade of darkness, accompanied by yowling winds, thunder and pummelling rain that skittered and bounced upon the rooftops. For anyone unfamiliar with the storms, it sounded as though the world around them was tearing itself apart.

The winds had begun stirring restlessly at dusk, the village's only warning that something was afoot. The temperature soon plummeted, the unbearable stickiness of those early-summer nights replaced by an ominous chill, hurrying people away from the tea shops to their homes, to wait. The storm quickly gathered momentum, and before long it was prowling through the village, ripping apart trees with murderous, moaning cracks. Tin and bamboo roofs were splintered apart, the pieces dragged into the vortex of the squall, before being angrily discarded.

Kalima had lain awake for some time, listening to the sounds outside with a muted alarm and, closer, to the steady breaths of her granddaughter Iffat, curled beside her. She had seen enough of the *kaalboishaakhi* to know that her house would hold, but she was fretting that the pen for her ducks, which she had carefully weighted down, might nonetheless topple over or be crushed under falling debris. She resorted to a familiar comfort, murmuring verses from the Quran – the skipping Arabic words that she did not understand but had learned by heart soothing her, nudging her towards sleep – before her thoughts sharpened once more at the screech of buckling metal.

Her mind flew to her son. Riyaz lived apart from the main homestead in a one-roomed shack on the edge of the clearing, with his wife Roshini and their three small children. Its recently constructed walls were roughly hewn and brittle, not like the thick foundations of her own home, which had stood in this exact spot since the village was first settled. It had been her father's before hers, her grandfather's before that. Riyaz may have understood the contours of bricks and steel, but he had not yet refined the older art of coaxing natural materials to come together to form a structure. She listened, straining her failing ears against the rush of the wind, anxiety blooming in her chest for the son she adored, in spite of everything. There was nothing.

The next morning the *azaan* rang out at dawn as it always did, when darkness was still blanketing the land, the stars slow to take their leave from the bruised sky. The village awoke tentatively to survey the damage. Later that day Kalima would wonder why she had not checked on her neighbours sooner. When she learned that their house had been destroyed and offered to take care of the children – six small scraps of dirty skin and torn clothing, who raced around the clearing in a tangle of games with her own four grandchildren – she thought to herself how lucky it was that no one had been hurt. Standing, hands on hips, fingers tensed as though inadvertently searching beneath the cotton folds of her sari for the comfort of her ageing bones, Kalima shook her head, marvelling both at her neighbour's misfortune and at her own impulsive generosity. She spat into the dust. She would give them three days, she decided, that was all.

On the other side of the clearing, Roshini also watched the children. Three were her own, those precious beings whom she guarded fiercely, whose names when she called them ran together like water droplets down the edge of a battered metal tumbler: Shhhaahhharrraaa, Sssuummaaaaayyyaaa, Saaaiiiiiiddddd. The fourth, Iffat, was their cousin and a bastard who, despite her shameful circumstances, was obviously Kalima's favourite grandchild. The other six children belonged to their neighbour. Roshini now silently and, she conceded, unfairly resented them, knowing full well that the temporary burden of their care would fall upon her shoulders. Kalima may have banished them from her home, unable to accept that her favourite son had indulged in the scandal of a love-marriage, but Roshini nonetheless remained where an obedient daughter-in-law belonged, pinned beneath her mother-in-law's heel.

Her husband Riyaz had been roused at daybreak, his mother's cries pulling him from sleep to confront the devastation that littered the clearing between their houses. They had all walked around, dreamlike, tiptoeing on the palm fronds that covered the ground, cautious of what might have slithered or scuttled beneath. They had spent the morning clearing the debris, Kalima ordering Roshini to gather the twigs and smaller branches that carpeted the floor whilst she squatted on her haunches, her gnarled hands deftly stripping them of their leaves, the inner ribs tossed into a pile. Riyaz coaxed his younger brother, Asad, into helping him shift a severed tree bough and then mend the wheel of the bicycle that had bent and buckled in the wind. When they had finished, it was as though the storm had barely grazed them.

Roshini had not slept during the night, terrified that their hut would be torn from the ground, or that a tree might crash down onto their roof. As the winds abated, she had unshackled her thoughts from panic and allowed them to drift. Lately she had begun to imagine running away, although a glance through the darkness of their hut to the three tiny shadows asleep in a tangle on the floor soon reminded her of the impossibility.

Instead Roshini daydreamed, filling her days with fantastical journeys beyond the edges of the courtyard. As she ferried slopping buckets of water from the pond, sieved rice and lentils until her slender arms ached, and scoured pans whilst crouched in the cool, sticky mud alongside the water, she thought only of the future, a time when her children were grown. After which she would twist her few possessions into a bundle and walk out of the village, away from her husband, away from her mother-in-law, tracing a path defiantly back to her father's village, where she knew she would always be welcomed. Home.

More than buildings had come apart in the storm. That morning Bashira loomed behind the cluttered counter of her family's tea stall, cradling her swollen wrist and staring distractedly into the harsh white glare that jarred against the gloom of the shop's interior. Gingerly counting out change with her right hand, she recounted in her deep and rasping voice to inquisitive customers exactly what had happened. How there had been a power cut, the current absent, as it so often was after nightfall. How the sheer force of the wind had knocked her back. How she had slipped on the concrete step behind the shop in her haste, coming down hard on her wrist. The pain had caused her to cry out, a sound swallowed hungrily by the night, by the agitated whispering of the trees and the persistent drumbeat of the rain.

Both too poor and too proud to visit the local hospital, Bashira fashioned a makeshift splint of twigs and red twine to hold her wrist in place, but it struggled to contain the swelling. The flesh became engorged, as though determined to break through the temporary bindings and subsume all traces of the bones beneath. Bashira was stubborn, dismissing her daughter Rani's plaintive requests to try one of the cheaper, under-qualified doctors in town, and ignoring with a hiss of disgust the muttered prognosis of her mother-in-law,

Maryam, that if she did not get someone to look at it soon, her whole hand might eventually fall off.

Bashira, Tabina, Maryam, Rubina, Rani – the Lohani women moved as a pack. Yet, though bound together by blood, they were distinctly different animals. Bashira was like a tiger, physically imposing, larger than almost everyone in the village, including the men. She bristled, enduring only the company of a select few, prone to snarling acts of violence when provoked. Her sister-in-law Tabina resembled a jackal: smaller, agile and with an amiable shrewdness that enabled her to come out on top in almost every situation. Both in their early forties, the arduous years of raising young children behind them, these two women were forthright, and they behaved in ways that only men normally dared to, chewing *paan* and speaking in gravelly voices that suggested strong opinions and dirty jokes. Their relationship could be fiery, but they would also often be found sitting in the throb of the afternoon sun on the steps outside Tabina's house, combing out the knots of each other's hair, splitting apart the lull of the day with their raucous laughter.

The matriarch of the family was their mother-in-law Maryam, a greying wolf, a widow approaching the end of her life. Though age had cowed her, curving her spine and causing her to hobble with the aid of a stick, there was a nobility to the way she bore her years. Just beneath that disarming patina of age remained a glint of the power and cruelty she had once possessed. She disliked her daughters-in-law, and they despised her in return, though over time they had reached a tolerable stalemate. Were anyone to threaten the family, they closed ranks. Amongst these powerful women, it was no wonder that Bashira's youngest daughter Rani struggled to find her place.

It was Tabina who had managed to talk Bashira round. In the past,

Tabina had spent an unfortunate amount of time in hospital, rendering her a reluctant authority on the subject. Just the year before, her husband had been injured whilst driving his rickshaw, the roads more treacherous and deceptive at night, and now metal plates filled the gaps between his shattered bones. She knew only too well the whimpers of agony that rumbled beneath his skin, the ricocheting aches that gathered momentum until he became speechless with the pain. Although he had regained some use of his arm, he was no longer able to drive for long periods. This meant shorter shifts, which meant less money.

Maryam claimed to have been forewarned of his accident in a dream. Her fears were bolstered by a visit from the imam, who confided in her that her son was evading the obligatory Friday *namaz*. Maryam believed in a vengeful God; she understood a reckoning was due. When the rickshaw crash happened a week later, she had not gone to the hospital, resisting the calls of others and the maternal pull to her son's bedside. Instead she had devoted herself to prayer, promising Allah that should her son be spared, she would ensure that he once again fulfilled his religious obligations. He had survived and now attended the mosque every Friday, under the narrowed gaze of his mother.

Though she fully placed her trust in God, Maryam was not exempt from worldly misfortune. The next blow came when her ration card was damaged. This small oblong piece of laminated card was the only thing that guaranteed the poorest access to a range of subsidised foods each month: litres of cooking oil, scoops of rice and lentils measured out on rusty scales by a vendor assigned by the government, who, depending on the individual, would skim off either a little or a lot of the allocated amount. The lamination had been done haphazardly, the plastic edges beginning to curl up and in on them-selves, taking with them the last two digits of the long identification number. For weeks Maryam had been unable to claim her rations, straining her already fractious relationship with Tabina, from whose cooking pot she currently ate. When she had gathered enough of her dwindling strength, Maryam resolved to visit the local government office again, to try once more to rectify the situation.

Aside from fretting about her mother's wrist, Rani was preoccu-pied by another accident: that of being born a girl into her particular family. Since becoming a teenager, her once-smooth forehead was often drawn into a deep furrow, and the glint of her front tooth flashed white against her plum-coloured lip as she tugged at it absent-mindedly. Even in familiar company (the only kind to be found in the village) she was overcome by a crippling shyness, speaking in her low voice at such an unnatural velocity that everyone struggled to under-stand her. She had grown tall, like her mother Bashira – her broad shoulders awkward on her narrower frame – the unhappy occupant of a body that felt hopelessly out of step with her mind.

Her sister Rubina was in trouble, her predicament causing grow-ing disquiet amongst the entire Lohani family. The village was not a place where one could get away with anything. It was little more than a handful of shops flanking the tarmac road, which even Rani could recall as a bumpy rock-strewn track. There were two butcher's carts, their lean, unknowable carcasses hanging amidst the flies and the heat; the barber's shop, which was just a beaten-up barber's chair around which men would loiter, smoke and chat. There were a couple of tea stalls, like the one run by her family, offering *cha*, snacks and conversation. Next to their stall was her brother Faraq's internet shop, a room of dilapidated equipment adorned with cobwebs that was shut most of the time. Instead of working, Faraq would be found outside in the shade of the concrete verandah, where a permanent and impenetrable card game with an ever-changing cast of players took place – a circle of five or six men, watched over by spectators, their calls for drinks, *paan*, a new set of rules or a change of player, and their lingering cigarette smoke, seasoning the breeze.

There were two tailors, providing alterations, hemming and made-to-measure garments. The primary school alongside the large banyan tree was separated from the decrepit high school by a brick path and a playing field of scorched, withered grass. There were three mosques, the largest being across the pond from Rani's house, a smaller one nestled further into the village, and the third on the other side of the tarmac road at the village periphery. And that was it. Just houses and ponds and vegetable gardens and jungle and empty fields, all joined, encircled and intersected by narrow, earthen paths.

Rani had always behaved more like a boy, innocently playing cricket and tag and racing through the fields that surrounded the village. But, at fourteen, these were no longer suitable interests. She had started to draw the flicker of a glance from her mother each time she excused herself or explained where she had been, and she knew it would not be long before these pursuits moved from pointedly ignored to outright forbidden. All she wanted was to spend time with her best friend, Nadia, whose family lived directly opposite the tea shop and seemingly had no problem with their daughter tearing around exploring and getting up to mischief. But Nadia was two years younger than Rani – an age in the lifetime of a girl.

It might also have been said that Nadia's mother, Sara, was unusual by the standards of the village; she was regarded both as an outsider and as one of the lucky ones. She was certainly one of the most striking, her plump heart-shaped face resembling a perfect Kashmiri apple, with sculpted cheeks tapering to the gentle curve of her chin. Where most other women grew their hair long, only to twist it into straightforward knots at the nape of their necks, Sara cut hers to just below her shoulders, basting it in henna so that it took on a glittering crimson sheen, and sometimes wearing it loose so that it danced alluringly along her back and brushed against the tops of her arms. She wore lipstick and sunglasses, and painted her fingernails the sunken colours of overly ripe fruit. The problem was her audience. For the most part, no one even noticed her efforts. And those who did vehemently disapproved.

It wasn't a coincidence that the family into which the glamorous Sara had married was one of the most wealthy and well connected in the village. Though perhaps still poor by wider standards, they enjoyed a level of comfort and stability that others who rubbed alongside them could never imagine. They lived in a *pukka* house, one of just a handful in their surroundings, painted an eye-watering shade of pink and set back from the roadside down a tapering brick path. Inside were luxuries: a slumped, threadbare sofa, a large television set and even, it was rumoured, an indoor bathroom. Sara lived there with her husband Khan, mostly absent as he worked in the city; with their son Hasan and daughter Nadia, their daughter-in-law, Parveen, and a cherished grandson, Aryan.

Sara had little time for superstition. She had been born a Christian, converting to Islam for marriage, and she viewed the irrational practices of those she now lived amongst with bemused disdain. But she could not help feeling concerned by the current spate of bad luck in the village. Exactly a year before, her two-year-old grandson Aryan had almost died.

It was twilight, and Aryan had been left unattended for a moment, as children here so often are in the rush and grind of chores. Clambering down the concrete step that led into their home, he tottered with one hand along the wall of the house, keen to explore the bowl of shimmering clear liquid that was placed deliberately away from the door. Gazing onto its surface, he was startled at the bark of his name, and turned and fell backwards into the bowl. It contained carbolic acid, intended to ward off the snakes from a house in whose cool concrete floors and darkened corners they longed to hide.

It was the sound that Sara could not forget. Standing in front of the mirror in her bedroom, she was wrenched from her reflection, the glass bangle she had been admiring against a new sari falling to shatter on the floor. The world slowed as she moved towards the door. Parveen's sobs and wails as she crouched over her son, his body writhing in the dust. Her grandson's shrieks of pain. Her neighbours too would remember the sounds, though it was Sara's screams they would recall, their awful insistence drawing them towards the tarmac road where, in the gloamy evening light, a figure stood with a twisting bundle cradled in her arms.

Sara had stopped a passing car, her body blocking the road, and demanded to be driven to the home of a man in a nearby village who, she knew, drove a taxi. She called him from the car, telling him what had happened and to be ready to take them to the hospital. She was not someone people ever refused lightly. The journey to Kolkata took more than three hours and, as the minutes passed, Aryan's cries subsided into moans as he slipped from the battle lines of agony to the constrictive embrace of suffering. The silver car wove across the tarmac to avoid potholes and animals on the dark road. Sara's hand clutched Parveen's tightly, and across her lap lay her grandson's small, burning body.

Aryan had survived. He had scars along his back; from the curve of his right shoulder to the arch of his left buttock his skin was like a lizard's, or the softly cratered surface of the moon. He was still confident, cocky even, and possessed the kind of chubbiness that everyone viewed as delightful good fortune. Occasionally he would cry, as his tightened skin struggled to accommodate the quick and thoughtless movements of a child. But for the most part he was content. It was Sara who would lie awake at night, rising to steal silently to the room Aryan shared with his parents next door, standing motionless for long minutes in the doorway, checking for something – anything – to be amiss. It was Sara who would curl on her side, tracing the outline of the bangles around her wrist, eyes open, the sounds of darkness outside unable to dull the echoes of the screams that still rang in her ears. It was Sara who worried that misfortune would come once again.

As summer gathered pace, the days becoming insufferable, Nura harboured concerns of her own, not that she had anyone to share them with. Where so many women filled the lonely corners of their lives with female camaraderie – friends, sisters-in-law, neighbours – Nura did not. She was an odd woman and it wasn't easy to warm to her, the volume and grating timbre of her voice making conversations with her difficult, as did her propensity to stray into the realms of prophecy, the time beyond death; the unknown. Had she a friend or confidante, she might have been able to explain to them what was truly behind her growing fear of nightfall, or perhaps she would not.

Nura had not always been afraid of the dark. Darkness was familiar company on the island, a place huddled close enough to the equator that twenty-four hours was almost always evenly divided between the day and the night. Unlike many of the women who arrived after marriage, Nura had been born on the island, her father's village being just a few kilometres further south. She belonged to this place that gave little thought to the pulse and light of the city; after all, it was only seven years ago that electricity had arrived. The current remained capricious, fleeing the island at dusk and slinking back to the mainland, plunging the village into a blackout. Before long, lights would begin to burn, the flickers of gas lamps drawing soft outlines or the glare of electric lanterns whose stark beams caused shadows to leap away from them.

In Nura's home beneath the stoop of the banyan tree alongside the road, the occasional glare of headlights would interrupt the darkness, sweeping across the walls in blinding arcs. The road was the central conduit on which outsiders passed through, and the proximity of Nura's newly constructed dwelling to this external channel led many to believe that her family was simply asking for trouble. Sometimes the intrusion was only a neighbour, returning late from the bazaar, though on other occasions it might be a stranger, asking for help with a punctured bicycle wheel at the roadside. Some evenings Nura realised, with a start, that the person who had crept up on her was one of the vagrants who roamed the island, their lives unravelled, begging for a glass of *cha* or a handful of rupees with a dirty, outstretched palm.

It was not those who had lost their way that Nura feared, however. She had learned to be wary of her husband, Mahir, and his temper, always unsure of the mood he would be in on his return from work. Fastidious and a hard worker, Mahir never finished before the evening had settled in. After he had shuttered up his bicycle-repair shop, he would rely on the moon and starlight to guide him home as he cycled slowly past the black fields.

Things had been particularly tense of late, the ongoing dispute with Mahir's brother who lived next door rankling once again. A grievance festered between them that could not, it seemed, be laid to rest. It concerned the earth beneath their feet, the allocation of ancestral land in a place where few other assets existed, inflicting irreconcilable wounds. One or the other of them was always picking at the scab of their disagreement, threatening to tear it off. Although the popular view muttered, out of earshot, was that Nura's family had done better out of the arrangement, Mahir had never cared for the opinions of others.

In the darkness Nura would wait, her sons murmuring in their room next door, her daughter Radhia asleep on the cot beside her. Sometimes Mahir would not utter a word when he got home. He'd kick off his sandals before climbing the mud step, push open the tin door to their tiny, crowded room and collapse on the vacant side of their bed in exhaustion. But on other nights, his anger could not be so easily tamed.

Up the mud path than ran behind Nura's home, Aliya too was often awake in those shadowy hours. Her troubles had begun long before the latest spate of accidents, accumulating imperceptibly like the grey mud and silt slapped onto the banks at the edges of the island, building up in incremental drifts until they almost overwhelmed her. Her days were always long now, any appetite for sleep suppressed by the gnaw of worries that knotted in her stomach. Exhaustion had long ago consumed her, carving deep sable-coloured moons under her eyes and dulling the aching muscles of a body that so rarely found stillness. Her mind was keen, however, even as her limbs slowed into the repetitive movements of the menial embroidery work that she accepted with the resigned dignity of someone who knows both that they have no other choice and that they deserve better. 'The work is not difficult,' she would say whenever anyone expressed sympathy for her ceaseless undertakings. 'It is boring.'

Her dogged labour was hardest at this time of year, when even at night the heat failed to retreat. Although the earthen walls of the *kacca* houses such as Aliya's were designed to breathe, the tin or bamboo roofs packed with straw trapped the sultry air. Even outside on the verandah, Aliya could feel the sweat begin to creep across her neck as she sat hunched over, her eyes aching with the strain of looping tiny iridescent beads onto shimmering threads. There was a kind of peace to the nights; the landscape softening around her, the stars littering the sky. Aliya was one of the only women who had learned, for the most part at least, not to fear the dark.

On an evening uncomfortable even for summer, a few weeks after the storm, there was another job that demanded her attention. The proud cultivator of one of the most impressive gardens in the village, Aliya had a clutch of mango trees and pragmatically divided her fruits three ways: those to sell to others; those to be eaten raw and teeth-suckingly sour, as she preferred them; and those to be allowed to ripen, before being gathered in the soft sling of a worn-out sari and taken to the outhouse kitchen, where a large and battered pot awaited them.

Sitting on the earthen floor, Aliya peeled and sliced the mangoes. A faint glow troubled the gloom of the kitchen, silhouetting her fingers as she coaxed the soft fruit from its leathery, flaccid skins, scooping it into her cupped palms. She was careful to add each splash of juice to the hissing pan, into which she also dropped handfuls of sugar, salt, chilli powder and intuitive mixes of whole and ground spices. She sat as the hours drifted past, only her arm moving over the slow-burbling cauldron, making sure that the syrupy mixture did not catch on the scratched and scoured bottom.

Behind her on the cot bed, her husband Kabir stirred. They had slept apart for so many years – he alone in the outhouse, she in the main house along with the rest of the family. Aliya paused, listening, waiting. His laboured breathing resumed slowly, subsiding into soft snores. Her shoulders unclenched, and she allowed her arm to move once again in rhythmic circles. Her thoughts trailed away to other things beyond the kitchen walls: to the boundless sky beyond. She had been watching these nights as the silver moon fattened, its heaviness drawing it low in the sky so that it sat almost atop the trees. She would watch in the coming days as it would begin to diminish, carved into a dwindling angular crescent before it would vanish momentarily, the faintest curve then reappearing to begin the cycle once again. When the cycle had been completed once more, the month of Ramzan would commence.

Chapter Two

The Slowest Month

Nura gasped as she surfaced in the grey-green waters of the pond. The morning was white-hot, one of those strained and expectant mid-June days when it feels as though everything is holding its breath, anticipating rain. Ensuring that her clean sari was carefully positioned, the dirty one tucked under her arm, she climbed slowly back up the bank, the water dripping from her toes leaving dark footprints on the baked earth. Glistening droplets clung to her skin as she ran her hands over her face, savouring the water on her tongue. Soon she would have to be more careful.

Nura was determined to fast every day of Ramzan this year. For those thirteen long hours – yawning from the first light of dawn until the sun met the horizon once again – she had resolved that nothing, not even water, would pass her lips. In preparation she had begun to skip meals occasionally, small abstinences that nonetheless showed her what she might be capable of. It was only the fleeting moments of free time that were a problem: a stolen minute idling over a cup of *cha* whilst she caught her breath, a few seconds languishing in the cool depths of the pond when bathing. In the absence of friends, the nagging demands of a busy household were more than enough to fill the days. When there was so much to be done, it was not hard to keep busy.

All of her previous attempts had somehow been frustrated. Her father's lenience had excused her from fasting as a child, as had the swift transition from a girl of twelve to a married woman of thirteen. Long, repetitive years of pregnancy and breastfeeding had made keeping a fast impossible. Like other women, she had quietly enjoyed her temporary exemption – her sex – for once allowing her to forgo an obligation.

Last year she had come close, although she had been thwarted by illness. The month of fasting had fallen at the height of the monsoon; and the thick mud, the pools of standing water and the impossibility of keeping anything dry or clean meant that sickness was rife through-out the village. On three occasions she had surrendered to the remedy of clear water from the pump on the roadside, boiled furiously before salt and sugar were added, to combat the other flows ebbing from her weary body. This year would be different. This year she would be ready.

As she walked along the path winding through Aliya's vegetable garden, Nura felt the water's revival evaporating from her, the burn-ing sun once again revealing her tiredness. In these days before the moon was sighted, she got up with the first call to prayer at around half-past three. Whereas normally she would roll over, returning to a thick sleep before rising quickly for rushed prostrations before the dawn, she now spent this hour and a half dutifully praying. When Ramzan began, these liminal moments would become even more precious – a window in which to eat, before the amber glide of sunrise. Other, stricter households would get up even earlier, wanting to eat before the first call to prayer, though Nura's husband Mahir had forbidden this. They were believers, but not like the bearded ones.

Throughout the village a few fires would be lit, though in Nura's house they would not bother. Overnight, battered aluminium pots of leftover rice would steep in cloudy water. This *panta bhat* would be scooped from bowls in quick, hungry gulps with a plate of salt, chillies, some thinly sliced red onion and perhaps a squeeze of fresh lime, if Mahir had remembered to bring some home from the bazaar. The parents and the two of their four children who were old enough to fast would sit on woven mats around the wavering gas lamp, eating purposefully before washing, performing their prayers, then returning to their beds, bellies full, to snatch a few more hours of sleep.

Nura had never been slender like her sisters. Even when she was a child, her father had joked that her sturdy figure reminded him of the buffalo he lovingly tended, which provided his seven children with a daily glass of warm, frothy milk, an extravagance that belied the family's poverty. Though short, she had always been strong, her thick and muscular arms able to haul large bundles or hoist heavy pails when helping her parents with the manual chores that dominated their existence. In a smooth, round face, her wide, deep-set eyes and generous mouth, which struggled to conceal that she was slightly buck-toothed, lent her a permanent expression of surprise. Nura was not greedy, though perhaps she might have been, had circumstances afforded her the opportunity. Nonetheless, as she eased herself onto the mud step of her house now, in order to comb her thick black hair, damp and knotted after its submersion, she thought only about dates.

Poverty meant that the breaking of the fast each evening was not a grand affair for most in the village. The fabled trappings of the *iftar* meal were enjoyed only in the luckiest houses such as Sara's, where slices of apple, orange segments, pieces of guava and pudgy dates would be spread on delicately patterned but mismatched china plates. For most, a simple bowl of *muri* or boiled *chana* would suffice, enough to revive them after many hours of fasting. This year, however, Nura had set her heart on dates.

This fixation on breaking her fast in the way advised by the Prophet was the kind of subtle change that was noticeable in Nura since the Tablighi Jamaat had arrived in the village. The reformists – once striking with their full beards, pale *kurtis* and short, ankle-length white pyjamas – had long become a familiar presence. These outsiders brought with them new ideas about the proper ways in which Muslims should behave, gentle at first, but coercive nonetheless, towards a reframing of Islam and an Arabisation of familiar practices. Now, almost all men who prayed in the newly remodelled *boro masjid* wore similar attire for Friday prayers or occasions of religious importance. The organisation had paid to transform the mosque from a squat earthen structure into an incongruous towering building of marble, glass and electric fans, with the improvements arriving as the funds did, bit by bit. Yet with the building almost completed, in recent years it was the women to whom the reformists had turned their attentions.

A girls' madrasa school was in the nascent stages of construction on a muddy stretch of earth alongside Aliya's vegetable patch, envisaged to enable future generations of females to receive their own, segregated religious education. Most Sundays the women's madrasa meeting would take place in a low oblong building adjacent to the mosque, in which a rotating cast of invisible male presences took turns to describe female lives in instructive tones from behind a bamboo screen. The women would listen as they were told yet again that a woman's life is a path fraught with the dangers of sinful opportunity.

The true ways of Islam were outlined, as was just how lucky they were to have been lifted out of their former ignorance. The thick black coverings of female modesty had begun, in the last decade or so, to appear around the village. Once viewed as strange and impractical, this attire was now regarded by many as a prized marker of faith and religious commitment. In an inverse motion, partaking in the festivals of other religions had begun to dwindle. Some, in quiet defiance, still maintained annual excursions to the *Durga pujo pandals* that flourished across the island every autumn – their many-armed goddesses enthroned within, their glimmering lights dancing through the trees – or to the Christmas fair with its jostle and fireworks, held in the main town each year.

Nura was often there at the madrasa meetings on Sundays, accompanied by her small, fidgeting daughter, Radhia. It was a social outing not dependent on having friends – one that granted her a coveted slip into the hallowed world of prophets and angels. She would process the short distance up the road, a dark scarf draped over her head and shoulders. Her husband had refused her requests to buy her a *burqa* or a *hijab*, baulking at both the unnecessary expense and the ideology behind them. She had managed to persuade him to buy one for Radhia, though, who giggled and spun, arms outstretched in her tiny black *chador* with its amusing unfamiliarity.

Now, as Nura looped the damp coil of her hair into a thick knot and secured it at the nape of her neck, her thoughts hovered on the month ahead. Who else would be keeping the fast this year? Though almost everyone in the village claimed to be committed to observing the holy month, almost everyone in the village was also capable of lying.

'Have they seen it yet?'

Kalima dropped her bags against the outside wall of the house, her fishing poles and whatever she had caught still damp, the smell of pond water clinging to them. She was always keen for knowledge, furtively collecting it in scraps to be tucked away out of sight for use at future opportunities. The moon was expected, this everyone knew, and when word of its sighting at Mecca reached them, Ramzan would begin. In Kalima's limited imagination, which was ignorant of distances and time zones, this could happen at any point and she was anxious to be kept informed.

'I don't know, my sons will tell me later. They have the phone,' Nura replied, heaving herself off the step with a sigh. Mahir would soon return after a long morning at the shop, simmering with hunger and expectation.

Sensing no further conversation, Kalima clicked her tongue and turned away. She gathered her bags to her shoulder as she made her way up the path behind Nura's house, picking her way nimbly through Aliya's garden towards home. She stopped to greet her neighbour, who was as usual hunched over the fabric of the sewing frame. Aliya barely raised her eyes, her needle moving all the while.

'Fish?'

'Some.' As one inherently adverse to generosity, Kalima was careful not to elaborate. 'It doesn't get any easier, you know,' she said with a sigh. 'Particularly when I have no daughter-in-law to help me.'

'And how is that going?' Aliya asked quietly, careful to avoid specifying whether her enquiry referred to Kalima's quest to find her youngest son Asad a bride, or the troubled situation with Roshini, the daughter-in-law she already had, whose home was almost certainly within earshot.

'Autumn, after the monsoon,' Kalima responded, making it clear that she was speaking about the former. 'I have told him it has to be this year – who knows how many more winters I'll see? You'll help, of course?'

'Mmm,' Aliya assented, unable to refuse the obligations of both neighbourly and distant family proximity, or the valuable chance to earn a few extra rupees. Everyone in the village knew of her family's difficulties, though Kalima knew more than most. Seeing Aliya's concentration, eyes fixed on the outline of an intricate teardrop that she was painstakingly embellishing in golden beads, Kalima's resolve softened.

'I'll put a fish for you over here; just a small one, mind, I have my own mouths to feed.'

Aliya looked up for the first time, her mouth curled into a small smile.

'The children will be happy.'

Sighing and raising her eyebrows, Kalima moved off, walking around the side of the house to the large clearing where her own homestead lay. Two days later the whisper of a crescent moon was sighted in Mecca and the fasting began.

Kalima liked to watch the rain dance. A week into the month of Ramzan, she sat on the long verandah that spanned the length of her rectangular house as a storm brooded. The space was covered, protected from the rain, but the bamboo-slatted walls permitted the tremors of a breeze to enter. She enjoyed the forced contemplation that the holy month demanded, her prayer mat always nearby, draped carefully over a length of twine that she had strung up from two hooks gouged into the earthen wall. On these turgid afternoons when rain and fatigue made venturing outside an unappealing prospect, Kalima would sit, doze and sometimes do something useful like mending blankets or sieving rice. On this particular afternoon she was making *roti*, bringing together the dough, kneading it again and again with the firm ripple of her knuckles. Her position allowed her to keep half an eye both on her grandchild Iffat, playing quietly in an inner room, as well as the occupants of the shack that lay just across the clearing.

The month of Ramzan was guided by the moon, the lunar calendar out of sync with the solar, causing the dates to move back by around 10 or 11 days each year. This year they were unlucky, the fasting falling during the first stuttering weeks of the rains, when the weather alternated between ferocious downpours and a sharp, blistering heat. Pregnant clouds stole across the land. Ponds swelled and the jungle around the village turned a glistening green, only for the sun to reappear, baking the earthen paths that snaked amongst the houses into a thick, congealed mud. As the days slowly slipped by, the rain became incessant. Even for someone like Kalima, who was more comfortable than most with the challenges of the monsoon in a place such as this, she was sure it was worse than usual. Everything was damp, mould blossomed on clothing, thick mud streaked the ankles and legs in pale-grey licks.

Kalima had seen out most of her holy months here. Although in the event of marriage women were almost always uprooted from their father's village, she had been lucky enough to return. This was not for the usual trio of ignominy: divorce, death or destitution. When he was alive, her husband had worked on the railways, being absent for long stretches of time, regarding home as a fleeting place of uncomplicated family existence. So after sixteen unhappy years spent in Kolkata with his family, they had moved back to the island, her beloved *jonmostan*. The surrounding landscape was a cluttered museum of her memories. Each tree root, coconut palm, path, clearing or tangle of forest cradled a story from her past. Much had changed in the fifty-six years she had been alive. She had seen many pass through, ushered out by marriage, opportunity or death. As she approached her own twilight years, Kalima dwelled comfortably among the ghosts.

The world she inhabited was lit with religiosity. She prayed often, her exchanges with Allah enjoying the relaxed intimacy of friendly conversation. An early madrasa education meant that she was able to read the Quran in Arabic and, though she could not tell you what the individual words or sentences meant, she derived from this a great sense of peace and fulfilment. Like Nura, she would often attend the women's madrasa meeting on a Sunday afternoon. Once there, she was as happy interrupting those around her as she was listening to the details of the sermon. For her, being in that space surrounded by women in *hijabs*, *chadors* and *niqabs*, none of which she owned herself, was enough to confirm that this truly was a place of God; that they were on the right path.

Her favourite night of the year was that of *shab-e-barat*, when the living brought food, candles and flowers to the graves of the deceased. In all-night vigils, prayers were recited for the souls of the departed in the hope they would be released at last from the burden of their worldly sins. As an ageing widow, Kalima was one of the few women able to partake in the ritual, taking food to the graveyard, a place beyond the boundaries of the village and otherwise forbidden to women. She relished every aspect of the occasion: the murmur of impropriety, the presence of the supernatural, the sense that one could reach with outstretched fingertips to brush against those of the dead.

If her relations with the departed were intense, then the same could be said of her worldly intimacies. As the dough softened under her attentions and the rain began to fall harder, Kalima could just about make out a light in the small hut of her favourite son, a stone's throw away from the family home and a bitter reminder of their lingering animosity. Of her six children, only two remained in the village. Her eldest son worked as a labourer far away on one of the Andaman Islands and her three daughters were married and living with their in-laws. Now there was only her youngest son, Asad, whose name meant 'lion' in Urdu, belying his selfish and cowardly nature, and Riyaz.

Riyaz could hold up the world with his smile. It was one that his handsome face struggled to contain, his large white teeth flashing, his bright eyes crinkling at the edges. It mirrored what was for the most part a deeply easy-going nature. He could stop at almost any household in the village for a chat, his affable manner wooing into conversation even the most reluctant of interlocutors. He was desperately interested in outsiders, often standing at the roadside to watch when a gleaming coach lumbered through the village, bearing its passengers to the *ghat* at the bottom of the island, from where you could catch a boat winding further into the Sundarbans. Riyaz would wave at the blurred and unsmiling faces as they passed by, unable to understand why they never waved back.

He had a game he liked to play when he encountered new people, or at least those who were unfamiliar with his past: the *jamaatis* who visited every Tuesday, say, or relatives who came to stay with other families in the village. One morning, just before Ramzan, Riyaz had sat opposite a visitor whom he had jovially cajoled into a chat. His small son Said was cradled in the loose fabric of his *dhoti*, swinging happily in the makeshift hammock, bravely eyeing the stranger before scrunching his small body into a ball and burying his face in the cloth.

Riyaz's wife, Roshini, glided soundlessly around the clearing. Her face was hauntingly beautiful, with large eyes, a high forehead, full lips and sticking-out ears, behind which she tucked her veil in a way that lent her a slightly goofy appearance. She handed round *cha* and a plate of stale biscuits, before retreating to a place by the stove where, though she was not part of the conversation, she could nonetheless hear what was being said. Examining the biscuit pincered between his thumb and forefinger, Riyaz had then looked up.

'What do you think of love-marriage?'

The visitor had smiled, demurred, skilled in the art of avoiding difficult discussions with someone with whom he was not well enough acquainted. Such questions were petrol, prone to start uncontrollable fires between even the closest of friends. Roshini stared at her husband, her expression looking as if she had just been slapped.

Kalima had also witnessed this moment from the other side of the clearing. Hearing her son's words, she felt as though someone had punched her in the gut, removing the air, leaving her fighting for breath. It had taken everything in her limited powers of self-control to turn away from Riyaz and the stranger and continue scattering the odds and ends of vegetable peelings and rice onto the ground, to be eagerly pecked at by her ducks.

Now, as she set the perfectly kneaded dough aside and placed a damp tea towel over the bowl to let the mixture rest, her anger at her son swirled heavily inside her. As someone for whom secrets were held like a hand of cards, clasped tightly against her chest, it was unthinkable for Riyaz to be so brazen. All here were resistant to *asanti* – the lack of peace that fluttered in the heart when relationships turned sour. Although almost a decade had passed since his original defiance, she still nursed an unshakable bitterness, where there had once been love. It was bad enough that Riyaz had embarrassed her, disgraced their family by marrying out of something as foolish and fleeting as love, but to be so flippant about his past with a stranger, it was as though he was deliberately trying to create unease.

She glanced across the clearing, where the rain and the darkness were both drawing in.

'*Badmash chele*,' she muttered, 'despicable boy', shaking her head.

Kalima knew that the open hearth that his family cooked on would be unable to catch a flame this evening, even if the rain eased up. She sighed. The whole of her family would break their fast together tonight.

Two weeks later the call from the *muezzin* split apart a swampy mid-morning. It was a different call, longer than the usual call to prayer, the tone instructive. The men stirred into movement, replacing their tattered everyday clothes with those now understood to be necessary for undertaking any religious actions – Allah witnessed everything, after all. Water was splashed across faces, fingers rubbed hurriedly across teeth, hair flattened beneath prayer caps. They left their homes, moving quickly towards the smaller mosque, where a crowd was already gathering. Someone had passed away, their elderly body unable to bear the effects of the unrelenting fasting.

Dying during the holy month was highly auspicious, everyone understanding that it would guarantee immediate passage of the soul to *Jannah* or paradise, though in keeping with custom there was nonetheless a need for immediacy. As Muslims, they believed that the deceased should be buried as soon as possible, ideally before sunset on the day they died, the whispers of the earth calling out for bodies before they have turned cold.

Hunched over her sewing on the verandah, Aliya heard the calls summoning the men to honour the dead. She did not struggle with fasting; poverty made hunger familiar company, the ache in her stomach spurring her on. If anything, the absence of a lunchtime meal to prepare meant that other less taxing, long set-aside chores could be considered. This was an opportunity to repair the *kacca* homes that most people lived in, which were made from an alchemistic mix of natural materials and demanded time and care from their occupants. Dung cakes that had been baked to a brittle snap would be packed into spidery cracks along walls and then sealed with wet mud. Inner floors would be sopped with a bubble-strewn mixture of earth, dung and water, left to harden and seal into a smooth crust. Old, musty thatched roofs would be removed and replaced with thicker bundles of thatch that had only recently been dried. Those fortunate enough to own a lumpen mattress would wrench out tufts of sullied straw, before repacking the threadbare casings with fresh, coarse handfuls.

In courtyards, slices of *holud*, limes and whole red chillies spread on trays would lie to blister in the heat of the sun, drying into lustrous husks to be bartered or used in later months when weddings and festivals returned. Palm fronds would lie in piles waiting to be dissected, the leaves stripped and dried into kindling, the spiny middles bleached into firm spokes to be bundled together and used as brooms. Some parts of the village would be strangely still, with men and women seeking piecemeal work sowing the summer crops out in the fields. A dedicated worker known to be in need of the money, Aliya was often called upon, slipping out before dawn and entrusting her daughter Amal with the care of her three younger brothers.

In an effort to keep spirits buoyant in the last tortuous days of fasting, Aliya's household, along with all the others, began to focus on the day of Eid itself and the food they would prepare. There would be fish, of course, a unifying religion for all Bengalis, irrespective of other varieties of faith. There would also undoubtedly be meat, most likely beef for any family able to afford it. This was something prized above all else on festive occasions, understood by those in the village as the essence of Muslim celebration. Sweet things – indulgences usually absent from their lives, due to their cost – would be abundant: *mishti-doi*, *sondesh* and *rosogolla* from the bazaar, the last of the mangoes and special desserts prepared just for the holiday.

Aliya's neighbour Kalima was famous for her *shimai*, the vermicelli pudding made with sweetened milk. Above a blistering fire she would swirl oil around a pan, before placing in handfuls of broken vermicelli, the pale strands dancing in the golden fat. In another pan milk would be urged to a juddering boil, and large scoops of sugar thrown in, before it was tipped into the bubbling oil and covered with a lid. There it would dwindle and soften into an unctuous pudding that, once cooled, would be adorned with a scattered handful of burnished cashews. Aliya's children asked in barely muffled whispers whether Kalima might share some with their family this year, prompting giggles in their mother, who tried her best to frame delicately her neighbour's miserliness.

There was also the matter of presents. Since the embroidery work had first begun in the village two decades before, women had been exchanging myriad hours and uncountable stitches for small packets of rupees. Touted by local microfinance organisations as a straightforward solution to the problems of endemic poverty, the reality of the situation was inevitably more complicated, as Aliya understood only too well.

Women became ensnared by debt, the draining and badly remunerated work yet another chore to be shouldered by their exhausted bodies. In many homes it had now fallen to them to earn the additional money for Ramzan presents – typically a set of new clothes for each family member. The hopping anticipation of excited children was infectious, and the cramped hours hunched over grubby polystyrene bags of sparkling beads was thus rewarded. As she moved the needle in its infinite see-saw, up-down, up-down, adorning the clothing of others, Aliya wondered whether this year she would have enough money to buy her children a gift. She knew deep down that she would not.

The luckiest of the women – those with husbands willing to overlook what some men in the village might deem an unnecessary outing – were allowed to go to the bazaar to choose their presents, often in the reassuring company of a neighbour or a sister-in-law. They enjoyed the thrill of entering one of the few shops with a glass door and a rumbling air-conditioning unit, the frigid wave that greeted them causing goosebumps to rush across their skin. The eagerness with which they accepted the offer of the free drink, and the length of their deliberations, revealed their meagre circumstances. As they walked home laden with purchases, making their way in busy streets past the piles of rubbish and the mangy stray dogs snapping at fleas, the bazaar was almost beautiful.

Nura was not allowed to visit the town. It was not that her husband had explicitly forbidden her; she had just never asked him. She couldn't see how such an excursion might be possible, given the various demands of her four children and a household, replete with the lurking presence of her judgemental in-laws next door. She was sure he would say no anyway, and preferred to avoid having such an uncomfortable truth aired. She was content to allow him to go on her behalf, or to wait for the travelling saleswomen who would pass through the village from time to time, selling bangles, costume jewellery, hair clips, scent and make-up.

This year she felt as though she should ask Mahir for a *salwar kameez* as her Eid gift – the single present she could expect all year. Several times in the women's madrasa meetings the problem with wearing saris had been mentioned, the strip of flesh revealed through the habitual folds of material a visible impropriety. But for most of the women in the village the sari was more than a garment; it was an identity. Whether they knotted them whilst working in the paddy fields during the harvest, or hitched them up to navigate the sloppy earthen paths during monsoon, or fashioned them into colourful screens whilst bathing in the ponds, their very existence was wound up in these five-and-a-half metres of cloth. Nura thought saris were beautiful, Aliya found them practical and Kalima could not imagine wearing anything else. After deliberation, Nura had asked Mahir for a sari instead.

For her, as for all the women of the village, the day of Eid would begin just like any other. Breakfast would be made, eaten, the plates washed, the inner room tidied and then the real work of preparing the feast would begin. Dicing, chopping, shredding, peeling, frying, simmering; the kind of cooking that involved weighing grains in an upturned palm, and judging by smell, by the colour of the spices toasted and ground into a fragrant paste the colour of rust. Once the food was ready, there would be the sweeping and mopping, before the women could finally submerge themselves in the pond to slough off the streaks of dirt, the lingering smells of the cooking fire and the tang of sweat. The women would then put on a new outfit, the fabric almost coarse to the touch, the scent an absence as opposed to a presence.

The remainder of the day would mellow into eating and laughter, and visiting the houses of neighbours. In the days that followed, for the nine women there would be both joy and disappointment. Some would keenly anticipate a trip home from their married daughters or sisters – those who had been wedded long ago to others in far-flung villages and localities – bringing with them grandchildren and cousins. Others were forced to accept that visits would not be possible, with pangs of longing reaching out to the women they loved whose new lives and circumstances made their returns too difficult. For Nura, she would be the one returning, having the longed-for excuse to visit her father's home for an afternoon and be amongst the buffalo again.

Chapter Three

Underwater, Under Threat

'*Chaaallll! Chaaaaaallllll!*'

The rice seller slowly wheeled his ancient bicycle down the tarmac road, its form as rusted and battered as his own. He was forced to keep to the main roads now, to the slivers of tarmac that unfurled across the island, branching out into two sharp points that lapped the southern river's edge, from where onward journeys required a boat. The earthen paths that ran between villages had lately become impassable except on foot, as water fell, pooled and stole boldly across the island, hungry for new territory.

This year's monsoon had transformed the landscape into one of unimaginable liquidity. Although the showers were always expected for three or four months between June and September, in a single month they had deposited more than an entire season's worth of rain. Rani was too young to remember the terrible floods of the past that had wrought similar shifts, though could clearly recall the devastation of Cyclone Aila five years before. Howling winds had torn apart houses, wrenching trees from the earth, whilst the churning seas had breached the island's mud banks, with saline water eagerly invading the landscape in a silent, poisonous film. But this current devastation was solely the handiwork of the rain.

After an initial hesitation, the monsoon had entered its stride. And then it had not stopped. Each morning the village awoke to a persistent patter, or to the oppressive gloom of dark, heavy clouds, almost close enough to skim the tin and bamboo rooftops. The paths became treacherous, thick mud grasping at the limbs of those who unsteadily picked their way through, flip-flops in hand. The ponds around which life in the village was centred overspilled their banks, water rising until it was almost impossible to find patches of land that had not been engulfed. The paddy fields turned to lakes, soft and shimmering. The fragile stalks of recently sown rice, upon which so much depended, struggled to raise their heads above the water, like drunken patrons bowed beneath the effects of an evening's liquor. For farmers, the longed-for rain had, after its initial relief, brought with it a calm despair. There was little to do except sit and watch as their crops drowned and the year's profits disappeared – sunk slowly, centimetre by centimetre.

The weather made everybody fractious. Sickness crept around the village, revealing the impossibility of drawing boundaries here: inside and outside; clean and dirty. The veils of respectability that many worked so hard to maintain disintegrated in the ceaseless onslaught of the rain. There was no way to get clean, dry, with the mud on everything, the water everywhere. In murky pools of standing water bacteria flourished, droplets sliding seamlessly in rivulets across the earth, or attached to the ankles of those making their way to the ponds that people bathed in and drank from. Bodies creased over, twisted in agony; vomit clung to the backs of hands, and excrement slid down legs in uncontrollable surges. Bodies itched, with small bumps erupting in patches across skin unable to tolerate the shift from an incessant heat to a continuous, inescapable damp. Worse still, they all knew it would be at least another month before the monsoon would start to abate.

Further inland they were no better off. In parts of Kolkata the water stood waist-deep. Newspapers traded on images of families huddled on the roofs of shacks, their possessions submerged or swept away by the filthy water overflowing from the city's ancient drains, unable to accommodate the constant deluge. Car lights peeked perilously above the swirling water, which they crawled through at a hearse's pace, whilst cycle rickshaw-wallahs bravely navigated the depths through which rubbish, debris and rats swam and bobbed. A six-month-old baby had been washed away from his family in the middle of the night, when their makeshift home on the pavement running alongside one of the city's main thoroughfares became inundated with overflowing water, his small lifeless body later being found washed up on an adjacent street.

The rice seller paused by the covered verandah of the tea shop. The two wooden benches were crowded with patrons, damp bodies huddled over cups and conversation, seeking a distraction from the rain. Behind the clapboard counter Rani stood next to her mother, alerting her with a softly spoken 'ma' to the seller's presence. Bashira glanced up from the bags she was unpacking and sighed. The sight of the bedraggled man, whom she knew had eight children and a wife to feed, provoked from her an unusual display of sympathy.

'Give him tea,' she said in a low growl, returning her eyes to the sacks of potatoes and baskets of onions clustered in the cool shade of the shop floor.

Rani lit the stove, the flame a bright spark in the dim light of the shop. She muffled its brilliance with a dented pot filled with water from the pump, watching as the tiny bubbles began to rise to the surface. She flicked her thumbnail over a piece of ginger, peeling back the skin to reveal the pungent nub beneath. This was an affectation – the ginger – something Rani had once overheard Sara request and had been awed by this unusual marker of sophistication. She sliced it clumsily, brushing the slivers from her palms into the water, followed by tea leaves shaken from a broken tin and several generous scoops of sugar. As it came to the boil, Rani shut off the flame, tore open a sachet of milk with her teeth and poured it into the saucepan before allowing the mixture to steep.

At fourteen, she belonged in a classroom. But the tea stall needed looking after, and her mother was often absent from the village, spending long mornings at the bazaar in the nearby town, sometimes even going back there during the freshness of the evening. The responsibility had fallen to Rani, even though she was the family's third and youngest daughter. Her eldest sister was married and living far away in the capital with her husband and daughter, where she laboured as a domestic worker cleaning middle-class houses. Rubina, who fell between them in age, was somehow exempt; it seemed that the worse her behaviour became, the less she was asked to comply.

Rani knew she was falling behind in her studies. She had never been particularly bright, but she had approached her work with the same methodical patience with which she now made *cha* or counted change. Her parents no longer paid for any kind of extra tuition – an absolute necessity for any pupil here, so poor was the quality of the teaching at the ramshackle high school in town. The family had no money; only the dog-eared ledgers kept under the counter and filled with increasingly depressing columns of figures showing the extent of their financial difficulties. Besides, they would say, you'll be married soon, so what is the point?

There was a point, Rani would think silently – knowing far better than to try and argue with her mother – for at school she had grown to love athletics. Almost everything about this was incongruous, and to some almost amusing: a girl, a Muslim, poor, living in a village where the few televisions didn't even have the cable-channel subscriptions necessary to watch something like the 400 metres. And yet she loved running; loved the way her body moved around the scrubby track; loved that she was at last able to move her body at all. She thirsted for the wind that flew into her face, drowning out the sounds of the world around her, rendering everything but the path in front of her a blur.

Having won all the local races on the island, Rani was automatically selected to take part in the subdivision championship, for the best of those from all the islands and the stretch of the mainland as far as, and encompassing, the town of Canning. The family travelled the forty-five minutes there for the race, crammed excitedly into the rickshaw jointly owned by her father, Ali Tariq, and his brother. It was the furthest away Rani had ever been from the village, save for the single occasion when her family had caught the packed local train that snaked wearily into Kolkata, for a day out. Although longing for a pair of running pants, leggings or even shorts, she had been forced to wear a pair of baggy, ill-fitting boy's trousers several sizes too large for her under her tunic. She had still won.

There were further competitions, races against girls from other subdivisions, before the possibility of representing the whole district in athletics meetings with competitors from all over the state, but after Canning, Rani didn't run any more. It was neither religion nor tradition that had swayed her parents, as the Lohani family was not conservative or pious, but rather it was inertia. Like so many mothers and fathers, they battled to picture a world for their daughter beyond their own experience. Unable to see a positive outcome – athletics was a financial burden that was unlikely to be repaid – they instructed Rani to withdraw from the championship. She would soon be married and the responsibility of others anyway.

'*Ei! Bitu!* Give me a tea, and strong, not too sweet.'

Rani winced at the use of her *dak nam*, the private, silly name used only amongst family members and close friends within the confines of four protective walls.

'Who are you, to be talking to my daughter like that?' Bashira shouted, unable to stop the smile from creeping into her voice.

'Her favourite auntie,' Tabina said with a grin, gesturing impatiently for those on the bench to move apart, wincing as she lowered her body onto the seat. She spat over her left shoulder. '*Brishti* . . .' Such a beautiful word for the rain, said with so much venom.

Fishing into the top folds of her sari, Tabina removed a beaten-up tin and placed it carefully onto her lap, prising open the lid with an agile forefinger. She scooped a generous pinch of tobacco and betel nut between her fingertips, thrusting it high up into the back corner of her mouth against the gum. She raised an eyebrow at her sister-in-law, who in response curled her fingers into her palm, beckoning. The tin spun, glinting through the air, and Bashira caught it in her outstretched hand.

'And where are you off to?' Bashira asked, eyes focused on the contents of the tin.

'*Onchol* office,' Tabina replied. 'My contact says there is going to be some flood relief for farmers.'

Bashira smirked, the brazenness of her sister-in-law impressive, even to one as bold as she. Tabina had never farmed; she had also never missed an opportunity.

'How much?'

'Up to ten thousand rupees apparently. I don't know, let's see.'

For a moment there was a break in the thick grey fug of clouds, the sun startlingly bright, the rays dancing briefly across the slippery tarmac. Finding no customers, with the crowd thinning as attention was drawn elsewhere, and his cup now empty, the rice seller moved on, his cries disappearing into the lightly falling rain.

Each morning, long after her husband had left to begin driving passengers up from the island to Canning, or down to the *ghat* in the opposite direction, Tabina would take her time to uncurl herself from the painful knots of sleep. Gingerly she inched herself up the cot bed, emitting an occasional private whimper, her aching back searching for the firm security of the overstuffed pillows. Safely bolstered, she would feel the discomfort slowly abate, her body supported by the flimsy mattress and the hard wooden frame beneath. She would reach up and, with rippling, inquisitive fingers, ease the tin of *paan* and tobacco from the slender wooden shelf above the bed. Once the parcel was pressed between her jaw and her cheek, she could relax, allowing the warmth to spread across the roof of her mouth and her saliva to run thick, staining her lips the colour of blood.

Though she awoke most days in pain, two weeks of visits to and from town in the back of overcrowded rickshaws had caused her body to stiffen and protest more than usual. She was only forty, but, concealed beneath the magenta fabric of her sari, Tabina's abdomen was criss-crossed with the ridges of scars from three operations in the hospital down the road. A ruptured appendix, an ovarian tumour, a hysterectomy – her body now laboured under these unhappy absences.

There would be no journeys required today. After hungrily pursuing the possibility of government relief for those who had suffered income loss, due to the first of the monsoon floods, the paperwork was finally all in order and had been submitted on her behalf. She had copied what felt like hundreds of pages, after hours jostling for her turn at the photocopier that gulped down her money and spat out shadowy copies of the proof of her existence. Tabina, Tabeena, Tobinah, her name was spelt differently on every document she was required to replicate, though as she was unable to read, she had not noticed.

She had paid the necessary bribes to the local official in charge of the paperwork, given tea, cigarettes and *paan* to those guarding the door to his office. She had smiled and lowered her eyes and appeared anguished at exactly the right moments. Satisfied that she had done all she could to ensure her family's inclusion on the list, now she just had to wait and see whether her efforts paid off. That they neither owned no land nor farmed was, to her mind at least, entirely irrelevant.

This moment of calm was temporary; Tabina's thoughts had already begun to flit towards another opportunity. Whilst at the *onchol* office one day the week before, the same local official that she had befriended had mentioned to her a new welfare scheme, whereby the government was giving out 100 days of guaranteed manual work for R100 per day to the poorest people living in rural areas. And were they not some of the poorest? Ears pricked, Tabina had pressed him for details: where was the work? What exactly would they be doing? Above all, how could she shoulder her way to the front of the queue?

When she had returned, fizzing with excitement and keen to share the details with her family, she had found only her mother-in-law sitting on the floor of the concrete verandah, laboriously slicing crooked fingers of okra into neat, thumb-width disks. Maryam had listened to her in silence and then, without even looking up, had asked how she could ensure that she would be paid at the end of a day's work. Tabina had glared at her and curled her lip, a jackal baring its teeth.

'At the end of the day, if he doesn't give me the hundred rupees . . . I will climb out of the hole, put my feet on his chest and demand the money!'

Recalling Maryam's face this morning, she smiled; she delighted in upsetting her mother-in-law.

Truce would be too generous a word to describe the current relationship between Tabina and her mother-in-law. Though the passing of time and Maryam's encroaching frailty had poured cold water on their earlier blazing disagreements, hostilities had not ceased. Rather, both parties were simply too exhausted to fight with the intensity they had previously mustered. Now they eyed one another, flinging out an occasional infraction, neither willing to lay the past to rest.

Little frightened Tabina, and what adversity she did encounter she tackled with a knowing snarl. Yet in the first years of her marriage her mother-in-law had terrified her, sending her scampering back to her father's home on more than one occasion. Maryam had repeatedly accused her of being a thief, doing her best to turn her son and her husband against her, hounding her out of their home. When Tabina had denied the accusations and fled, she realised that Maryam had cursed her with black magic. Even now, on the cracked underside of Tabina's right foot, was a circle of whitened scars – a reminder of the halo of nails that she had stepped on in the courtyard of her father's house, placed there, she was convinced, by the demonic conjuring of her mother-in-law.

Maryam's own experience differed, of course. Hers was of a pernicious upstart who had come into her home and caused nothing but trouble. Tabina had played innocent, when in fact she had watched her mother-in-law furtively, stolen money from her secret hiding places and then denied all knowledge of her treacherous acts. They spoke about each other with words used for the most devious of beasts: crafty, sneaky, underhand. Whatever the truth behind their grievances, as a widow now in her seventies, and thus dependent on her sons to support her, Maryam had become Tabina's responsibility.

Tabina was forced to concede that Maryam had been smarter than many of the older generation, bluntly refusing to assign control of the land on which they all resided, when her husband had died. Instead she had kept ownership, stating that it would not be transferred until her demise, thereby removing any possibility that the family could simply dump her on a cot bed and forget about her, as so often happened with those who had become a burden. Also unusually, Maryam chose to live separately from both of her sons, in a tiny one-roomed structure that had once been used for storage, and under which animals were penned in to protect them from the night or the rain. But as she was unable to undertake all of the laborious preparation of meals for herself, Maryam depended upon her sons and their wives for sustenance.

Her presence at their hearth had come to embody success for the two Lohani brothers. Where Maryam ate depended on whose family was doing better, who could afford to feed an extra mouth when there was already so little to go round. In previous years this had been Bashira's responsibility, one that she accepted with an irked resignation. But as Tabina's family fortunes had steadily begun to rise, so those of her sister-in-law's family had plummeted.

The two were intricately related. The brothers' fates had become intertwined when they made the decision to go into business together, taking out loans to buy an autorickshaw with which they would ply the route between the island and Canning, working in shifts to ensure a constant stream of passengers. The business flourished, the loans were almost repaid and it seemed for a while as if their families might achieve the kind of financial security that so many could only dream of. Yet the enterprise had now fallen solely to Tabina's husband, in spite of his accident. When asked, Bashira would say that Ali Tariq could no longer drive, plagued by an ongoing and seemingly untreatable eye problem. No one dared to question her further, though everyone in the village knew the truth. He had been stopped by the police, failed a breathalyser test and was subsequently banned from driving. Tabina shook her head at his stupidity. This was how her success had blossomed whilst Bashira's had shrivelled and died.

As her mother-in-law would probably now be her responsibility for the foreseeable future, one of Tabina's most pressing bureaucratic concerns was to get Maryam's name onto the food-security bill. This particular government provision ensured additional subsidised foodstuffs for the most vulnerable, from official vendors in the town. At a time when the island was waterlogged and work was scarce, such assistance was even more significant. Familial obligation might mean that she had to feed her mother-in-law, but Tabina certainly did not want to have to pay extra for it.

*

Watching the monsoon transform the land around her, Maryam remained unfazed. She had witnessed floods before, from the rains or from cyclones, and trusted that time would see balance restored. For her there was little difference in the days, her existence having already slowed to the steady, though monotonous pace of old age. The damp made her bones ache, however, causing her to take the road more carefully in order to avoid the sharp knife of pain that would shoot from cracked heel to wasting hip. She brandished with additional fortitude the large stick that she used to support herself whilst walking, making her way home from the jungle where she wove amongst the trees, gathering wild plants to boil into a tea, the sound of her moving down the road: pat . . . pat . . . crack!

When one became a widow here, time changed. Traditionally it marked a stripping away, of status and identity, as well as of the visible signs of marriage. Bangles smashed, nose studs removed, the enforced wearing of white, as though transformed to a pale imitation of the previous life from which the colour, along with a husband, had seeped away. Although such proscriptions were no longer imposed, Maryam had changed nonetheless. She only occasionally wore a sari blouse now, often simply draping the fabric across her chest, her body coming full circle, once again innocent and unthreatening to others. She was no longer head of her household, relegated to the role of onlooker when it came to matters of family significance. She was starting to forget things – her memories blurring, the golden light of nostalgia casting its soft glow across the parts of the past that she had chosen to carry with her.

As she limped along the other side of the road from the Qazi's house, there was a line of impatient petitioners, the rain-dictated lull in work and other kinds of activity giving legal matters the space to bubble to the surface. This nondescript homestead was in fact the legislative centre not just of the village, but of all the Muslim villages on the island; it was where the local arbitrator of Muslim Personal Law resided. Marriage, divorce, land ownership, family fractures and disagreements were all governed by the Qazi's decisions. Decades earlier, Maryam had her own marriage certificate signed within its walls by the current Qazi's father, the role being one that was handed down habitually from fathers to their sons.

The lawmaker's was an old family in the village, and a vast one. Its happy maintenance of polygamy in the face of changing times meant that its many members' names and faces belonged in some way to almost everybody's story. There was a daughter now married to the imam with six children of her own, and a son who was one of the main sari brokers in the village, familiar to many of the women as a boss of sorts, who exploited their labour and demanded an unfeasibly quick turnaround. Rani was one of his clients. Silly girl, thought her grandmother, but what kind of man would exploit the work of one so young?

Shouts from the house opposite caused Maryam to pause. It was the Qazi, she was sure, but with her failing senses she struggled to hear his words. She could hear the names of two of his younger sons – two useless boys known for doing little but lazing around with other equally useless young men outside tea shops, playing cards, smoking and sniggering.

'And why are they not in the fields, seeing what can be done? Am I to do this job and to try and save the crops as well?' The voices came closer; two figures pacing the corridor, one of the Qazi's wives shoved into the road with the instruction to go and discipline her pathetic offspring. Children always belonged to their father, until they failed to live up to expectations.

The Qazi stood framed in the doorway, rubbing a hand forcefully across his forehead as though to dislodge the troubling thoughts. He turned to speak to those at the front of the queue, a group of middle-aged men standing beside the small figure of a woman entirely veiled in black. This was not a marriage, Maryam thought; the woman's presence thus could mean only one thing. She strained to hear what was being said, catching only the Qazi's brusquely delivered questions, unable to grasp the responses of the woman, who, she observed, was composed, speaking firmly, her elegant hands making clear and precise gestures. There were no children with her, her cloaked body still slender; she was young, Maryam thought. The Qazi told her to take a week to think over her decision and that, should she feel the same way in seven days' time, he would grant her a divorce.

The group moved away reluctantly, looking down the road for a passing driver with whom they might barter a ride back towards town. Maryam stood watching, slowly shaking her head. Though unsure of her actual age, having been asked to choose it many decades ago when she was first registered for a voter ID card, she was old enough to view divorce with an unbridled incredulity. After all, had she not had to endure her own husband? And now her intolerable daughters-in-law?

Watching them depart in a crowded rickshaw, with a final shake of her greying head, Maryam continued her journey towards home, a look of disdain darkening her features. She had always had a remarkably open face, round, bright-eyed, eager-looking even in her dwindling years. When she smiled, her eyes crinkled and her few remaining teeth could be glimpsed, and there was something almost encouraging in her countenance, as though to draw out more silliness, an even better story, a further joke. But it was a face that betrayed pain or anger all too easily, flaring with shadows, like clouds drawing across the moon.

She shambled on down the road, past the tailor's shop where she exchanged pleasantries with the elderly man hunched over his dilapidated sewing machine. The tailor, slender, wizened, with sparkling eyes, even older than her, had been close friends with her husband. They now shared an almost familial intimacy, enjoying the removal of the prohibitions of gender in old age. They had spoken properly only last week, when he had been the first person to mention to her the strange presences that had begun to appear in the village.

'You know, *didi*, the CID have been here?'

'Who?'

'C.I.D. CID . . . Central Investigative Division. Police.'

'*Chi!* What are you saying?'

The tailor then told her a story. One day he had noticed a man, an outsider not from the village, sitting underneath the large banyan tree by Nura's home. Filthy and dressed in rags, the man was acting crazy, muttering faintly to himself. They were all familiar with these desperate figures who roamed the island, neglected shadows whose lives had been derailed by alcohol, drugs, mental illness or tragedy, with no net to catch them.

Yet something about this man had given the tailor pause. There was something in his movements, his mendicancy, that did not ring true. Others were similarly struck, so could he be an infiltrator of some kind? They noticed him watching intently, moving around the village throughout the course of the day as though searching for someone, something. He sat outside the *boro masjid*, observing the men gather and perform the five o'clock prayers, his limbs jerking in an unwitting mimicry of their prostrations. That evening, having ascertained that no one had seen the man eat all day, the tailor resolved to bring him some food. Finding him still sitting by the mosque, he placed a tin plate of rice and leftover potato curry in front of him, with a cup of water. The man looked up and held his gaze. Finally he murmured, 'Thank you, uncle.'

The next morning, he was gone.

'But why would he come *here*? What do the police want?' Maryam had asked, leaning into her stick.

'Isn't it obvious? It's because they are spying on Muslims, *didi*! Well, I hope he reports what he has seen!'

Today Maryam did not stop for stories. She had given her word to Tabina that she would peel some potatoes for lunch, and she intended to keep it; besides, what the tailor had told her had unsettled her. She was old enough to remember the years after Partition, when many around her had their lives torn apart by the violence that erupted between Hindus and Muslims, their beloved land cleaved in two and her fellow Muslims suddenly conspicuous, as though on the wrong side of the border.

Things they had seen, things they had lost, things that had been done to them or to those they were acquainted with, or that they had done to others; and worst of all perhaps, the things they had not done. It was as though everyone carried with them fragments of a shattered world, splinters of a past that no longer existed. There only had to be a whisper of *jonghi* – terrorists – lurking along the borderline and suddenly all Muslims were under suspicion. The idea of undercover policemen in their village, or that unrest could erupt again, was unnerving.

'Oh, Allah. When will it be over?' Maryam muttered, fixing the sky with a lupine stare, unclear whether she was asking about her life or the task at hand.

She continued down the road towards home: pat . . . pat . . . crack!

A week later Rani found herself spending another listless afternoon in the tea shop, staring out into a mist of rain. The light was already dwindling, the traffic steadily picking up along the road heading into town. Outside the Qazi's house the veiled woman was there once again, waiting patiently for him to finish his lunchtime nap before deciding her fate. She had thought over her decision and she had failed to change her mind.

Two factions milled around her, like packs of dogs snapping over a contested piece of meat. The men were composed of her husband's family and her own – her side better represented, a handful of men identically clad in blue *dhotis* and white *kameez*. At last the Qazi appeared, to visible excitement, and they began tussling over a sheaf of yellowing papers. As page after page was examined, then cast aside, the look on the Qazi's face distilled into one of disdain; the original copy of the marriage certificate was missing.

The husband's side erupted in anger, his father slamming his hand against the door frame and declaring that he would never accept a copy.

'What if this *girl*,' he spat the word like a curse, 'was to turn around one day and claim that a divorce had never been granted?' He was scared she would take further advantage of their family; after all, hadn't her character already proven her to be more than capable of something like this?

The girl's side was outraged. They had travelled for hours to be here on the appointed day at the appointed time. Besides, why would she even contemplate such a thing, when it was *she* who wanted a divorce in the first place?

After fraught negotiation back and forth, a bribe was quietly suggested by the Qazi. Just a couple of hundred rupees that could enable him to overlook the slip-up and remove their names from the marriage register, in the absence of an official wedding certificate. The young woman's father, initially irate at the suggestion, consented, placing two dog-eared notes on top of the pile of paperwork. Their names were removed and with that the marriage was ended, their separate journeys home and onwards, now before them.

The woman's father boldly met the eyes of those walking past on the road – the unashamedly curious, always alert to strangers in the village. They stared at the woman, who wore a full veil, lingering on the side of the tarmac, clutching a small grey suitcase that contained everything she owned. If only the shame and stigma that would hang over her for the rest of her life could be so easily packed away.

The shop phone, a battered Nokia that was kept by whoever was in charge, vibrated on the wooden counter. Rani answered, to hear her mother's voice snarling over the sound of traffic in the bazaar. There had been a fight at the *onchol* office in town. A crowd of more than 10,000 people had turned up in order to obtain one of the flooding-relief application forms, when there were only 2,000 forms available. The strum of good-natured anticipation had soon turned to a desperate anger as the crowd realised what was happening. Fights broke out, with people shoving neighbours and companions out of the way, while others were pushed to the ground as the crowd surged forward and outstretched hands sought to snatch one of the coveted pieces of paper, which would, they believed, secure them some kind of future – the paper-thin barrier between survival and starvation.

'Be careful, *meye*,' Bashira warned, 'people are angry.'

As the evening drew in, Rani saw the bloodied shapes limping down the road, purple shadows returning to their own villages further south. Figures slowly disappearing into the dusk.

Chapter Four

The Path

'A woman's life is a path upon which she must struggle to walk straight at all times; sin lies in wait on either side. Every single footstep represents a risk.'

The voice brushed against the bamboo screen that shielded the speaker from the audience and hid the listeners from the very possibility of his gaze. The air was almost fetid inside the low-slung building, adjacent to the mosque, that on Sundays served as the women's madrasa space. The monsoon had at last begun to ease, retreating to the occasional heavy downpour, as though the sky were emitting its last ragged sobs after months of ceaseless crying. With the dwindling rains the fierce heat had emerged once more, a silent observer who had been there all along. Hands were fanned in front of faces and *dupattas* were tugged away from the body, dispelling the warmth that nestled closest to the skin.

This Sunday almost all of the nine women were in attendance, sitting in a loose group towards the back of the room, amongst the fifty or so others who had gathered for the meeting. Kalima and Roshini were seated close together, though facing determinedly in different directions, invisible strands of tension quivering between them. Nura sat cross-legged, her brow creased in vexed concentration, with her daughter Radhia – at only four unable to sit still for long, yet also too young to have been left behind – next to her.

Aliya sat with her back against the wall, her serious face passive, her piercing green eyes closed. Beside her was Maryam, the threadbare straw matting failing to cushion her elderly bones comfortably from the concrete floor. Sara was there, relishing the performance of piety out of boredom more than any religious conviction, staring disinterestedly at the ceiling, oblivious as her daughter Nadia whispered to Rani, their heads drawn together in an arch of girlish intimacy. Bashira and Tabina were nowhere to be seen.

The sermon had started late, the additional half-hour of waiting enabling the heat in the room to build to an ever more uncomfortable pitch. All, save the oldest of the women, had covered their heads, the loose fabric of scarves, sari ends or *dupattas* settling in gentle ripples across their slackened shoulders. Some wore *jama-kapor* – what they were told each week was, unlike a sari, appropriate clothing for the devout. Others sat cloaked in full black *burqas*, a few going as far as thick black gloves and socks, concealing even those slivers of flesh from the eyes of their friends, neighbours, sisters. In a strange inversion of the typical uses of garments of piety, when the meeting was over and the women spilled out into the late-afternoon sun they would discard these layers, like chastened butterflies eagerly emerging from stifling cocoons.

The speaker sounded bored. It was almost certainly one of the men from the village as opposed to an outsider, the sermons of strangers usually possessing the benefits of verve and nuance born of both practice and unfamiliarity. There was the predictable focus on *purdah* and modest appearance, delivered with the lack of conviction of one who knew only too well these women's love for their saris. The disconcerting presence of CID agents in the village was mentioned once again, drawing shared glances and concerned mutters from some of the audience. A lot was said about children: how they are a mother's responsibility; how she must ensure they grow up to be good Muslims and part of the *Ummah*, the pan-global Muslim brotherhood; and how the burden of their failures, in the eyes of Islam, will be placed directly at their mother's small, weary feet. *Nadi . . . Nabi . . .* the words for 'river' and for 'the Prophet', peace be upon him, winding around one another in a lilting song.

Kalima was bored. She danced a gnarled hand over the matting to tickle the outstretched feet of Radhia, who shrieked in delight, snatching her legs back and scrabbling to hide behind her disapproving mother. Kalima then began to whisper to Rani, pointing out those who had fallen asleep or who sat slack-jawed, their faces assuming a piscine slouch, attempting to make her laugh. The smart navy sari and emerald-green blouse that shrouded Kalima's ageing body glittered in the gloom, causing her eyes to spark, so dark as to be almost unnerving. There were hints of how beautiful she must have been in her youth, although her now-black teeth and sour breath made Rani recoil slightly.

The relaxed press of hot limbs was a reminder of the unrestrained closeness of the women, whether they wanted it or not. Shoulders were leaned upon and those falling asleep were gently prodded awake. Limbs that jerked in spasms of pins and needles were rubbed and massaged by firm and eager fingers. Murmurs of affirmation rippled through the crowd at certain moments, like rip currents swirling below the surface, tugging disparate bodies in a uniform direction. Sighs were uttered, thoughts strayed to the world beyond the rattan-covered windows, to homes, to piles of plates and utensils adorned with the hardening crusts of lunchtime scraps, to children who would need to be corralled from games of cricket in the fields and forcibly seated in front of fraying exercise books before school in the morning.

It was hard to know what Roshini was thinking. Her face was like a mirror, impassive, reflecting back to anyone who spoke to her what they themselves were feeling. As she sat unmoving in her purple *salwar kameez*, with her matching scarf closely framing the oval of her face, her large, doll-like eyes did not reveal whether she was focused intently upon the sermon or whether her thoughts were drifting, like so many of the others.

Though facing away from Kalima, Roshini could also smell her mother-in-law's breath, causing a creeping heat of repulsion and shame. She shifted in her seat, neatly crossing one leg over another in a way that a body less lithe than hers would have struggled to accomplish so gracefully. She always wore a *salwar kameez* – at twenty-two, she was of both an age and a disposition where this was normal, rather than an expression of particular adherence to the instructions of the Tablighi Jamaat. Her seven-year-old daughter Shahara sat alongside her in a child's imitation of her outfit. The little girl struggled to emulate the straight-backed stillness of her mother, instead engaged in intently picking off the nail polish that she had spent hours clumsily applying just days before.

Roshini was no stranger to losing herself in her thoughts. If anyone had bothered to ask her what her happiest moments were, she would have answered that they came when she was alone – as alone as it was possible to be in the tiny one-roomed shack that she shared with her family. She preferred it when no one demanded anything of her: no shouted orders from Kalima to fill a pot or peel some potatoes, no slurred regrets from her husband Riyaz when he returned home drunk in the moonlight about how stupid they had been to marry for something as volatile as love.

She longed for the night, when Riyaz and her children were sleeping, when she could lie in the darkness and allow her mind to fill deliciously with nothing, gazing at the ceiling, tracing patterns in the cracks. Now she enjoyed a similar lull, gently pushing aside the thoughts that crept uninvited into her mind. She was not without faith, but nor was she ignorant of the challenges women faced. She knew only too well the narrowness of the path on which she was walking, so much so that she sometimes struggled to place one foot in front of the other.

Nura too grappled to keep impatient thoughts from wandering in, though hers were of stories from her past. The sermon's focus on the fickleness of a woman's path reminded her of a tale her father had told her about her great-uncle. He had been a spiteful and petty man, from a time when certain men resented their wives for praying too often, particularly when there was so much other work to be done. Her great-aunt, an especially pious woman, was nonetheless committed to her prayers and covertly ensured that she managed to perform them as often as she possibly could.

One evening, when her husband returned home from the fields, he had found the house empty, his wife unusually absent. Walking around the side of the house to the courtyard at the back, he found her kneeling, praying peacefully and grazing the earthen floor with her forehead. He was outraged, furious that she had so flagrantly disobeyed him. In anger he had kicked her and, as she hit the ground, her neck broke, killing her instantly. Three days later he too had passed away suddenly in the night. Once they were both buried, her father had told her, her great-aunt's grave had been generously tended and visited frequently by those beyond the family who were impressed with her piety and dedication. Her husband's grave, however, was ignored, and his name slipped willingly from their prayers.

Nura's father told her the story as a warning. It was a reminder of the cruelty of some people, those who could be so blinded by their own deep-rooted ignorance and uncontrolled anger that they could take such reckless and unreasonable actions. It was also a good illustration of why a woman should always obey her husband. Nura, though, had taken a different meaning. For her, it was undeniable proof that it did not matter what happened – Allah saw everything.

Eventually the sermon concluded, and Nura was pulled by the voices and movements of those around her to face towards the west, the direction of Mecca, and offer her prayers. She placed her forehead against the mat, searching for the chill of the concrete floor beneath it, savouring these final moments before life outside would take over once again.

'The path' was something the nine women thought of often, and even those who did not attend the madrasa meetings regularly were aware of its significance. The idea belonged to the Tablighi Jamaat, whose influence had manifested itself so gradually, so imperceptibly and over so many years, that it now coated them like a spider's web. Most were unaware of the silky threads until they were fully entangled. As to whether life had become better or worse since the reformists had arrived, opinion was – perhaps predictably – divided.

Some enjoyed the madrasa meetings; others found them tiresome, yet another obligation on the one day of the week when there was a moment of respite. All held a childish kind of pride that their village was now somehow deemed worthy enough for visitation by these religious outsiders, although several were uncomfortable with some of the new understandings and interpretations that they brought with them. At no point were these troublesome beliefs more prominently on display than at an event a few days after the women's madrasa meeting, one that the Tablighi Jamaat had introduced to the village a few years before: an annual religious book fair.

The Islamic *boi mela* fell at the start of September, as it did now each year, when it was hoped the worst of the monsoon rains had passed. On this day hundreds of *jamaatis* from the surrounding area, as well as further afield, streamed into the village for two days of prayer and sermons. This was the kind of convivial and communal event that the Tablighi Jamaat were renowned for – the reorientation of Muslims towards an older, simpler way of embodying their faith, in which the education of one's Muslim brother, both by discussion and by example, was paramount.

Religious books and pamphlets would be circulated and sold, and these prized objects were regarded with the utmost reverence; they were both Islamic and from outside, from places far beyond the island. Any that were purchased would not be displayed, but wrapped in bags or pieces of fabric, stored away carefully in metal chests or locked cupboards, along with other most precious possessions.

In spite of their enthusiasm, the women were instructed largely to keep hidden. Bashira paid no notice, manning the tea stall herself for the entirety of the two days and delighting in the roaring trade they were enjoying. Kalima volunteered to host a few of the visitors at her home, fussing around them on the long, covered verandah where she had permitted them to sleep. Her age and the presence of her sons granted her the freedom to take such liberties, and to wander around and speak to these exotic strangers.

Other women enjoyed the excitement greedily from afar, careful to avoid the scrutiny of the men they knew from the village. This was a time when familiar men became strange, no longer offering greetings as they passed along the roadside, no longer smiling at the women they knew so well. Instead they ignored them, or glared at them disapprovingly when they strayed too close to the proceedings, or in some other way failed to conduct themselves appropriately within these new standards of propriety. Brothers, sons, fathers and husbands changed before the women's eyes, becoming abrupt, impersonal shapes who wore the same pale blue and white as the outsiders, no longer recognisable as the men they knew intimately.

Sara had been spared the transformation of her husband. Khan had not even been present in the village when the *mela* had happened, unwilling to be part of an event that he had no interest in. Aside from his infrequent attendance at *namaz* when he happened to be at home, he paid little attention to the goings-on at the mosque. The family he came from was one that prized politics over piety and he rarely wore Islamic dress, being far more comfortable in the pressed slacks and short-sleeved shirts that resembled his police uniform, bearing a comforting, neutral authority.

Sara guessed that Khan would have chuckled, had she relayed to him the rumours about undercover CID officers that she had heard at the madrasa meeting. She was sure he would have told her not to believe such ridiculous stories, as if the special investigative division had nothing better to do than spy on the inhabitants of this out-of-the-way and irrelevant place. Yet when they had spoken afterwards, she had forgotten to mention it. And in the week that had since passed, something far more tangible, and far more concrete, had been giving the villagers cause for alarm.

She had not seen the writing, but Sara knew what had been going on, recognising it as part of a wider awakening. Whilst idly scrolling through the TV channels, tipping palmfuls of *muri* into her mouth, trying to unwind after a day of teaching as her daughter-in-law Parveen prepared their supper, Sara had caught glimpses of protests awakening in other parts of the country concerning the practice of eating beef.

'*Bou ma, dekho!*' she had called, urging her daughter-in-law to come and look. Parveen hurried in, her face falling when she caught sight of the images on the screen.

In Rajasthan, where Sara had fleetingly lived as a teenager, the slaughter of cattle had been banned long before the current divisive Prime Minister had come to power. But Bengal was different, or so they had all thought. And yet now, in the nearby bazaar, butchers were arriving to open their stands in the peaceful morning haze to discover that words in bright-yellow paint had been daubed across the ground in front of them: '*gorur mangsho khao na!* – don't eat cow meat'.

She told her husband on the phone about the writing. Khan paused, an audible inhalation through his nose. Sara imagined the humid air tugged into his nostrils causing the hairs of his moustache to quiver; the thick moustache he wore made him look more like a Bollywood action hero than the Muslim police officer he was. He exhaled and, with a smile in his voice, dismissed it as the foolishness of bored young men, riled and with nothing better to do than try and cause trouble.

He had eaten beef only days before, Khan told her. He had finished a shift in Howrah before crossing the bridge with his colleagues over the vast, sluggish Hooghly towards the city centre, seeking out a dripping beef *kathi* roll from somewhere with a glamorous name that whispered of Persian roots and a regal past, such as Khadims, or Nizams, or Arsalan. She could picture him in the bustle of Park Street – a place that she knew more by name than by experience – as college students, occasional tourists and eager families walked by, bathed in the yellow lamplight, making the most of a break in the rain to escape into the streets.

This thought made Sara inexplicably sad. It was no secret to those who knew her even slightly that she imagined a different path, a life outside the village. In this way she was not so different from many of the women; Nura often spoke of her desire to move into the town by the bridge, to be away from her husband's family with whom the grim feud rumbled on; Rani dreamed girlishly of a life in which she lived somewhere – anywhere – without a family to determine the course that her life would take. Yet Sara had in fact tasted what so many others had not: life beyond the island, beyond the district, beyond even the state. She had escaped, travelling to study at a theology college in Rajasthan, where she learned reasonably good English. She had glimpsed a life that would be different from the one she had grown up in. And then her trajectory had stopped.

Sara was one of the only converts in the village. Had she ever truly become a Muslim? She believed in one God and in a heaven that was open to all, but these things were also a part of the Christian faith of her childhood. There had been no official conversion process, no tests of scripture or recitation, no drawn-out procedures whereby time and time again she was asked to prove her commitment to her newfound religion. All that had been required was for her to profess her love for a Muslim man and a willingness to enter his faith, confirming in doing so that no pressure had been placed upon her. These clauses had been listed matter-of-factly in a single document that she had signed on the day of their wedding.

The ease with which she had slipped into her new life was quite remarkable, as was the openness with which Islam and Khan's family had embraced her. Yet she was not so strange to them, coming as she did from her father's home, just some fifteen minutes away down the other fork of the tarmac road. She had even known some of the people in the village before she came to live here – from school, from shopping trips to the bazaar, from the natural overlapping of lives in a small community.

The only other condition of becoming Muslim, that of changing her name, in practice never truly happened. It had always struck her as perfunctory that her conversion came down to that, although in a place where a name could mean so much, it was hardly surprising. In the village they were all painfully familiar with the secrets that one's name could betray: a religion undoubtedly, but also a state, a caste, a class, one's financial circumstances or whether you came from the north, the south, the east or the west. Her new surname alone would have been enough to convey that she was Muslim, but it wasn't sufficient. On the day she became a wife she also officially became Saleha Begum, a suitably Muslim name, though everyone just continued to call her Sara. It was as though they could not accept this decree, and many still referred to her as Christian, a constant reminder that she was not one of them, that she was different, although in the ways that mattered most, she wasn't different at all. Sara she had been born; and Sara, it seemed, she would remain.

*

Unlike Sara, Aliya laboured under no illusions of escaping the village. She knew that every path available to her was somehow circular, ushering her back to where she had begun. Her life was only work now: the uncountable hours tethered to the sewing frame, harvesting crops in the fields of others or kneeling amidst her own plants, hands deep in the loamy earth. As she toiled, what Aliya yearned for was change of two kinds: for development to improve life in the village, and for her daughter Amal to have the opportunities that she herself had never even been able to contemplate.

In the days after the book fair, the rains once again returned. The sky was leaden, with brutish clouds that had emptied only that morning masking the sun. Although it was lunchtime, Aliya sat working by the light of a gas lamp. She was, as usual, beside the bamboo sewing frame, a burst of citrus-coloured cloth pulled taut in front of her, onto which she was looping a border of intricate gold beads. Work was picking up again, now that the monsoon was at last drawing to a close and the cooler autumn months ahead of festivals and weddings were promised. She might make R100 for a day's labour of sixteen or seventeen hours, or a little more, if Amal or her daughter-in-law helped.

Aliya had always prized education. But of the four of her six children still young enough to attend school or college, all of them were intelligent, and all of them were struggling. English-medium school was out of the question, the costs unassailable. As the extra tuition needed to stay afloat in the government school became over time an impossible burden, she had watched her children slip. From first or second in their classes, they were now much lower in the rankings, sometimes even sinking to the halfway mark. Her youngest son had begun to get into trouble, missing lessons, preferring to ride his rickety bicycle around the fields behind the houses that clustered along the paths. Aliya did not know that her children were embarrassed by their second-hand books, embarrassed by the poverty denying them the few rupees to buy some snacks for their tiffin. She did not know that Amal saved up any money she was given by her mother, siphoning off a few coins each week so that her younger brothers were allowed, momentarily, to forget.

Aliya was known for her pragmatism, but she nurtured a private resentment of anyone who had the opportunity to advance themselves but who chose, nonetheless, not to pursue it. Frustration simmered within her on each occasion that Kalima complained of the lacklustre careers of her sons Riyaz and Asad, a day-labourer and aspiring van driver respectively, when as the wife of a man who had worked for the Indian Railways, Kalima had had more than enough money to send them to an English-medium school, but had chosen not to. Though she had always liked Roshini, Aliya similarly watched dismayed as time and again she let Sahara and Sumaya skip their morning school, instead racing around the clearing with a raggedy bundle of other truants. Had she not learned through her own mistakes that this was the only chance they had?

Had Aliya been given an offer to improve her lot, she would have accepted hungrily. But whilst she heard about elusive state-sponsored jobs cleaning toilets, cooking school meals or laying bricks on the road as the sun scorched their backs, where were they?

Anxious thoughts distracted her as she struggled to focus now on the golden thread. All the time there was tension. Before their troubles had started, they had been *boro lok*, big people, with a large house, land, livestock and the vegetable gardens that became her territory as soon as her parents-in-law realised they had been fortunate enough to acquire a wife for their son Kabir who was not only good-natured, but also naturally green-fingered. Where Aliya came from on the mainland, everyone had these skills: how to train the twirling spirals of the *kumro* vines, how to nurture the deep greens and blushing purple reds of the *shaak* leaves against the snap of winter, how to nestle the tomatoes so that they greedily bathed in the sun all morning and received enough shade in the shadows of the fruit trees in the heat of mid-afternoon.

Although they had once enjoyed status, her family had sunk far below the poverty line. Now they were small people, and they could never regain their affluence. Public meetings were held in which new schemes designed to help those in trouble were announced: the construction of toilets, contributions towards *pukka* houses being built, or proposals for municipal infrastructure such as water pumps to offer clean drinking water and brick paths to replace the unreliable earthen tracks. And then nothing happened. Unless one had the money with which to pay a bribe, even being considered for inclusion in such projects was little more than a fantasy. Places were reserved for those closest to the people currently in power, or with enough money to buy their way into favour. Aliya knew this better than anyone; she had once been both.

If one even made it as far as inclusion, there were further costs to pay, endless forms to complete, pages to file, documents to copy. All this required money: the notes they were forced to slip into the middlemen's palms, coins for the photocopier, and the lost hours that could have been used productively to earn money elsewhere. The local officials at the *onchol* office would demand a portion of the funds when they were received, for advancing the case, for doing the legwork to ensure someone's inclusion. She was sure that Nura's husband must have paid a large bribe in order to have the new concrete bathroom constructed beside their house, topping up the funds with the good money that he earned from his cycle-repair shop. Despondency dragged Aliya's shoulder blades down her back; at least he worked hard for what he had.

The path that snaked away from the mud verandah where she was sitting, down through the vegetable gardens and back past Nura's house to the road, was another example. It had become almost impossible to navigate over the months of heavy rain, the centre a permanent river of grey liquid mud, the edges sticky and squelching, eating up into the grass as people inched further and further to the sides to avoid getting dirty. The head of the local *panchayat* had promised to lay down bricks after the last monsoon when things had not even been this bad, but again nothing had happened. Aliya knew that if she were able to pay a bribe, it would happen tomorrow.

Her path had in recent years come to represent a political bargaining chip. During the elections, she worked as a vote-capturer. This was an arrangement she had made years ago, when she was truly desperate. She had been recruited by a new political party headed by a grim-faced, though impressive woman. It was a straightforward task: to persuade everyone who used her path to access the main road. Aliya knew that she could be convincing, and in truth this new party did have a lot to offer, particularly for women. She also knew that political allegiances were stubborn old things, like knots in wood, which often did not make sense, but were rarely abandoned.

The party had told her that she could threaten her neighbours to prevent them from using the path if they did not agree, not that it ever came to that. Aliya had talked them round, and in return she did not receive any kind of financial benefit, but instead was offered political protection. She certainly needed it.

Her gloomy thoughts were broken by the tinny cheeriness of her phone. Her stomach twisted at the name on the screen.

'Hallo? *Hai bhai.* Yes . . . yes. I haven't forgotten, but something has happened. It's my son. He was kidnapped . . . I know, and I am trying so hard . . . I understand. When the money is here, I will give it to you.'

The caller hung up. Aliya placed her phone back on the floor. She was amazed by the ease with which the falsehood had slipped from her mouth. Her son had not been kidnapped. She had no money to pay the moneylender. By her calculations, it was now at least R10,000 that she owed. She looked out over the garden. The air was heavy with the smell of the rain that had fallen that morning, everything gleaming in the sombre light. She picked up her needle again and began to sew.

PART TWO

Autumn, Secrets and Lies

Chapter Five

Rumours

It is a sorry state of affairs to have the best days of one's life assuredly behind one. But that is how Roshini found herself, crouched low next to the cooking fire, the acrid smoke from the straw stinging her eyes and drawing tears that she felt no urge to wipe away. Even this was a battle, the slow and frustrating process of mastering the outdoor oven that Riyaz had built for them out of mud and clay. It was fickle in its temperament and hopelessly inept at handling the changeable and often inclement weather.

Growing up on the outskirts of a town, Roshini's mother had always cooked over a gas burner, quite unlike the capricious mud cookers used by many in the village. Though Kalima favoured her outdoor oven, she also owned a gas burner to use during the monsoon season, when it was almost impossible to keep a fire going. Many times Roshini had struggled alone, the damp straw refusing to ignite, when out of the corner of her eye she had seen the confident orange flame dancing on her mother-in-law's verandah. She stubbornly persevered, but knew all the same that if her family were to eat a hot meal that day, she would eventually have to concede defeat and ask her mother-in-law for the use of her gas cooker. She hated asking her for anything and, knowing Kalima, she would probably charge them a couple of rupees for the gas. Now that the rains were over, things had at least become a little easier.

Roshini had few friends in the village. Her aloof nature was in part to blame, the kind of calculated and protective coldness that comes from having a past that one is sure others will uncover. This reserve was matched by the reluctance of others to allow the stain of her shame to seep into the public selves they struggled so hard to keep pristine. For those who had next to nothing, a reputation might be their most valuable possession. Being avoided was the price that Roshini paid for defying convention, for marrying out of love, for arriving in the village so abruptly and unexpectedly, swathed in a cloak of rumours.

Roshini could well imagine what the villagers said about her. Thus, instead of losing herself in idle talk, she had become an expert at enjoying her own company, stealing away from the present by retreating into her mind: those cherished moments at night when she allowed her thoughts to dissolve into nothing, as though floating on her back in a dark ocean, or the slow minutes watching the dance of the cooking fire. Now, as Said played quietly by her side as she went about the preparations for lunch, Roshini thought of her mother-in-law as she split onions and forcefully pounded *holud* and garlic into a paste.

It was almost Eid. The festival of Eid al-Adha, or Bakr-Id, falling two lunar months after Eid al-Fitr, was one that everyone in the village looked forward to, their mouths watering and bellies aching at the promised transformation of freshly slaughtered meat. Though it was known by many names, the day was frequently referred to as Qurbani Eid, or even simply Qurbani, the Arabic word for 'sacrifice'.

Being drawn from the word *qurb*, or 'near', everyone recognised this particular undertaking as one of the special few capable of bringing one nearer to God. Falling as it did on the last day of the *hajj*, the annual pilgrimage to Mecca that should ideally be undertaken by all Muslims at least once in their lifetime, it was the culmination of offering. The killing of goats, sheep and cows had come to represent the willing sacrifice of a child, just as Allah had replaced Ibrahim's son Ishmael at the last minute with a ram, whose tender throat he then cut instead.

The sacrifice that gave its name to Qurbani Eid was a financial exercise as well as an emotional one. Only four or five families in the entire village could afford to buy an animal, raise it, fatten it, then offer it for slaughter and be willing to share a portion of the proceeds with the rest of the inhabitants. It was said that every single hair on the animal's body was a step closer to Allah. The vast majority could not manage such undertakings, and instead gave donations to the *masjid*, which pooled the money together and purchased animals on their behalf, in order to ensure that there was enough meat to go round. A cow cost R20,000, a buffalo 40,000 – eye-watering sums to part with – prompting many to speculate in envious whispers that perhaps it was the financial loss, as opposed to the temporary bond forged with their coddled beasts, that brought tears to the eyes of those handing over their animals. A few years before in a village nearby it was rumoured that a family had even sacrificed a camel.

Roshini's favourite memory from her short childhood had taken place on this particular holiday when, after feasting on beef curry until she thought her small stomach might burst, her family had made a rare journey into Kolkata. In the crowded and narrow lanes of Park Circus, a girl who had never before seen the city basked wide-eyed in the pulsing, busy, filthy, loud freneticism. Protectively her father had swept her up from the crowded pavement high onto his shoulders, as the family joined the steadily growing circle around a couple of street performers about to begin their act.

The magician's blindfolded assistant stood Messiah-like, arms extended, displaying a body blighted with tumorous lumps. In the shuffling dimness, it took Roshini a few seconds to realise that these bulges were potatoes, attached in neat lines to his *kurta*. To startled gasps, the magician unsheathed a huge knife and held it aloft like a proud schoolboy, the glinting blade catching the warmth of the lanterns and the fizzing, crackling street lights that illuminated the scene. Then, much to Roshini's horror, with a flourish he produced a further blindfold of heavy black cloth, asking a member of the audience to tie it tightly over his own eyes, concealing his vision entirely.

As the two men faced one another, and after a bellowing call for silence, the magician began to slice the potatoes on his assistant's body. At first he was slow, precise, his arm lingering at the end of each stroke, as though to savour the excitement building around him. As muffled gasps gave way to shouts, the magician's blows increased in speed and flare, and the cheers and stamps of the crowd grew louder. It was as though he was intoxicated, drunk on the swell of the people around him, spinning as he flashed the blade through the air, severing the three potatoes attached to his assistant's blindfold in a single, violent slice. There was only one potato left when the knife slipped, missing the target in the centre of the accomplice's chest and driving forward with such force that it emerged from his back, the silver tip visible in a darkening circle of blood. The magician stood motionless for what felt like hours, arm outstretched, before slowly raising his trembling left hand to tug the blindfold from his eyes.

The crowd was silent, the rumble of traffic and the blare of horns audible once more, and they stared, unmoving, suspended in a moment of horrified disbelief. Just as Roshini felt the swim of tears begin to waver at the corners of her eyes and a cry bubble up in her throat, the accomplice reached round, plucked the small silver triangle of the artificial blade from his fake wound and flung it at the magician, who in turn retracted his arm and stared quizzically at the bladeless knife in his right hand, before proudly brandishing the original weapon in his left. He took a lap of honour around the circle, thrusting his arms in the air and exhorting the crowd for deservedly rapturous applause.

Those gathered around roared in appreciation, turning to grasp one another in excited embraces of relieved disbelief, slapping backs and fishing in pockets, before showering the performers in glimmering fistfuls of small rupee coins that flew through the air like iridescent missiles. One landed on her knee. Roshini picked it up and ran her finger round the coin, tracing the smooth edges as they walked slowly back to the station, where they would join the packed train travelling south, churning through the darkened city towards Canning. More than a decade later, she still could not work out how the magician had done it.

Recalling this story as she always did in the days leading up to the festival, little did Roshini know that there would be a killing just three days after Qurbani Eid – vicious rumours causing a sacrifice of an altogether different kind. This would not happen here, but in a different village, in a different state, thousands of kilometres away, an hour outside the capital city of Delhi, where the consumption of beef was legal, but the slaughter of cattle was not.

The home of fifty-two-year-old Mohammed Akhlaq would be

surrounded at night by an angry mob, wielding sticks, bricks and knives. He was accused of stealing a calf and illegally slaughtering it. He was accused of disposing of the animal's head, abandoning the carcass fifty kilometres from the village. He was accused of storing ten kilos of meat in his tiny fridge. All claims, it would later transpire, that were false.

He was asleep when they broke in, dragged him from his home and beat him to death. His son, severely beaten too, would just about survive his injuries. They were the only Muslim family in the area, although they had lived there for more than seventy years. Those responsible had been their neighbours, associates and, in some cases, even friends. This death would begin a pattern of violence across India, of Muslims murdered in extrajudicial killings. They would become known only as 'the lynchings'.

In the village there were many more questions than answers.

Who was responsible? . . . Had they arrested anyone?

Why had an announcement from a nearby temple said that he had slaughtered a calf?

Did he have any beef? Even if he had beef, did this give anyone the right to take a man's life?

Men congregated on the verandahs of the tea shops, rapidly relaying the latest rumours, piecing together the shards of conflicting information, poring over shared newspapers, bellowing angrily for silence when something pertaining to the case was discussed on the hissing, dilapidated portable radio that someone had brought with them from home, speculating on what could happen, worrying about what might not. Like Agni, the Hindu god of fire, women wore their double-faces, a role with which they were wearily familiar: breezy projecting normality in front of the children, while urgently discussing the events with others in impromptu clusters along the paths. After dark, when the children were sleeping, their parents whispered in the lamplight, the warm glow masking the gravity of their words as they made quiet and impossible calculations as to their own security.

Roshini lay awake in the dark. With the happy mood following the celebratory feasting of the previous days punctured, she was once again on her guard.

Thirteen days after the murder of Mohammed Akhlaq, five days after the Prime Minister had finally broken his silence and obliquely called for religious unity across the country while failing to condemn the murder, a man died in the village, and everyone was talking about it. Of the countless jostling variations of a single narrative, certain underlying facts could at least be agreed upon by all nine of the women. The deceased was a young man. He had recently returned to his father's house in the village, where he had spent the last three months of his life. Before that he had been living elsewhere, though not for work, it seemed – something that was itself quite out of the ordinary.

Everyone knew that he had been ill. They had watched him ambling around during the long, hot mornings as they worked, often seeming disorientated. His skin was a sickly shade of yellow, a sign they recognised of a body eating itself from the inside out. It was known that his family had cast their net wide in the vain hope of finding a cure for what was troubling him. They had visited the state-run hospitals, they had visited the private experts in the city, with money scraped together from various begrudging family members. They had seen homeopaths and gnarled medicine men in their haphazard healing rooms. The young man had swallowed palmfuls of pills, drunk blessed water and slept with Quranic verses under his pillow.

None of these measures had been successful in slowing the inevitable march towards death. He had died on a Thursday morning.

The women's stories began to diverge around the matter of his cat.

'It was not a cat,' Nura stated firmly.

'Of course it was a cat!' cried Kalima, shaking her head in exasperation.

'It was much, much too big for a cat, more the size of a dog . . . and it was pure white,' said Nura, raising her eyebrows as she scratched a pattern into the dirt with a twig.

'It was a strange-looking cat, that is for sure, but a cat nonetheless,' demurred Aliya, perplexed as to how people could question something so obvious.

The cat had followed the man everywhere. On the morning he died, once his body was washed and bound in clean white cloth, the wailers gathered and began their mournful song. The women huddled close around the corpse, pouring out their grief into the thick incense-perfumed air, which it was hoped would disguise the smell of putrefying flesh. Their lamentations formed a protective circle around the deceased, one that would hold until the body was carried to the *masjid*. There the funeral prayers would take place, before the deceased was taken to the graveyard to be buried, all of which had to happen before sunset.

It was then that they noticed the cat. It had slunk its way into the circle, through gaps in the cluster of sari-clad legs, and stood just in front of them, as if surveying what had happened. Then it too began to wail.

'Whether it was wailing or not, who can say, but it certainly was making one hell of a noise,' said Sara, quietly appalled at the idea of this strange, shrieking animal.

Then the cat had begun to cry, huge tears falling from its eyes, making shimmering furrows in its silky fur and pooling on the earthen floor.

'Tears? Are cats even able to cry?' scoffed Tabina. Bashira nodded.

'*Chup!* You have no idea what you are talking about,' said Maryam, disgusted that her daughters-in-law could be so sceptical about the divine.

The cat had then walked towards to the body, curled up next to it and died. It had been buried alongside the man.

'It was an angel!' blurted Nura, as though unable to control the words that leapt from her mouth.

'A sign from Allah,' said Roshini, pulling her veil around her shoulders.

'That man was a drunk,' spat Bashira. 'Everybody knows that!'

'That is why he returned home to his father's house. That is why he was ill. That is why he died,' continued Tabina, only half interested, more concerned with the wad of tobacco she was rolling around her palm.

'But what about the cat?' Rani said, puzzled.

'Can't a cat feel love?' asked Aliya. 'It must have died of a broken heart.'

When death and immoral behaviour collided, rumours ignited.

Other strange stories were also circulating, whispering their way down the mud paths in hushed female confidences, slinking to the edges of the brackish ponds where the women hitched up their red and yellow and black saris to scour clean the rattling piles of dirty utensils, muttering softly to one another.

In a village nearby there was a woman who was said to have had improper relations with a man who was not her husband. When he had discovered her infidelity, her husband had hurled violent curses at her, beaten her, threatened to kill her and beseeched God to punish her accordingly. A few days later death had turned up in their house, too.

She was given a quick and frugal burial. There was no wailing, only the quiet sobs of the children, who were too young to understand that one should not mourn those who don't deserve it, and of family members who knew this, but felt their hearts breaking nonetheless. The woman was wrapped briskly in tattered pieces of cloth, thrown unceremoniously in the earth, facing to the west, and covered with the warm red soil. The village did not congregate. No prayers were said. They believed that the fallen woman's shame, like her stiffening body, would now be buried, out of sight.

A startled cry shattered the peace the next morning, calling people from their houses to learn that the woman's body had been dug up. The earth-stained cocoon lay on the ground beside the grave, a greying hand had escaped from the shroud, dirt under the broken fingernails, as though the corpse had dug its own way out of its confinement. She was hastily reburied, her restless cadaver now radiating the filth of a double-taboo: an improper relationship and an improper burial. And yet the next morning her body was there once again.

This happened day after day. The villagers grew increasingly horrified. The men called emergency meetings, and the women said urgent and forceful prayers. Imams and *maulanas* were consulted. All agreed that although they had heard such stories before, none could have predicted that a body of one so sinful would be refused permission by Allah to rot in the grave, paying again and again for its earthly aberrations. The body kept rising to the surface until one morning, in the eerie blush of the first breaths of sunlight, it was torn apart by wild dogs and eaten.

At a time of sacrifice, it was perhaps unsurprising that these rumours swam with such velocity through the village. Stories about the people one lived alongside were in constant circulation, everyone immersing themselves to some degree in the stream of gossip. There were alliances, grievances and confidences spilled. Exchanges were, by necessity, furtive because those under discussion would remain neighbours for ever, and the rumours often served a purpose – as an outlet, an example, a measuring stick. No one was under any illusion that what they were required to do was easy; they would be the first to say that theirs was a hard faith, a religion that, although it imparted huge strength, required a great many sacrifices. They all knew that following the way of God, particularly for a woman, was a fraught and dangerous exercise in which many were bound to fail.

There were rumours about who prayed and who didn't; who claimed to have kept a fast when they had not; who indulged their children, or mistreated their in-laws; and who wore excessive make-up, caring too much about their appearance in a manner not appropriate for a place such as this. There was talk, too, about who owed money, and to whom; who told lies, who stole, who gossiped; who spent too much time outside the village; who dabbled in black magic. There were stories about whose husbands drank, whose beat them, whose failed ever to visit the mosque, whose gambled and committed adultery.

The rumours of the most potent kind were those that, although perhaps unable to be verified, were known to be grounded in truth. These were events that had transpired in the past, things that had caused such destruction and pain they had become almost unspeakable. The stories about what had happened to Aliya's family were of exactly this nature.

She was not alone. The lives of each of the nine women were subject to rumours of one kind or another, some of them more than others.

Bashira was one.

Sara knew all about the rumour surrounding Bashira. She could not say when she had first heard the gossip about the woman who lived just across the road from her, the stern, familiar face from the tea shop. It centred upon a different kind of work that Bashira was believed to perform – another reason why she was always in town, another reason why she had managed to halt the family's slide into poverty.

Some claimed that she rented a small shop above the bazaar, where she went during the long, hot mornings and the sultry afternoons. It was said that men visited her there, and that the performance of unspeakable acts was how she really made her money, not the modest success of the tea stall. It would certainly explain her uncomfortable absences, and why no one wanted to marry her daughter.

Sara did not know if the stories were true although, as with all the worst kinds of gossip, the mere suggestion meant that the damage had already been done. Once or twice when she had returned home from teaching at the school in the neighbouring village, Sara had decided to follow Bashira, flagging a passing autorickshaw or waving down a lift from someone she knew. When she arrived in the bazaar she would pursue Bashira, seeking out her unusually statuesque figure as she moved unhurriedly through the market, eventually losing sight of her at a sharp corner or in the crowd gathered around a particularly popular stall. Sara supposed that she could simply have asked Bashira outright about the rumour. But even Sara – bold, confident and ensconced in a family with significant power – wouldn't dare.

Sara was undoubtedly lonely. As she relaxed into the sagging, half-hearted embrace of her sofa she sought to drown out the grumbled muttering coming from her son Hasan's room, echoes of the fight they had earlier. Arriving home after a long and frustrating day to find him sprawled supine on the cot in his room, his mobile in one hand and an unlit cigarette flicked nonchalantly between the fingers of the other, Sara had dropped her handbag in the doorway and rushed forward to snatch the phone.

'Again? Is this what you have been doing all day? Get up!'

They had fought, as usual, about his laziness and lack of ambition. In the several years since he had finished school with satisfactory, though uninspiring results, Hasan had spoken about starting some kind of business. Fruit and vegetables maybe, or a small shop servicing phones. Yet here he was, sitting in his room again, idle. And if he was not here, Sara knew he would be found in a tea shop, smoking, playing cards, perhaps even drinking, or in one of the fields behind the village, partaking in a ragtag game of cricket with friends.

She had never imagined that her son would be such a disappointment. In truth, her daughter-in-law Parveen had far more to recommend her. Soft-spoken and industrious, she was an excellent mother to Aryan and worked hard at her studies, well on her way to having her own form of coveted government employment as a nurse. She would be taking her exams next year, and provided that she got the necessary grades, they had already put aside a *lakh* – the R100,000 required to bribe the correct people and ensure a job at the end of it. Added to this, Parveen was compliant, yielding where Sara knew she could be hard and inflexible. Although the drab prospects of Hasan hurt, Sara was at least pleased with her choice for his wife.

The power cut out. The village plunged into darkness and the house itself seemed to shift, the groaning generator and TV falling silent. Sitting alone on the threadbare sofa in the dark, Sara felt a creeping claustrophobia, as though the walls she could just about make out were inching towards her, ever closer. Abruptly she stood up, running her right hand along the smooth wall of the living room to guide her to the doorway, the front step, then outside.

It was lighter out here. The sky was a mottled purple, faintly echoing the brilliance of the sun, which, only an hour earlier, had sent vibrant flashes of red and orange across the land. The stars had already begun to adorn the inky expanse and there was the faintest breath of chill in the night air, suggestive of the late autumn days approaching.

Sara dragged one of the red plastic chairs from the outdoor kitchen onto the brick path where she sat, legs extended. After a while she heard the light scuff of a footfall behind her, a tentative hand on her shoulder, and Parveen placed a chipped china plate of sliced cucumber onto her lap. Sara thanked her with a gentle squeeze on the arm, then sat there for some time, enjoying the refreshing tang of the salted vegetable on her tongue and allowing the sounds of the night to cocoon her.

It had been rumours that had driven them to build this house in the first place, rumours that had stoked an unquenchable thirst of greed. It had begun, as so many stories did, with two brothers, a pair whose fates were cleft by their own determination. Their father had divided his land equally between them, his parting wish that they do with it what they wanted. One brother laboured like an ox, working tirelessly, exhausting every hint of opportunity. He hauled his family out of poverty, not stopping until he had accumulated enough wealth and power to be more prosperous than almost any other man in the village. The other brother lazed in the shadows, doing absolutely nothing to improve his lot. He was content to subsist on the crumpled bundles of rupees paid to him by those who rented his land – money that he quickly gambled or drank away in the toddy shops. The first brother was Khan's father, the second was his uncle.

The troubles had started when Khan lost his only brother at just twenty-eight, a devastating blow for the family. Not much time elapsed before his parents too passed away, his father broken-hearted at the death of his favourite son; a few years later, his mother, worn out by grief. Their bones were spared the anonymity of the shared graveyard that lay at the southern edges of the village, instead being buried alongside one another in three neat strikes at the edge of the family's land. Khan was left with his parents' considerable wealth, and the responsibility for three boisterous and demanding sisters.

Things should have remained peaceful, but death had served to remind the wider family who had, and who had not. Rumours started, innocent enough at first, about exactly how much Khan had inherited from his father. Khan's cousins became all of a sudden keenly aware of the little they possessed, how starved their prospects were in comparison. There were five of them, each of them lazy to varying degrees, each of them avaricious and, above all, each of them intently jealous of the money that had been left to Khan by their hard-working uncle. It wasn't long before they began to make trouble.

They started coming by at night. They crept along the side of the house, making a racket outside the bedroom window, loud enough to wake the family with a start, but not so loud as to draw out those who lived nearby. Things began to go missing. These were, after all, houses of earth, bamboo and tin, with exposed courtyards, open verandahs and outdoor kitchens from which items could easily be taken. Sometimes the stolen items would reappear days later, causing Sara and Kahn to doubt themselves, although deep down they knew they were being toyed with. With Khan away at work in the city for long stretches of time, and two young children at home, Sara began to feel scared when they were left alone. The cousins' homestead was just across the clearing, behind the tangle of forest, only striking distance away.

Things had come to a head when their son, still a boy at the time, had been playing by himself in the courtyard. The five men had sloped out from the matted jungle that divided their land and formed a circle around him. They had begun what had at first seemed to be a friendly conversation, but it soon veered into laughingly delivered threats. The boy was only young, and later he would stammer to remember exactly what his uncles had promised to do to him, recalling only the terror of their threats, delivered with artificial smiles.

Khan's response had been swift. There was a piece of land they owned that lay dormant, an overgrown stretch of grass where children from the village played football. On it they had quickly constructed a *pukka* house, firm in its concrete and bricks and its obvious intentions. This was a house that would not be breached, protecting a family that would not be intimidated. Where before the proximity to the main road and neighbouring households had seemed an unwanted inconvenience, now the simmer of traffic and other people's lives were welcome reminders of their closeness. They had found safety in being near others. The walls of the house were thick.

Sara was never sure, but after peace had been restored, she too had heard rumours. She knew her husband's nature, and knew that he would never allow a son of his to be threatened without consequence. Although Khan would never tell her, she believed the stories that he had paid a visit to the five brothers, after which all of the troubles had ceased.

Rising now, Sara walked up the path to the roadside. The traffic had mostly died away, save for the occasional orange beams of a too-fast car and the intermittent brush of bicycles and their riders navigating the road by the moonlight. Across the road she could see that they had lit the stove at the Lohani tea shop; Rani stood behind the counter, silhouetted in the light.

Sara called across, 'Where is your mother?'

'Alipore.'

'Why?'

'They have business up there.'

'What business?'

A pause. 'You'll have to ask her.'

'I suppose I will,' Sara murmured to herself. There were only two things of interest in the faded grandeur of the Kolkata suburb of Alipore to people in a far-away village such as this: a crumbling zoo, home to a sorry collection of dejected, emaciated animals; and the district's courthouse. Sara hazarded a guess that Bashira would have been visiting the latter.

A week or so earlier Sara had been enjoying the slow preparation of some *muri* alongside Parveen, dicing cucumbers and tomatoes, breaking dried lentil sticks into small shards, savouring the comfortable female silence, occasionally punctuated by snippets of conversation. It was early evening, the day slipping away into a soft lilac haze, the road busy with those returning home, and the orchestras of the night beginning their humming preparations. From outside there had been a screech of brakes and then a thud, then an unmistakable rasping shout: Bashira.

Sara had rushed outside to see her neighbour standing in the road, a boy sprawled on the tarmac in front of her, his bicycle lying beside him with the wheels still frantically spinning, as though unaware of their rider-less predicament. She would later learn that Bashira had been waiting for him to return home from school. When she saw him, she strode quickly into the road and, with a single thrust of her powerful arm, knocked him clean off his bicycle, splaying him across the tarmac, to shouts of dismay from his school friends who skidded to a stop, and to shocked gasps from the women and children queuing for the water pump nearby.

'You! Get up!' Bashira yelled, towering over him. 'Do you know who I am? Are you so tough now? To be saying things like that to my daughter? I should clean your filthy mouth out!'

Those who had gathered to watch shook their heads in disgust, appalled to see a grown woman behaving in such way in public, but intrigued as to why she was so angry, and possibly a little satisfied to see a young troublemaker get what he deserved.

'If you ever speak to her again, I'll do worse than knock you off your bike! Hey! Do you hear me?'

Tabina, behind her, gently pulled Bashira back towards the tea stall.

'Okay, it's done now. Let's go.'

'Nothing is done! He should be ashamed of himself! Stupid, irresponsible boy.'

No one could be sure what the boy had said to Bashira's daughter, Rubina, at school that day to provoke such a violent reaction. After all, Rubina was a troublesome girl, headstrong and fiery, exactly like her mother. And, like her mother, she was someone around whom rumours lingered. Sara guessed, like many others who had witnessed what had happened, that the boy had probably called Rubina a whore.

Chapter Six

The Matchmaker

At last it was October and a beloved daughter was once again return-ing home. On the sixth day of Navaratri – the nine nights celebrated all over India in which good triumphs over evil – she would make her way down from the snow-capped peaks of the Himalayas, whose name in Sanskrit underscores their status as a dwelling place of the divine, an otherworldly house of snow. Leaving behind her husband, Shiva, in their mountain abode, she would descend into hundreds of thousands of temporary households erected specially in her honour. Once there, she would take her place astride a lion, surrounded by her four celestial children, her smile serene, her ten arms outstretched, brandishing ten different glinting weapons.

The homecoming of the goddess Durga would be joyous: prayers recited, gifts and sweets exchanged, a myriad of favourite foods pre-pared in quite frankly unnecessary quantities and shared at the long-anticipated reunions of family and friends. The air would be thick with incense, heady with the scent of an abundance of roses, jasmine and carnations, draped in luscious garlands over the necks of the divine visitors and carpeting the earth with fragrant petals strewn at their feet. There would be laughter, and new clothes, and gossip, and staying up too late, and music, and the singing of the old songs, and dancing, and the beginning of romances. Tears of joy would be followed by those of sadness at the prospect of parting.

Evil defeated, the world saved, on the tenth day Durga's visit would be over and the goddess would once again depart, making her way back to the mountains, where she would remain for another year. She would leave behind bereft, weeping women calling out to her the familiar Bengali farewell, *'abar asbe!'* – 'come again!' – their faces smeared with the red of *sindoor*, embodying their wish for a marriage as happy and fulfilling as her own. Though a daughter, Durga was also a mother, and children desperate for a final touch of her feet or the delicate curve of her face would scuffle anxiously alongside her. With the solemn sound of drums, the staggering multitude of her temporary bodies would be hoisted onto men's shoulders and taken to the water's edges, where they would be submerged in the Hooghly, the Ganga, the Yamuna, the Arabian Sea or the Bay of Bengal, sinking slowly beneath the surface, out of sight.

On the island the goddess was also anticipated. Her arrival would prompt an influx of many visitors, those wishing to make the most of the extravagant stretch of nineteen days of public holiday, leaving behind their towns, cities and even other states to take overcrowded trains, buses and rickshaws to the dusty villages and eager families they had left behind. The island itself would transform, with scores of temporary structures dotting the landscape, their twinkling lights calling out to those brave or foolish enough to navigate the treacherous roads by night. Behind the flimsy bamboo walls and shabbily curtained entrances, figures of goddesses and gods sat proudly, encompassed by the smoke of smouldering incense, awaiting their human visitors, and their offerings.

During the days of the festival, Rani found herself on the cusp of enjoyment, still just young enough to be enchanted by the holiday. Although Durga was a Hindu goddess, and thus not a part of her own religious life or beliefs, Rani nonetheless found her a worthy focus for admiration, given her reputation for extraordinary strength and bravery. She was equally thrilled at visiting the *pandals* at night in her uncle's rickshaw – the marquees that impressed with their elaborate decorations, and the speed with which they appeared and then vanished. Rani appreciated the rare opportunity to stray beyond the boundaries of the village after dark; once night fell, a woman's place was at home, safe from the danger of violence and the danger of supposition. Though childish enough to be restlessly excited for days before the promised excursion took place, she was well past the age when, for girls at least, night had become the enemy.

On the evening of the outing, Rani, her sister Rubina, Sara's daughter Nadia and a clutch of other girls and their appropriate chaperones crammed into the rickshaw and set off down the darkened road. The pulse of music throbbed through the evening, blasted too loudly from outdated speakers that crackled under the strain. Crowds milled around outside the entrances to the *pandals*, waiting for their turn to enter whilst being accosted by eager vendors selling balloons and cold drinks and *pani puri*, whom they either gratefully welcomed into their midst or dismissed with an abrupt wave of a hand.

Inside were the collections of beautifully crafted statues, always of Durga, but also of other gods and goddesses. Some were arranged in daring tableaux, while others sat simply, garlanded, with space for alms to be placed at their feet. The elderly regarded this year's idols with a weary scepticism, unable to prevent themselves from recalling the superior creations of previous *pujos*. Clusters of girls giggled and shoved one another playfully, before posing austerely for unsmiling photographs in front of the divine, whose fixed, painted eyes reflected their naïve, yet somehow defiant stares. In the days to come, Rani knew that these deities would also meet a watery end, deposited in the turgid waters surrounding the island where crocodiles and sharks lurked, and on whose banks not too long ago a crab fisherman had been taken by a tiger.

The days of the festival had served as a welcome respite from the tensions in Rani's household, where a beloved, though recalcitrant daughter was causing trouble. Her older sister Rubina had once again started to disappear from school, riding her bicycle to the deserted fields between villages, where Rani imagined her texting furiously on her tiny phone whilst smoking the cigarettes she had seen Rubina sneaking from the shelf at the back of the tea shop. Rani hated her sister's absences, and the burden they placed upon her. When she came home without her sister, she tripped over her mumbled attempts to evade the questions as to why they were not together, citing different classes and missed encounters in the bustle of the end of another school day.

When Rubina's truancy was inevitably discovered, Bashira had dragged her into the courtyard at the centre of their homestead, seething with shouted threats to finally beat some sense into her. Rubina, defiant, had shouted back. With a yelp of triumph she had managed to wriggle free from her mother's bruising grip and jump on her bike, pedalling furiously down the path away from the village and returning only once it was dusk. Even she knew better than to stay out after dark.

Their home felt restless, as it had done before. In the evenings Rani found herself consigned to one of the interior rooms with Rubina, their sister-in-law Mira and her two small children, whilst urgent late-night conversations took place between her parents, her elder brother Faraq, and Tabina and her husband, all observed in watchful silence by her grandmother Maryam. Rubina would sit sullenly in a corner of the room, refusing Rani's whispered attempts to draw her out of herself, building up the invisible fences between them that, after the last time Rubina had been in trouble, had taken so long to dismantle.

There were things that Rani knew, things that she did not know and many things that she knew but was not supposed to know. What was certain, once again, was that Rubina needed to be found a husband.

Though the legal age for marriage was eighteen, the sad reality was that girls could simply not be trusted. Marriage was many things for a girl's family: a significant and frequently financially ruinous expenditure, a worrisome negotiation and the inevitable loss of a daughter, who would be for ever transplanted into a new household in a different village, often hours and hours away. It was also a preventative strategy, an action to take before their daughters had the opportunity to damage their future prospects.

All the families of young women were terrified of love. Parents fretted that their girls would go to school and fall in love with just about anyone, disregarding the crucial strictures of caste, class or even, in some cases, religion, dishonouring their parents and their hard-earned right to choose who they would marry. Without the option of single-sex education, girls in the village were often withdrawn from school before tragedy could strike, despite their tearful protestations that they were there to study and nothing else. Had an alternative existed, like the private single-sex schools found in the city, those in the village would have been unable to afford it anyway.

Even the girls whose days had been confined to the duties of sewing and housework while they awaited an inevitable match were not immune to risk. Rani knew of several 'wrong-number romances' that had flourished in the village, in which girls had struck up telephone relationships with men they had never actually met. Across the road from her house, down towards the rundown village school, lived a family where a girl had been promised to a boy only the week before. Little did her parents know that her devastation at the match was not due to the chasteness of youth, or their poor choice of husband, but because she was in love with a boy who worked in a bag factory in Kerala. He had dialled her number by chance sometime last spring, yearning to hear softly-spoken Bangla from an imagined pair of lips pressed close against the phone. Another couple from a different village on the island, who had met at the local high school, had just eloped to Bombay, arriving in that hulking metropolis with no one but each other, and nothing but their love, at seventeen years old.

There was a defiant bravery but inevitable hardship for those who fought for love. Rani knew as well as anyone that Kalima's dislike for her daughter-in-law Roshini stemmed from the fact that hers had been a love-marriage. Even Rani's own sister-in-law Mira, the quiet and docile girl whose babies were unable to anchor themselves in the moorings of her womb, had made a love-marriage to Faraq. Bashira had surprised them all by eventually giving her blessing, although grudgingly, seeing in her son's choice the qualities that she herself would have approved. Although Mira may not have been perfect, Bashira understood there was little to be done when two people saw one another and fell in love.

This fraught inevitability was why Rani had no interest in marriage. She pretended to ignore Tabina's smirking digs regarding the time when it would be her turn, her blushes betraying both her shyness and her discomfort. Instead she remained determined to become a police officer, asking permission from her father every night to go and watch television at Sara's house across the road, where she would beg the family to turn off the WWE wrestling matches and instead watch any detective shows that happened to be on. This was also why she had begun, at just fourteen, to take on her own sewing and embroidering work, saving each crumpled rupee note and wanting – needing – more.

Like Rani, Aliya also disapproved of girls being married underage. She was disgusted by families who married off their daughters too young, whilst also understanding that for many parents, caught in the trap of poverty, it was an easy way to offload some of their burden. As the eldest of nine siblings, Aliya knew that in her case her parents had simply had no other choice, although this did not lessen the ache she still felt after so many years that she had been plucked from the studies that she was excelling in and married off to her husband at fourteen. Selfishly, parents freed themselves from a significant spring of worry, able to sleep better, safe in the knowledge that the money had been saved or borrowed, the exorbitant dowries had been paid and their most precious possessions would be taken care of. Or, if not taken care of, then at least no longer able to be disgraced or defiled.

Aliya's daughter Amal had been spared that fate. She was eighteen and in the midst of finishing Class 12, with various important exams fast approaching, for which she studied diligently, when not required to help with the sewing work that was the family's only regular income. Often Aliya would glance at her daughter, painstakingly threading slippery beads onto a needle although her mind was so clearly on something else, and gently tell her to go and study, knowing that her leniency would mean a long night of work with only shadows and spools of thread for company. Amal was desperate to continue her education after high school, nurturing plans for college, where she would study Bangla, art, maybe even philosophy. As she amicably, yet forcefully, petitioned her mother daily with this dream, Aliya could not help but smile. Where she would scrape together the money to realise her daughter's desires, she did not know.

Often neighbours would sidle up to the verandah where Aliya was sewing, their faces fixed in masks of breezy concern, slick with their faux-camaraderie.

'*Didi*, how are things? How are Amal's studies going? Eighteen now . . . almost too old to be married! You should think about it soon, *na*? Weddings are expensive, and everything with her father . . .'

A gesture to the room in which Kabir was lying, prone on the cot.

'But then for you there will be one less mouth to feed . . .'

'It is not our way,' Aliya would say firmly, holding with a steely gaze whoever had served up their unsolicited opinion. She was determined to make a new tradition for her family, one that she would also generously assign to her husband. *Our* way.

Aliya had no problem being different. Over the past seven years she had made many decisions that others questioned or struggled to understand. Though she undoubtedly did things her own way, what they could not fault was her tenacity, or the unflappable manner in which she just got on with it. Aliya was a navigator, always observing the behaviour of those around her, weighing it up in her mind before plotting her own course of action. She did not gossip, she had no time for the cruel and speculative dissection of the lives of others, but she learned. She knew better than anyone that although her family had once been fortunate and comfortable, the path they were now walking had narrowed. She could not afford a misstep.

Kalima's family served as a significant source of caution. The hasty marriage of her second daughter to a deeply unsuitable man from the city had resulted in a terrible, ongoing fallout. After several years the marriage had begun to break down. He had been an alcoholic. He had also been violent. With Kalima's support and that of his disappointed though agreeable family, her daughter had divorced him and returned with her own daughter, Iffat, to live in the village in her mother's home.

If an unmarried daughter was a worry, then a divorced one was an even greater concern. With difficulty, Kalima had managed to arrange another match for her, to a strange and pious man, a *maulana* who lived in Murshidabad, long hours away from any potential gossip or insinuations regarding her daughter's previous wifely incarnation. To this end, however, there was a single condition, and a not-uncommon one. Her daughter from her first marriage must be left behind. Aliya had always taken pity on the sad, hunted-looking little girl who was cared for roughly though lovingly by Kalima, hundreds of kilometres away from her own mother.

Perhaps the greatest struggle for the parents of daughters was the dowry. Although the demand for a dowry had been illegal in India since 1961 – the idealistic step of an independent, secular government determined to bring about gender equality – it remained an insidiously ubiquitous practice. In truth, it was not even a Muslim custom, but a Hindu one. But the allure of extravagant sums of money for the families of boys had been too great to resist and, step-by-step, the demand of a dowry had now become unavoidable.

'*Meyera khub dami!*' the imam of the smaller mosque would smilingly lament, watching his young daughters play with one another in the shade of the courtyard. It was a familiar complaint, one uttered by all the parents of the village who were unlucky enough to have been blessed with a daughter, sometimes even two or three; or, in the case of the elderly madrasa teacher, seven – the kind of misfortune that would have made a different kind of man lose his faith in God. Girls were very expensive.

It was unclear how the exact figure for a dowry was agreed upon; it was one of those unspoken, inscrutable alchemies that possessed significant consequences. The generally accepted amount on the island was currently around a *lakh*, or R100,000. Sometimes paid partly in cash, more often than not it was composed from a list of scrupulously considered demands from the boy's family: a glass-fronted cupboard, cooking utensils, a gas stove, a new cot bed, blankets, plastic chairs and crockery that would inevitably be locked away and never used. There would be saris and jewellery for the female members of the household, watches, gold chains and made-to-measure clothes for the men. In richer families the demands were even more extravagant – items such as fridges, TV sets, bicycles and motorbikes. For those who dwelled in the shadows of poverty, a dowry was an ardently awaited windfall.

Aliya was grateful that only two of her six children were girls. Amal's older sister had been married at nineteen with little fuss, two years before. Aliya had arranged the match herself, prioritising the dual qualities of intelligence and kindness – those that she found to be the most important in people – when searching for a potential suitor.

After consulting her relatives, she had managed to find someone informally studying the practices of nursing and medicine in a town almost two hours away, who after a couple of years had managed to land a respectable job in a nursing home. His family had been flexible, understanding of their financial circumstances and had compromised on the dowry. Now there was just Amal to pay for.

Finding a wife for her son had involved considerations of a different kind. He worked outside the village in the town of Diamond Harbour, three bumpy hours away on broken, back roads, and returned home infrequently and only when his job permitted it. This meant that his wife was more often than not seated beside Aliya at the sewing frame, and was thus more her responsibility than her son's. Yes, there had been some silliness to start with, but once they had smoothed out these early rumples they had enjoyed a warm and uncomplicated relationship. Now Aliya longed for a grandchild, teasing her daughter-in-law that surely it was time for another little one to join their household.

On those empty days following the wild celebrations of *Durga pujo*, another visitor arrived in the village. A tall man sat on the wooden bench in front of the Lohani-family tea shop, rolling a cracked earthen cup between his palms. He had sought out the most comfortable spot, his back resting against the perpendicular beam supporting the tin roof, his long legs outstretched. Along with a short-sleeved brown shirt and pair of pressed though faded blue trousers, he wore the calm sense of impermanence of someone who was used to being a stranger. The man was a matchmaker and he was here for Rubina.

On the floor beneath the bench he had placed a small leather satchel and a worn briefcase. These two unassuming bags carried all that he required for his life on the road: the former, a couple of personal essentials for overnight stays; the latter, his files. The man was from a place on the next island down, although he would confess with a sad smile that he spent little time at home. Instead he had spent the last thirty years on the road, moving from village to village, town to town, on the lookout for girls who needed to be married.

He had begun life as a builder, a profession in which he had enjoyed a similarly itinerant existence, rejecting a place in the crush of other day-labourers clustered on misty roadsides each morning anxious to be picked for work, and instead choosing to go from house to house, enquiring about small jobs or repairs that needed doing there or elsewhere in the area. Unwittingly he had begun to weave a web of intricate relationships of exactly the kind necessary to begin his new undertaking. In his long and fruitful second career, which had seen him travel thousands of kilometres, as far away as Uttar Pradesh even, he had successfully found more than 3,000 girls a husband.

The *ghatak*, as he was known, had a kind face, which concealed a strong sense of what was acceptable in this game and what was not. He would not arrange marriages for any girls that he deemed 'not good', such as those who had enjoyed romantic relationships with others in the past. He would not suggest partnerships in which there was an imbalance, having worked hard over time to hone the skills required to produce good and long-lasting matches, in which appearance, education, skills, circumstances and background were all given their own invisible though precise weighting. He would not take risks; his professional reputation depended on it.

That evening he planned to stay with a relative nearby, before travelling onwards in the morning to Canning, to Metiabruz and, after that, who could say? He would accept requests for visits, though sometimes other opportunities presented themselves, tugging him in a different direction. His mind cradled the complicated network of longing, supported by the pages and pages of notes and photographs that he kept with him at all times, the paper renderings of matrimonial desire. To engage his services, the *ghatak* asked the girls' families for R300 up front. This was to cover the costs of his time on the road, travel, food, occasionally accommodation, in pursuit of what all hoped would be a suitable match.

He placed his earthen cup on the bench and, retrieving his bags, made his way down the path beside the tea shop to the Lohani family compound at the back. In the courtyard that lay in the centre of the crumbling, earthen buildings stood four plastic chairs placed in a line. On them sat a boy, his brother-in-law, a friend and the last one was taken by the *ghatak*. The boy was handsome, assured, and as his companions chatted amiably to each other, his eyes roamed around the clearing, absorbing the surroundings.

Inside one of the cramped rooms of the main house Rubina stood in the centre of the floor, her appearance reminiscent of a scrappy decoration. Her gauzy synthetic sari in bright red, yellow and green was the focus of Tabina and Mira's attention; they adjusted her blouse and carefully refolded the pleats of the sari before leaning backwards to take an appraising look at their handiwork. Rubina shifted uncomfortably from foot to foot, arms stretched out awkwardly from her sides as she received thrusts of bangles from her aunt. Bashira, deadpan, scraped her daughter's frizzy hair away from her face into an unfamiliarly severe knot at the nape of her neck. On the bed Mira's seven-year-old daughter stood rearranging her own outfit and admiring her reflection in the cracked mirror that hung on the mud wall next to an out-of-date calendar. Beside her, Rani was staring down at her nervously twisting fingers.

In the courtyard Faraq appeared, bearing a wobbling tray of cups of *cha* for the guests, accompanied by two plates of broken biscuits, their sugar crystals glinting in the last rays of the afternoon sun. Next Bashira came out from the house to check things were progressing smoothly, fixed a smile to her face and, in unfamiliarly soft tones, beseeched the boy to come away from his companions. On the other side of the clearing they spoke in hushed voices, her forced playfulness hiding her impatience as she tried to find out more about the man to whom she might marry her daughter. The boy was composed, possessing an ease of movement that suggested a laid-back disposition, and his blue-and-black checked shirt was smart, though not overly so for such relaxed and casual surroundings. From a sly peek through the window, Tabina pronounced him very attractive, to the stifled snickers and playful pushes of those inside.

Finally Rubina emerged. Her face was mostly concealed by the sari that her mother had carefully positioned over her shoulders. She stepped slowly, awkward in the unfamiliar garment, her eyes on her shuffling feet, a white plate of delicately folded packages of *paan* gripped between her palms. She was followed outside by the older women, Tabina pushing Rubina gently into the chair opposite the boy, whilst Mira took the plate from her lap, placing it on the floor in front of the line of chairs. The plate was picked up by the *ghatak* and offered amongst the men, before being returned to the floor. There was a pause, and then the questions began.

Her name?

What did her father do?

What school did she go to?

What grade is she in?

Could she cook?

Did she pray?

To each query Rubina blurted out a short reply: Rubina; rickshaw-wallah; in town, Class 10; yes; yes. Bashira, standing behind her, would frequently provide addendums to these staccato answers, a frustrated artist adorning the simplest sketches with colour and shade. Later, once the boy had left and before the crucial discussions took place, Tabina would have the whole family in stitches with her impersonation of Rubina, the answers darting from her mouth like bullets, all the while seated so precariously at the edge of her chair that she looked as if she might leap up and run away at any minute.

Once the questions had trickled to a stop, the men conferred in hushed tones. Seemingly satisfied with her answers, the boy stood up and crossed the dusty courtyard. He reached a hand into his pocket and presented Rubina with a small roll of rupee notes, as was customary, dropping it into her cupped palms, taking the greatest care that their fingers did not touch. Placing her hands against her chest and inclining her head slightly in gratitude, Rubina rose from her chair, before turning and making her way back inside the house. Her eyes had not left the floor once.

Her departure marked a notable lightening in the atmosphere. The boy's brother-in-law and Bashira began conversing quietly whilst leafing through the crumpled Kodak packets of photographs that she had been holding in her hands, some from the photo booth in the nearby town, others from Mira and Faraq's wedding day: stern likenesses of the girl he had briefly encountered. Bashira was careful to underscore her daughter's best attributes – her fairness in one image, or the poise with which she carried her niece in another, evidence no doubt of the beautiful wife and caring mother she could become.

All the while her husband, Ali Tariq, was strangely quiet, standing at the edge of the clearing, occasionally absenting himself to check if there was a customer waiting at the tea shop. He was perhaps reserving his judgement for later that night when, by lamplight, the elder members of the family would gather and come to a decision about the boy.

Both during the afternoon meeting and into the evening discussions, Maryam shrewdly observed the events surrounding her granddaughter. Her age meant that her views no longer carried much weight in the fray of family politics and, although she was content to offer up an opinion whether asked or not, her words fell like seeds on stony ground. She had long ago lost patience with her granddaughter, snapping at Bashira each time there was a further mishap for allowing her daughter to grow up as she had, for failing her as a mother. Although Rubina had undoubtedly besmirched her own name, the flaws of her family were a further stone around her neck: Faraq's accident, Ali Tariq's drink-driving ban, the rumours about Bashira's absences from the village. Although they all assumed that Maryam was too old or too naïve to know the things people said about her daughter-in-law, they were wrong; Maryam witnessed everything.

She had watched Bashira and could tell that she liked the boy, from the bubbling enthusiasm that she failed to hide in her normally harsh voice, to the feeble wings of hope beating once again behind her eyes. She also knew that there was no way her son and his wife could afford the boy's family's demands for the dowry, which she had heard included a large cot bed and mattress, gold rings and a sizeable sum of money. On the few occasions Maryam did interject, it had been to stress her own sadness that she could not help them financially. She was well aware of her daughter-in-law's muttered protestations that Maryam was secretly sitting on money, bundles sewn into her mattress or hidden away somewhere – she who now owned only two worn-out saris, and who still foraged in the jungle that surrounded the village to help supplement her meagre meals in the home of Tabina and her husband.

As the chill of night began to encircle the clearing, Maryam retreated from the discussions, making her way falteringly towards the worn steps that led to her tiny single room. Beneath the old storehouse that was now her home, squinting into the darkness, she could just about make out the feathered gleam of her two alabaster ducks, their necks wrapped around themselves as though to embrace their own warm bodies. There had been chickens too before, but they had died – poisoned, she suspected, though by whom she was both too bitter and too wily to say.

Placing her stick on each step, Maryam began to climb in a shuffling hop. At the top she fumbled with the knot of rope that she used to hold her flimsy door closed during the day, looping it over the wooden hook. The warmth of the pent-up air swept past her, as though expelled by the hut in a peaceful sigh. She stooped to find the gas lamp and struggled to light the flame. In the gentle glow that at last illuminated her room, Maryam leaned her stick in one corner and jerked the door shut. She placed a hand against the smooth earthen wall and slowly lowered herself to the floor, extending her legs, groaning with pleasure as her feet were finally able to rest.

It had been decades since her own wedding, though Maryam still recalled with a smile what her father had requested as a dowry for her; things had been far more straightforward back then. For a start, it was the family of the bride, as opposed to the groom, who were able to make requests of the other party, and they had lacked the greed and perhaps the imagination to make the kind of lavish demands that people did today. Her father's request had been simple: ten kilos of *sondesh* sweets to be delivered to the family when they came for the ceremony, to be distributed amongst the guests at the wedding party over the following days.

When her future husband and his male relatives arrived on the eve of the wedding, it became apparent that they had arrived empty-handed. Where were the *sondesh*? her father had asked, unable to keep the tremor of expectation from his voice.

The visitors began by claiming that all of the *mishti* in the small local bazaar on the island had already been sold. This was not altogether unimaginable; the island was very remote after all, but her father was not convinced. Surely they must have been able to purchase something?

The visitors exchanged glances. They went on to concede that yes, there had been some *mishti*, which they had been fortunate enough to purchase. However, when they were crossing the first river, chugging their way up slowly from the islands, the boat had jolted and the package went overboard, lost to the swirling depths, providing only a sweet offering to those that lurked beneath.

Maryam's father remained sceptical. What he suspected (and it would later transpire to be the truth) was that on the long journey spanning some fourteen hours the visitors had grown hungry. As the hours ticked by, he felt certain that they had either eaten the sweets or bartered them, in desperation for some water or a meal. Appraising the exhausted visitors with a scrutinising gaze, he was almost sure he could detect the faintest dusting of white crumbs in the beards and on the tunics of those who now sat, deflated, in front of him.

Having explained themselves, and finding the normal prompt and generous offerings of a host to be absent, the visitors eventually asked whether it might be possible for *cha* to be brought, to slake the thirst they had accumulated over the long hours of travel. Maryam's father had simply raised an eyebrow and said, 'Oh, sorry. We don't drink tea here!'

Maryam's eyes watered at the memory: her amusement at her father's irreverent nature, which still tickled her so many years later; and the hint of residual sadness of a well-worn loss, in spite of the fact that her father was now long dead. He had never let her husband forget their inauspicious start, teasing him whenever they met about where he might have hidden the *mishti* on that particular occasion. In the shadows, Maryam reflected that her life was now – like her father's – almost over. It occurred to her that this was something she did not mind. In the courtyard below, the murmuring continued. She blew out the lamp.

Chapter Seven

Years Past

Bashira sat on a low wooden stool with her back against the wall of the tea shop. She closed her eyes and rested her head against the exposed brickwork, strands of her coarse dark hair catching on its roughened contours. She allowed herself a few moments of respite from the chaos around her, and from the impending confrontation that she felt in the twist of her stomach was coming. She knew that one could not outrun the past. Sighing, sated, she rubbed a firm palm across her face and returned her focus to the papers once again.

Sheafs and sheafs of pages were spread out before her, a loose sheet occasionally escaping the ordered stacks and drifting onto the floor as she riffled urgently through the piles. Like so many women in the village, Bashira was barely able to read, particularly when the language was the strange and unfamiliar English, but she had devised a system to get around this. She looked for dates, as numbers were something she could easily recognise, and studied the stamps that graced official documents: blue for the police, purple for the courts.

'*Didi! Cha hobe?*' someone called from beyond the counter.

'What do you think!' she snarled, shifting on the stool and craning her neck to see who had interrupted her. 'Can't you see I'm busy? Come back in fifteen minutes.'

Bashira looked down at her hands, flipping them over to seek comfort in the familiar cup of her palms. Snaking lines ran brown across the faded cream, like muddy rivers hacking through fields. She had always been awkwardly conscious of her hands – not that she would ever have said anything to anyone about it. She had learned to conceal all signs of weakness, tamping down any fragility like soil in the gardens that she had been forced to work in, from as soon as she could walk. Her hands felt cumbersome somehow, masculine, as though they didn't quite belong to her own body. She deliberately grew her nails long to counter this, filing them into ovals that pointed defiantly over the tips of her fingers, the juice from the *paan* that she chewed staining them a faded red.

There were many things that Bashira despised; it was easier to single out what she did like, as opposed to what she did not: the kick of *paan* as she ground the nut between her back teeth; an excellent story; the achievement of intimidating a pathetic bureaucrat into doing exactly what she wanted – these were some of the few things that gave her true enjoyment. Like all mothers, she also took great pride in the triumphs of her offspring, though in recent times there had been scant opportunity. Today held no such possibilities. Instead it promised two of her most hated dislikes: criticism of her family, and submission to others.

Although she had a sense of what the day would hold, Bashira could not quite yet conjure the sensation of what it would be like to experience it; to travel to the house of strangers and present one's past to be pored over and intimately examined. They had arranged it that way this time, in an attempt to prevent the scandal escaping before they had the chance to explain. The reliving of painful revelations in a public setting over which the family had no control was something she had failed to anticipate properly, though she had bitterly learned to tolerate the shame and disgrace that would be dredged to the surface once again.

She was not sure she had found what she wanted in the papers, and if she had, they were after all such flimsy crutches. It hardly mattered, she could not help but think to herself as she began to tidy the pages away, because she would have given little credence to the opaque references of such staid bureaucratic documents, were she the mother of a boy looking for a wife.

The uncle of the first boy whom the *ghatak* had proposed for Rubina had rejected the match outright. Bashira suspected that he had asked around and had heard the stories about her daughter, needing little time to excavate something of such irreparable damage. Whatever he had found had prompted an immediate withdrawal, the reflexive snatch of a hand away from something that might burn. Thus the boy who had visited their home a few weeks before – the coolly confident boy in the blue-and-black checked shirt on whom she had stupidly pinned her hopes – would not even consider her daughter.

Today's meeting was, therefore, a different proposition. They had been forced to try again. This new boy was far less educated, a day-labourer with infrequent work, and the family was significantly poorer, although the matchmaker had suggested that such limitations might make them more willing to overlook other things. He knew the situation of course, or the version of events they had told him, the whole truth being known only to a handful amongst the family, burrowed, hidden further within.

Ali Tariq peered round the door to the tea shop. When he caught sight of his wife seated low to the floor amidst the piles of papers, his eyes were pitiful, his expression more an apology than a smile.

'*Cholo*,' he said quietly. 'Let's go.' Bashira heaved herself up, clasping a single sheaf of papers under one arm, smoothing down her hair and glancing quickly in the blackened mirror that hung on the back wall of the shop. She straightened her *bindi* and flicked away the kohl that had begun to creep into the lines around her eyes.

'*Cholo*,' she replied; they were ready.

The boat was waiting at the *ghat*, bobbing gently in the swirling brown waters when the autorickshaw pulled up. Ali Tariq stepped out, lit a cigarette and strolled round to the driver's side to confer with his brother. He was followed by the matchmaker, Bashira, Faraq and his small daughter, who leapt from the vehicle and rushed to hold her grandmother's hand. Bashira led the way towards the boat and shouted a greeting to the boatman, a lean shadow in his faded yellow short-sleeved shirt. An explosion of laughter followed their quick and incomprehensible exchange. She turned, encouraging the others to step carefully into the pitching vessel, paying particular attention to her granddaughter. The little girl hopped in, worming her way through battered fuel cans and coiled lengths of rope to a desirable seat near the bow.

As the launch slipped away from the bank, the engine began to grumble, spewing black diesel fumes into the air, which was already shimmering with the heat. The sun was rising steadily towards its highest point, blazing onto the murky water, flattening its surface and causing the reflections of the passengers to bounce and warp. The boatman was relaxed, though clearly concentrating; the channels that ran between the islands were famously duplicitous, shallow silt banks stretching far out into the open water or occasionally manifesting themselves as treacherous punctuation marks in the middle of fast-flowing currents that could pitch those unfamiliar with them into danger.

At the other side, the group disembarked. Ali Tariq lingered behind on the flimsy wooden jetty to arrange a time for the boatman to collect them later on. Up the mud bank waited another vehicle, its driver distantly related to Bashira, who greeted him with a hoarse shout of familiarity, '*Oh!*', her face breaking into an easy smile. They began the gentle chatter of extended family members whose numerous connections always allowed for relaxed and inconsequential conversation.

'And how are you? How long has it been?'

'Too long, as always! We are well, thank you, *didi*. And you?'

'Oh, you know, can't complain. Tell me, has your eldest daughter married now?'

'Last winter, and now a child is coming.'

'Wonderful! And the rest? How is your uncle? The one who was unwell.'

The driver sat astride an ancient red motorcycle that had a wooden cart for passengers attached to the back, onto which the group now clambered. Ali Tariq paused to make his own greeting, before saying pointedly, 'We don't want to be late for them.'

The driver agreed, gesturing to Bashira with a backwards tilt of his head that she could sit on the edge of the platform, so they would be able to continue their conversation. Once she had hoisted herself up and rearranged her sari, they jolted off, bouncing down the brick paths and winding away from the water.

It was a smaller, more peaceful settlement than their own village. The houses were arranged more generously, the spaces between them like grateful inhalations, allowing perhaps, Bashira thought, for some semblance of privacy. They caught glimpses of the inhabitants who were at home – women engrossed in sweeping courtyards or sieving palmfuls of grain, who, as they sensed the eyes of visitors on the backs of their necks, stopped what they were doing, turned round and stared back.

Towards the end of the path was an earthen compound, baked pale and brittle by the absence of shade, surrounded for the most part by wheat fields whose stalks nodded knowingly in the lunchtime breeze. In the open courtyard flanked by several low-slung buildings, the visitors could see that plastic chairs had been arranged in a circle, with a heavy wooden bench set alongside them to offer some additional seating for the large group that would be in attendance. As the driver led them confidently towards the clearing, a small boy darted out from one of the inner rooms, skipping onto the path before spinning on his heel and rushing back, calling out, '*Baba!* They have come!'

The parties assembled awkwardly, shyness and formality stiffening their movements and making them strange even to themselves. A young woman in a rich *begun*-coloured sari stepped forward, nervously twisting the bangles that circled her plump wrists, and in a voice that burbled like a stream rushing over her words, anxiously beseeched the visitors to *please sit*. They had come such a long way in such hot weather, after all. The driver, bathed in the confidence of one with mutual connections and the least to lose, was the first to amble over to one of the chairs, kicking off his sandals and, with a sigh, stretching out his arms and legs to ease the knots in his limbs. Slowly the others followed, finding places around the circle.

On the left-hand side of the courtyard entrance was an outdoor kitchen, where pots rattled above a blazing fire, and where three women, including one who would transpire to be the boy's mother, sweated and fussed over the final preparations for lunch. Shortly, an old pink-and-green sari blackened from cooking smoke would be drawn across between the earthen walls to protect the cooks from the glare of the sun, a makeshift screen that enabled them to perform the graceless tasks of hefting heavy saucepans or splashing pungent gravies onto plates, unencumbered by the watchful eyes of strangers. Straight ahead was the main dwelling, where before long glasses of cloudy *mishti jol* were brought out for the guests by another young woman in a sari the colour of crushed marigolds. Drinks distributed, she quickly doubled back to the house, before emerging once again with tin bowls of crisps and stale *aloo bhuja*.

Names were not exchanged; all those present understood the invisible codes and conventions by which people could be so easily identified. The boy himself was absent. His two married elder sisters hovered over the visitors whilst casting anxious glances towards the doorway of the building behind them, flexing their newfound roles as the orchestrators of such events, as opposed to the forlorn and subservient puppets. Their husbands were seated on the opposite side of the circle from the Lohanis, along with the boy's father and a couple of young men who, the matchmaker explained, were the boy's friends from the village.

Eventually, after some more time in which the conversation dwindled to a choked and self-conscious silence, the boy sloped out from an inner room. He was a tall, gentle-looking young man, sporting a black-and-red polo shirt in a shiny synthetic material, his eyes determinedly fixed on the floor in front of him. He walked towards the group with his head down, the plate of *paan* that he was carrying nervously thrust with a murmured '*Salaam alaikum*' into the hands of Ali Tariq, who in turn gracefully received it with a nod, responding, '*Alaikum assalaam*', before offering the plate amongst the other visitors. Once the boy was seated, the driver caught Bashira's eye and, with an almost imperceptible nod, the questioning began.

There was the air of a badly rehearsed play; the actions known, tightly scripted, though performed under the guise of a laboured unfamiliarity. The questions were just like those Rubina had been asked a few weeks before: What do you do? Where do you work? What grade have you obtained in school? And the boy's responses were similarly shorn of any details – day-labourer; Kolkata sometimes; I don't know – although neither his father nor his sisters prompted him, the words hanging in the air.

Before long a scrap of paper was produced and the boy was asked to write his name in both English and Bangla. Grasping the pen as though unfamiliar with its slender shape, his thick fingers surely more accustomed to shovels and ropes, he slowly traced his name in both scripts, halting at unpractised letters before rushing through in eagerness to find himself once again on safe ground. The visitors stood up and fanned around him, peering over his shoulders to see what he had written, their faces carefully arranged to avoid revealing what they thought.

Bashira, for one, was recalling Ali Tariq's wary assertions the night before that this boy was simple, and to moderate her expectations accordingly. He was certainly nothing like the one before, with whom she had enjoyed an easy and friendly exchange; or the charismatic sportswear factory worker who had married her eldest daughter, taking her with him to Delhi, where they now lived with a daughter. Could Bashira honestly imagine Rubina being married to this boy? Did she have any choice?

The questioning broke up naturally, the golden-clad sister shyly suggesting a walk to the river to stretch everyone's legs before the lunchtime meal would be served. The group moved down a path in the opposite direction from which they had arrived and marvelled at how quiet it was, the peaceful fields rendering their own home a cosmopolitan hub by comparison. It was as though the river cradled the island, reappearing as a sluggish tributary that wove along the edge of the field, glimmers of tiny fish visible in its shallows as the shadows of birds overhead cautioned them to remain hidden within the cloudy depths. A hot wind blew through the fields, chastising the dust on the path and causing swirling clouds to circle around their ankles.

The meal was served separately: the men seated on mats on the floor of the shaded verandah, the women confined to a stuffy inner room in which pillows and bolsters lined the walls in an attempt to make it more comfortable. Bashira slyly admired the pillows, prodding them to test the sturdiness of the stuffing and marvelling at the way in which they maintained their shape, even as she leaned her considerable weight onto them. They were nothing like the flat, sorrowful specimens they had at home.

The food was provided in vast amounts: crisp and oily slices of fried *begun*, a fish-and-potato curry, chicken in a thin spicy gravy and steaming pyramids of rice. Bashira ate with gusto – her role as a visitor in another's home demanded it – although she was as suspicious of food prepared by the hands of others as she always was. All women were particular about food cooked by strangers. So much of their time was devoted to its preparation that an unusual marriage of oil, of spices, of aromatics, delivered by an unfamiliar hand, could be a truly noticeable distraction.

As the post-lunch lull descended, everyone wandered out into the courtyard once again. After a murmured discussion with Bashira, the matchmaker produced his phone, one that had a camera. The boy was instructed by his parents and smirking friends to pose against the wall of the house, while his sisters hurriedly straightened his clothing. His eyes reluctantly met the camera, as though happier to gaze upon the fields that lay beyond. Watching with a strained, almost desperate smile, his parents nudged each other over towards Bashira and Ali Tariq, saying softly as much to them as to themselves that their son was a good boy – he was simple, straightforward and they would have few problems with him.

The group had drifted back to their seats, the men picking their teeth, Bashira and the boy's father exchanging minor pleasantries, when Ali Tariq stood up and began to speak. He did little to draw attention to the fact that he was talking, although it quickly became apparent to everyone that what he was saying was significant. There was a quiet assurance to his words and soon the courtyard fell silent as he spoke.

Bashira turned to watch her husband, as though properly taking him in for the first time that day: his unusually smart blue-and-pink checked shirt, his dark-grey suit trousers turned up at the ankle, his thick moustache and the special lenses of the glasses that he wore growing darker in the glare of the sun. She kept her eyes on him, tuning in, over the echoing beats of her own heart, to the words they both knew that he could not take back.

'We want to thank you. We like the boy very much; he seems sensible and calm. We have enjoyed coming here and meeting all of you, seeing where you live, and we know that our daughter would be very happy and comfortable here. However, there is one matter that I wish to speak of. This is something that we could keep quiet. But if this marriage goes ahead,' he paused, glancing at Bashira, 'as we both hope it will, if your family were ever to come to our village, then you might hear stories, rumours. You might hear people saying things about our daughter, making suggestions that she is not a good girl, that she has things in her past. People, as you know, will always talk.'

The boy's family members sought out one another's eyes fleetingly – their smiles shrunken, taut.

'This would not be good for either of our families,' Ali Tariq continued. 'Which is why I have decided to speak out. Last year our daughter Rubina was kidnapped. You will all know how these things happen nowadays – so many bad people out there trying to take advantage. One afternoon when she left school she was forced into an auto to Canning, and from there on a train to Sealdah, then Howrah and then all the way to Bihar. It was from there that she managed to contact us to tell us what had happened to her. We had already gone to the police when she had not arrived home from school, and they were sadly very familiar with such circumstances, so when she called us, with their help we traced the phone signal and worked out her location. They placed a call to their colleagues in Bihar and she was then rescued immediately. She was taken on one day and recovered the next.'

Ali Tariq stopped speaking, and Bashira bit down on the side of her cheek, terrified that she would lose control of her thoughts and that the truth might blurt from her mouth. 'Five days' were the words that repeated in her mind. Five days she had been gone. Five days when they had not known where she was, or even if she were alive or dead. Five days that, if revealed, would raise questions, for if it were known that this long had elapsed, then a person could get to wondering. An awful lot can happen in five days.

There was silence. Glances were exchanged amongst the circle. The *ghatak* spoke first.

'Things like this happen, as we all know. I am familiar with such cases, and have seen several of them before. What is important here is that there has been honesty from the girl's father, and I think we can all agree that this was very honourable. It should not be the case that this unfortunate event should impact on the girl's chances of finding a husband, and I am confident that a good match can still take place.'

The boy's sister spoke quickly.

'There has been a similar case near where I live with my husband's family. Just to be clear, how many days exactly was your daughter missing for? And was a report filed with the police that we might see?'

Bashira gestured with her head at the *ghatak*. He removed the sheaf of documents from his briefcase, passing it along the circle, where the pages were snatched by eager hands, examined with serious looks.

The sister's husband spoke authoritatively. 'We have very much enjoyed meeting you, and from what we have seen of the girl, we like her as well. We will now need to take some time to think things over and come to a decision. You can understand, no?'

All the while the boy's face remained impassive. It was not clear whether he was distracted, indifferent or whether he purposely maintained a careful silence.

For Bashira, what followed was strangely muted, as though she was hearing and seeing things from just below the surface of the water. Fumbling to follow the cues of those around her, she stood, thanked her hosts for their hospitality and moved thickly, as though through liquid, back down the path towards the van, turning to wave in a slow arc to the boy's family, who stood clustered at the edge of the compound, arms folded, watching the visitors depart. The dwindling sun behind them rendered them stark, shadowy figures and she could not make out the expressions on their faces.

At the *ghat*, while they waited for the boatman to ferry them back across the water, Bashira stood holding her granddaughter's hand, looping again and again the small cloth straps of the bag that she carried in the other, staring down into the water that was darkening in the late afternoon.

A few days later she received a phone call from the *ghatak*; the boy's family had rejected the match.

Across the island, preparations were beginning. They lived in the lands of the goddesses, a part of India renowned as somewhere these female figures were worshipped fervently, in a quite distinct manner and with reverence. Having bid goodbye just weeks before to their beloved daughter, Durga, Hindus were readying themselves to welcome a further deity into the fold. She was one who always bore a maternal prefix or suffix to denote her perhaps-unlikely celebration as a fierce and devoted mother: Ma Kali, Kali Ma.

When depicted as an idol or image, Ma Kali is almost always black or a dark midnight-blue, with wide eyes, fangs and long, untamed hair, naked except for a string of severed arms around her waist and a garland of severed heads around her neck. She is a goddess of the edges and the peripheries, of battlefields, cremation grounds and wild, desolate spaces. Long understood as a champion of the subalterns, Kali Ma had replaced Bonbibi as the one called upon to offer safe passage for many of those venturing into the forests of the islands further south – a more conventional and less problematic protectress. The personification of rage, she dances ferociously, red tongue outstretched, in what many misinterpret as a bloodthirsty cry of vengeance – though it is, in fact, an exclamation of surprise as she fails to spot her husband, Shiva, lying prostrate in her path. After all, it is not every day that one places one's foot upon a god.

The day of *Kali pujo* was greeted by Hindu families with the ringing of bells, the primal howls of wavering ululations, and the blasts of conch shells to mimic what was believed to be the first-ever sound: the sacred, universal *Aum*. Although in the morning Kali was welcomed, it was after dark that the celebrations of this goddess of the shadows truly took place. Coinciding with Diwali, the festival of light, the night came alive with the spit and bang of firecrackers, the stars graciously conceding to fireworks, with clay *diyas* filled with paraffin and stooped wicks wavering at the windows, lighting the paths and the doorways, guiding anyone who was returning home.

In the village, as Muslims, they did not celebrate Kali's arrival, although they eagerly anticipated the return of others: the husbands and brothers and sons who worked elsewhere and who used the public holiday to pay a coveted visit to their families. Though it might now be frowned upon to acknowledge the festivals of other faiths, many secretly prayed to their own God, Allah, for the message of the festival – the triumph of good over evil.

A week and a half after *Kali pujo*, an occasion prompted Sara to reflect upon the past. Birthdays were not often marked in the village. In truth, many did not know the day on which they were born and chose the date arbitrarily, when required to complete a government form of some kind. Birthdays and their celebrations represented a strange and anglicised import that captured the imagination of those in cities or towns who could afford them. But Sara, of course, was not like everybody else.

Her birthday fell on a Saturday this year and she had arranged a small gathering for the evening. Her husband Khan was returning from the city, spending Sunday at home with the family and not leaving again until Monday morning. She had asked his older sister, who lived on the edges of the village, to come along with her own husband, their son and his irritating wife, who everyone struggled to tolerate but who could not very well be left out, and their own precocious only son. Sara had purchased a new lipstick and had ordered a cake to be collected in the morning, adorned in crumbling white icing and decorated with looping patterns piped in green and orange, along with the swirling curlicues wishing her a *Very Happy Birthday!* If anyone had asked, she would have said, with what she knew was an alluring smile, that she was turning thirty-nine. A glance at her birth certificate would have revealed she was both forty-three and an excellent liar.

The evening was a success. Sara had spent the day cooking, taking the time to make *shingara*, her favourite dish, savouring the languid frying of the onions, the boiling of the potatoes and the browning of the mince, before these ingredients were folded into her perfect pastry and crisped in scalding oil. She made a pungent tamarind water to dribble into *phuchkas*, hollow pastry shells that they would fill with potato, onion, chillies and masalas before the liquid was poured on top – explosions of texture and flavour, able only to be eaten in a single mouthful. Sara loved food, losing herself in the flavours with a hunger both endearing in its childishness and that muttered of other yearnings.

They laughed a lot that evening, her brother-in-law regaling the guests with stories of extracting bribes from people when his wife had been the leader of the local *onchol* office. The TV was on in the background, and the children sat with their noses almost touching the screen as they watched a wrestling match, occasionally squealing with excitement. Reclining on the sofa, encircled by Khan's arm and the faintly coiling whispers of his cigarette, Sara felt almost happy.

She thought about when she had first met her husband. It had been autumn then too, with the promise of cooler days, countless festivals and long government holidays ahead. It was on one such vacation that she had returned home from Rajasthan, lured back from the harshness of the desert to her father's village on the island to delight in its verdant, lush familiarity. She had spotted Khan almost immediately in the bazaar. He was tall, noticeably so, with broad shoulders and a marionette-straight back, which, along with his uniform, conveyed discipline and authority. His thick hair was complemented by a generous moustache. He could have been too serious, almost intimidating, until she watched his face split into a smile so warm and gleeful that it made her want to smile herself. She felt her pulse quicken.

If she were truthful, she had no idea that he was a Muslim. Nothing about his appearance or his dress suggested to her that this might be the case. But when she discovered his religion, she had no problem converting. The leap from Christianity into Islam, full of recognisable prophets and familiar stories, hadn't seemed particularly intimidating. Besides, she had often admired Muslim women with their *salwar kameez* and their magpie love of everything gold, silver and sparkling.

It was perhaps only now that she understood what she had given up. Her studies had ended, abruptly, and instead of staying on or moving elsewhere, she had returned to the island to become a wife. The fact that she had studied to a high level – and, more importantly, that she had in-laws with political contacts – meant that with little fuss she was able to get a position as a primary-school teacher. It was a job that she didn't particularly want and even now didn't enjoy, finding her charges on occasion delightful, but for the most part deeply frustrating. As the years passed, her command of English had slackened, and she found that she could no longer remember the words or place them together correctly, unable to effectively wield the prize she had once been so proud of. Sara was different from those around her, but she was also different from the middle-class women in the city, and was now lodged uncomfortably in the centre ground, for ever an in-between.

As the evening of her birthday waned and her guests began to make comments about leaving, Sara's thoughts drifted to the family across the road. She had heard all about the failure of Rubina's two potential matches and had not been surprised; everyone in the village was at least to some extent aware of the troubles the girl had caused the family. With their homes being opposite one another and their daughters best friends, Sara was, through accidental intimacy, more familiar with the troubles of the Lohani family than most.

By her count, Rubina had been married three times before. On each occasion she had returned in a flurry to the village, her family swiftly claiming that there had been abuse or some other kind of mis-demeanour on the boy's part, annulling the union and filing cases for compensation against the other family.

First there had been the Hindu boy with whom Rubina had fallen in love at school and had married in secret. He was from a good family, but had been vehemently rejected by Ali Tariq and Bashira on the basis of religion – a fact Sara now knew they would be only too willing to overlook, were the family to have any interest in taking her back. Then there was an arranged marriage to a Muslim boy from a neighbouring village where Rubina had lasted just a single night, and who, the Lohanis latterly claimed, suffered some kind of hidden mental instability.

The final boy was the one with whom Rubina had run away, thinking that she was doing so for love, when in fact she was being lured into a well-worn, though no less effective trap. She had disappeared to Bihar for almost a week, before being rescued and returned by the police to the village and her frantic, devastated family.

The *ghatak* had been right, of course: these cases were, sadly, not unheard of. They followed a familiar pattern, one that relied on the paralysing naivety induced by first lust. A girl was identified, wooed, charmed. She was gently cajoled into doing the unthinkable and eloping, only to find that she was not in fact the object of another's affections, but merely an object – one to be traded, one to be sold. Some girls never came home to their families. Those who did were never the same.

Sara suspected that the challenges facing the Lohani family were greater than they admitted, having recently come face-to-face with Bashira without the comforting buffer of strangers around them. Sara had been alone in the house after work, enjoying a moment of silence when she had heard the faint, low call from the front door. Turning to see Bashira, she had stiffly invited her in, but the woman had remained in the doorway, unwilling to enter, thus drawing Sara reluctantly towards her. She sat down on the concrete step while Bashira squatted on her haunches a little way along the path.

These women were not friends, and they rarely indulged in the diversions of *adda*, the particularly Bengali practice of informal and rambling conversations, and certainly not with one another. So it had not taken long for Bashira to ask Sara for money.

'You know we are struggling. I am doing everything I can with the shop, but these things take time. It is only a small amount I need, just five thousand rupees, so that I can buy a gas stove for the house.'

'What is wrong with the outdoor stove you have? Many other families manage with it.'

'Do you know what it is like to cook over that thing?' Bashira paused, fighting back her sarcasm. 'Or maybe you don't, but it's hard and it takes a long time, especially now that the grandchildren are getting bigger and eating with us as well.'

'I can't give you five thousand rupees, *didi*. It's too much money, and how do I know you'll be buying a stove anyway?'

Bashira looked into her eyes, anger flickering at the corners of her mouth. 'It gives me no pleasure to beg from you.'

Sara met her eyes. 'And I don't want to refuse you, but I cannot help you this time.'

'I'll pay you back.'

'How?' Sara asked quickly, a hint of cruelty flashing in her eyes.

It had gone on for several minutes like this until, realising she was getting nowhere, Bashira finally relented. She stood up abruptly, looming over Sara, and spat into the dust before stalking back down the path and across the road without so much as a glance in either direction, disappearing behind the tea shop into her family's compound. Sara slipped back into her house, crossing quickly into her bedroom. She leaned against the concrete wall and felt the coolness against her back, its solid mass enabling her to feel the pulse of blood in her palms.

As one of the richest families in the village, it was not unusual for people to come to them for money, though Sara knew how much Bashira would have hated asking her. She must have exhausted all other options, and it showed quite how desperate things had become. Although she had not helped Bashira, it did not mean Sara did not pity her – a mother who, like herself, was tangled up in the disappointments of her children, and those of the past. The end of the year was fast approaching, the winter was soon to arrive, and Sara, like everyone else, guessed that Rubina would still be without a match.

Chapter Eight

Journeys

It was noticeable how the lives of those in the village so often moved in harmony with one another, yoked to the same landscape, caught in the same deeply local revolutions of time. The autumn gave just a passing glance to the island, a golden breath that swept them first into the embrace of festivals and then ushered in a period of fulfilling productivity. It was a time of balance, something of wonder in a place where the scales perpetually lurched from one extreme to another: the heat and the rain both often overstaying their welcome.

Although the days were pleasantly warm, the nights had grown noticeably cooler. Fragrant flowers blossomed, and in the morning the ground was carpeted with heavy dew that slid under the soles of those walking sleepily towards the roadside, where they would patiently await their turn to draw water from the pump. At the end of almost three weeks of public holidays for the Durga and Kali festivals there was a renewed briskness: marriages to be planned, rice to be harvested, and journeys to be made whilst the weather was still comfortable enough to do so, before the cold and the curdled fog of winter set in.

The tarmac road had granted comings and goings from the island in a way they could not have imagined before it existed. In a decade the village had evolved from a remote, cut-off outpost to a place that was, albeit somewhat haphazardly, connected. Each Tuesday morning *jamaatis* from the city and other villages would arrive, staying for a day of prayers and conversation, spending the night billeted in certain households or sleeping in the long, low stretch of the madrasa building, before leaving again the following morning. A handful of men now worked in the city, as tailors or on construction sites, returning each week on a Sunday, or every other Sunday in cases where work and finances refused to stretch.

The sari brokers – those who made a good living off the back of women's exploitation – would pootle out of the village on juddering, weaving motorbikes, weighted down with tightly bundled stacks of cloth. These would be deposited with a middleman somewhere like Baruipur, or perhaps taken even further to the city and the *boro bazaar* itself, where their price and quality would be aggressively haggled over. The brokers would hope to make R500 or R600 a piece – five or six times what they gave to the women. Although a handful of women had tried their hand at becoming sari brokers themselves, they rarely journeyed beyond the island.

For women, opportunities to undertake a journey were scarce. There may have been the occasional picnic and perhaps, for the most fortunate, a trip into the city or a visit to the sea, somewhere like Diamond Harbour, a dirty shrug of a place whose only real attraction was a concrete boardwalk from where the vast, listless River Ganga could be watched floating by. The only reason a woman would arrive in, or depart from, the village was for marriage.

The ultimate voyage – one that everyone dreamed of – was the *hajj.* This was the journey to Mecca, one of the five pillars of Islam, and an undertaking that every Muslim was obliged to perform at least once in their lifetime, although in reality it was a feat achieved by only a few. In the village no one had yet done it, though almost everyone had a tale of some distant relative, or friend of a friend of a friend, who had. For women this dream was even more implausible; if by some extraordinary, happy accident the funds were scraped together, it would undoubtedly be their husbands who would make the trip.

This was despite the fact that the *hajj* itself was named after a woman, Hajar, the wife of Ibrahim and mother of Ishmael. When Hajar was abandoned in the desert with her infant son, she kept her faith that God would provide them with water. She ran between two mountains seven times in a desperate, increasingly frantic search, before at last Allah spoke to her, commending her faith and causing a spring of beautiful clear water to burst forth from the ground. It is her journey that is re-enacted: resolute faith blowing across the sand.

Kalima would have loved nothing more than to perform the *hajj,* though she knew that time and money rendered it an impossible feat. Nevertheless, on a cool Monday morning she was returning to the village at dawn from another shorter and less satisfying journey. Deep lines had crawled their way across her forehead, and her shoulders drooped with fatigue under the weight of the bags she was carrying. It should have been a time of happiness; her eldest daughter Rupa had given birth two days ago, and to a much-coveted boy with startling blue eyes. But there had been trouble at the hospital, and Kalima had left in stunned anger that had followed her all the way back home.

It had started with a call early on the previous Friday morning; the pains had begun. Although this was not Rupa's first child, her pleading insistence, underpinned by the ripple of fear in her voice, had quickly coaxed Kalima from sleep. She hastily packed a small bag, barking instructions at Roshini to look after things in her absence, and made her way to the roadside, where she managed to flag down a packed autorickshaw travelling in the right direction. The driver took pity on the small, frantic figure hopping at the edge of the tarmac, urging his already uncomfortable passengers to squeeze even closer together.

At Canning, Kalima waited an hour for a bus to Park Circus, and then after three more swerving, lurching hours she alighted in the bustling, dreamlike streets, the beating Islamic heart of Kolkata. Green crescent flags ran between houses, minarets peeked out from the cluttered rooftops, and although now a stranger once again in the city, she felt unmistakably at home. From there she walked the ten minutes to the hospital, asking for directions several times, just for the chance to speak the lilting Urdu words that she had grown up with, knowing they would be returned in a familiar tongue.

When she arrived, things were not as she had expected. The contractions had eased off; her daughter was not in a labour ward, but in the crowded waiting area, calmly narrating what had happened so far. Eventually Rupa was called for an examination. The doctor was young, Kalima thought, and yet he leafed through the hospital notes with an assuring swiftness, tugging a stethoscope from around his neck to listen to her daughter's heart, before placing the glinting circle on her stomach, where he sought out the rapid swoosh of the one cradled inside. Straightening up, clearly satisfied that all was well, he said to Kalima, 'You know, auntie, everything is absolutely fine, but it will be at least three more days until this baby arrives, by my estimation. Why don't you go home and get some rest until it happens?'

Unwilling to be told what to do by anyone, Kalima had at first stubbornly dismissed his suggestion. But as the hours passed and the waiting room grew quieter, nothing happened, and the considerate doctor's words began to make sense. Where was she to stay whilst they were waiting at the hospital? Who would cook for Asad? Or her granddaughter Iffat, who, unlike her son, was most certainly too young to take care of herself?

As the night drifted once again towards dawn and her daughter and son-in-law nodded off to sleep, Kalima decided to leave. She made her way back down the echoing corridors and out into the city's pink daybreak, retracing her steps to Park Circus, where she caught a bus back down towards the islands, shedding the lights and the noise and the buildings for the soft expanse of fields. She alighted once again at Canning, savouring a quick cup of *cha* before catching a bus to the island. It was not until she had arrived in the softly awakening village, clambered onto the cot alongside her granddaughter and lain down to sleep that the phone rang with the news that the baby had come.

Kalima's thoughts grew frantic, struggling against the weariness of her body to form a coherent plan. She should be at the hospital; tradition held that a mother was obligated to be at her daughter's bedside, where she also desperately wanted to be. Yet there were presents to buy for both mother and child, domestic chores to consider, her family here to attend to and, at some point, a few hours of desperately needed sleep to be had. Her granddaughter stirred beside her. Kalima quickly decided that she would make tea, feed her animals, leave for the bazaar as soon as the shops were open to buy the gifts, return home and cook lunch for everyone, before heading back into the city to be at the hospital by dusk. It had almost gone according to plan; in the market she had found a beautiful dark-green blanket made of a soft, synthetic fleece, perfect for a boy and the coming winter; and after lunch was over, and she was packed and ready, she decided to lie down for just a minute, before beginning her journey.

She awoke with a start to the calls of the five-o'clock *azaan* drifting languidly across the ponds. Loudly cursing her family who had let her sleep, Kalima quickly realised that it was now too late to travel back that night, and she would instead have to leave early the next morning. But the next day was a Sunday, the one day of the week when most people in these parts took any kind of rest. The roads would be less busy and the transport less determined to reach its destination. By the time Kalima arrived on Sunday evening, Rupa was so furious that she could barely utter the bitter words that had clearly spent the intervening hours festering on her tongue.

Their fight ebbed and flowed. By the early hours of Monday morning it was apparent to all that a truce would not be brokered. In a final show of tenderness, Kalima offered the presents for her grandson. She admired his bright-blue eyes, which reminded her of a cloudless sky in summer; and then, as instructed, she left. Mother and daughter were now not speaking, and Kalima was too exhausted to care.

There was little time for her to dwell on family grievances. The following Sunday another journey lay ahead of her, a chance once again to leave the island that she so loved, her absence only serving to remind her how much she belonged at home. This was an annual pilgrimage, and one that Kalima greatly looked forward to – for the excitement of the new and, on her return, the chance to regale anyone she could collar with her tales of far-flung adventure.

The reason for the trip was the kind of bureaucratic idiocy that stank of a defunct and arrogant colonial system, one that had only become further entrenched and sprawling in recent decades. As her husband had been employed by the railway board of the distant state of Madhya Pradesh, Kalima was required to visit in person once a year to present the paperwork necessary to receive her widow's pension. Though it was an imposition, it was one that did not trouble her, unlike the cold demands as her husband was dying that she provide the railway officials with photographs of his corpse in order to prove her entitlement to the pension.

Kalima would never forget the images of his serene, greying body, the life so recently fled, yet the man she had known somehow changed entirely. In death, no one's face was their own. She still kept the photographs, hidden in an envelope inside a canvas bag inside a further plastic bag, tucked away, just in case she should ever need them again. Sometimes she felt their presence from behind the lid of the locked chest, the murmur of shame that defied at the deepest level her religious and moral convictions. Although she knew it was common for Hindus to photograph their dead, for Muslims it was an abomination.

With a free train pass, her journey would cost nothing, and whilst there she would stay with the friends she had come to know over the years. It was a shabby and ugly city, known primarily for the strangled lungs and twisted limbs of a horrendous industrial disaster – thousands dead, and hundreds of thousands more damaged and disfigured, the buildings turned black by pollution and bludgeoned by age. Kalima did not mind. She thought of the warm reception she would receive, the spicy dishes of meat that her friends would have prepared in anticipation of her visit, and the chance to sit idly and chat, with nothing demanded of her. Along with a small cloth bag containing her few possessions, she would take with her the large sack of young coconuts that she had gradually been accumulating in the weeks leading up to the trip. They did not get fresh coconuts like these in Madhya Pradesh.

As Kalima left the firmness of the tarmac behind, weaving her way down the earthen path towards home, she called in briefly to a house where others were plotting more permanent journeys, even farther afield. Once the news of her son's imminent departure had sunk in, Nura had developed the watchfulness of the hunted, although on this occasion it was not she who was the focus of her husband's attention. As her eldest son, Hafaz, moved around their cramped home, inspecting the breakfast pot in which the submerged rice had grown plump overnight, and gathering his things for school with the torpid inefficiency of a teenager, Nura's eyes followed him. She observed him with the pained hunger of one who would soon be deprived of the object of her affection.

Mahir was a calculating man. Others might have called him clever, and possibly he was, but in the twenty years she had known him, Nura had learned that above all he was calculating. He possessed the skill of fixing the present with a shrewd gaze, whilst turning his eye to the future, forever occupied with the infinitesimal strategic shifts and possibilities that presented and rearranged themselves before him. Mahir was driven and efficient with money in a way that so many men in the village were not, though the choices he made were cold, lacking any compassion.

It was in keeping with his artfulness that he had returned home one evening, radiating the satisfied certainty of having made up his mind. Kicking off his sandals at the foot of the earthen stairs that led up onto the small verandah, he announced that he would now have a conversation with his wife and his eldest son. Mahir was the kind of man whose violence was always preceded by such gentle instructions, and Nura hurriedly shooed away the three younger children to the interior room where, later on, they would fall asleep in a jumble. There had been these kinds of conversations before, notable not for their mutual exchange, but rather for the assertion of authority and domination, through which Nura would learn the course that her life would be taking.

Hafaz was at an age when school for boys like him no longer made sense. There were no white-collar jobs to be had, nothing that those extra years of tripping through staid Bengali texts or struggling to decipher equations could assist with. One did not need metaphors or mathematical symbols to haul bricks, cut patterns for clothes or patrol station platforms with tea and snacks. Though eighteen years old, he was just months away from taking his Class 10 exams – two years behind where he should be. This was not uncommon in a place where teachers were absent or uninterested, resources were scant, parents themselves were often illiterate and the pressures of the world beyond the dilapidated school walls often encroached uncomfortably into the children's lives.

'But what about my Islamic studies?' Hafaz had asked quietly, meeting his father's eyes.

'I know you enjoy going to the madrasa, learning Arabic and such, but what is the point? This country is changing – there is no place for this kind of study any more, and no money in it. It is time that you learned a trade, something useful. Like I did.'

The mountains of Kashmir lay far to the north, hemmed in by mist and restlessness. Yet in recent years a small number of people from the village had begun to make the journey to this far-off place, gliding from the humid clasp of the coast across the vast plains to the cool golden orchards and dark reflections of the lotus-rimmed lakes. Once there, they learned how to work with gold, taught by families who had devoted themselves to this art for as long as anyone could remember, and living amongst people with whom they shared neither language, nor culture, but faith. Muslim communities across India often comprised well-known artisans: the weavers of Varanasi, the *zari* embroiderers of Delhi and Hyderabad, the gold-jewellery makers of Kashmir – people seeking stability in their quiet and intricate arts. This, it turned out, was Mahir's plan for Hafaz.

After his exams in the spring Hafaz would travel to Kashmir. Avoiding the bitter winter was deemed necessary for a boy who had never strayed further than the city and could not even imagine the sensation of snow. He would spend six months working as an apprentice, returning to Bengal in the autumn, where perhaps he could find a low-paid position with a jeweller in Kolkata for a couple of years. One day, Mahir mused, Hafaz would be in good standing to open a shop selling bespoke gold jewellery in the local bazaar. Nothing like this currently existed; his would be the first on the island.

Carefully receiving these revelations with the subdued acceptance that she knew was demanded of her, Nura found herself over the following days filled with a mixture of anxiety, pride and a yanking disappointment. Though a fervent believer in the workings of God, she had never thought that he alone could be entrusted with worldly matters. She had always known the value of hard work, understanding that if one wished to eat a lavish meal, no one else's hands would provide the food or lovingly prepare it. She admired Mahir, and yet at times felt as though she lived only in the future, caught up in his single-minded push forward, torn away from the comforts of the present. She loved all her children, but had a particular affection for her youngest and her oldest. With Hafaz's imminent departure, Nura felt a further piece of her life drifting from her clutches, her world shrinking another centimetre.

She also wondered whether it was her fault. As she watched her son slip into his school shirt, washed so many times to the faintest lilac, and deliver a playful slap to his younger brother as they tussled over their backpacks, Nura couldn't swallow the knot of guilt that sat in her gullet. After all, she had told Mahir about the worries that had begun to gnaw at her, knowing it was not worth her while to keep secrets that he would uncover later. And they were concerning, the ideas that had started to trickle out of their boys' mouths, ideas that skulking outsiders were sowing in their heads.

It had started in the summer, just before Ramzan. The weather was blistering and sweat stung her eyes as she cleaned a fish for lunch, scraping off the silver scales, which drifted into iridescent piles on the mud floor. 'Boys,' she had called. They quietened their voices, but continued to talk. Again, louder, 'Boys! Come.' Slowly they emerged, the lanky forms of her two teenage sons: Hafaz, the self-possessed and thoughtful college student; and Yusuf, the skittish adolescent, a wispy moustache along his upper lip. Their brother Ibrahim, too young to be interested in their conversation, was nowhere to be seen.

'Where did you hear that?' she had asked.

A pause. 'Hear what?'

'What you were saying in there . . . about women not being allowed out without a man, about this not being a proper country for Muslims to live in?'

Hafaz had looked at Yusuf, silently instructing him to reveal what his younger brother was clearly hoping to keep a secret. Several moments passed, but at last he relented.

'The *maulana* – you know, from Ramalpur? The one who sells books. He was passing by once, when you were at the shop, and we spoke to him.'

A glance between the brothers.

'He was telling us about Saudi Arabia.'

At the time Nura had only been puzzled. 'You can be a good Muslim without living over there, *nah*? Look around you! We are good Muslims in this house.'

'Yes, *ma*, of course you're right,' said Hafaz, moving back inside the room to signal an end to the conversation. From Yusuf she had been met with a troubling silence.

It was only weeks later, when time had sifted through her thoughts, that what her boys had said began to cause Nura concern. This was followed by other things, small signs that gave her pause: their favouring of madrasa studies over school work, the pronouncement of previously enjoyed pursuits as immoral, and the way her sons had begun to gently chide her for her own Islamic failings. There was nothing wrong with adhering more strictly to the word of God, Nura thought, but the country around them was changing, hardening. The expression of these kinds of ideas, particularly by young men, overheard by the wrong people, could land innocent Muslims and their families in serious trouble. She had told Mahir everything, and they had agreed to be watchful. And now her son was to be sent away.

Nura knew that she would never be permitted to visit him. The costs would be too high, and her husband was reticent about letting her even leave the village, let alone the island. Days before this most recent announcement, Mahir had banned their daughter Radhia from his auto-repair shop. She was still too young to be left alone, which meant that Nura was no longer able to spend an afternoon in the shop, watching the soap operas that she adored. Her irregular visits made following the complicated plot lines difficult, so she spent the intervening days playing out the stories in her head, all the while looking forward to her next instalment, her only moments of entertainment and escape.

They were not allowed a television at home. Mahir believed it would distract his sons from their homework and his wife from her chores – concerns that he claimed were validated after they learned that their neighbour Aliya's daughter, Amal, had recently flunked three of her trial exams, as a result of spending too many hours absorbed in the tiny black-and-white television at Kalima's house next door. Failure here could never be kept quiet for too long.

His reasoning had been simple. On each occasion, as the shallow afternoon hours dragged by and Radhia began to lose interest in the blaring television set to which her mother was transfixed, she would tug at Nura's sari or her father's trouser leg, whining insistently for a tepid Mazda orange drink from behind the crowded counter of the tea shop next door. A bottle was R50, and Radhia never managed to drink more than half of it anyway, the orange drips sliding down her arms in sticky rivulets, catching on her faded pink dress and staining it around the collar, the rest discarded. It was an unnecessary expense, and a hassle that he had grown tired of, so they were no longer permitted to come. With this throwaway decision, Mahir had severed the only remaining excuse Nura had to leave the village and, just like that, she was trapped.

Her hunger for stories from the outside world burned inside her. When Kalima had stopped by earlier that morning to tell her of the fight she was having with her daughter, Nura had feasted on her words, as interested in the turbulence of the family politics as she was in the glimpses of the city that she could harvest from Kalima's tale. Nura had lived in a city once before, in Delhi, for the first year of her marriage, when she was only twelve years old. Her memories of it were hooded by childish shadows, and were largely confined to the tiny room they had rented in a rundown neighbourhood, where she was left alone whilst her husband went to work. It was when she was all by herself that uncanny things had begun to happen.

In her darkest moments, Nura sought to remind herself that she could not be displeased with her lot. She had four healthy children, whom she could feed and clothe and send to school, achievements not to be overlooked when so many others in the village struggled daily with these seemingly insurmountable hurdles. Mahir had worked hard and done well and, even better, she barely saw him. He was often up with the call of the first *azaan*, leaving the house by 6 a.m. in order to open the shop in time for the morning trade. Only occasionally did he return at lunchtime, and then only briefly, often content to take food with him in the morning and to rest at the shop, before opening once again for the late-afternoon rush and not coming home until late in the evening.

It was then that Mahir would hit her. Sometimes Nura understood why, as he would tell her before or after he beat her: an infraction that had happened that day, a poorly cooked meal, a failed school test, a dirty floor. Sometimes she did not know, and was left to lie in the heavy silence that swelled around her after they had blown out the gas lamp, listening to his breathing slow beside her on the cot. Gradually, as the boys had grown older, the beatings had lessened, ceasing almost entirely now that Hafaz was virtually a man. The boys were at that precious age when sons want to protect their mothers, not yet old enough to believe that such violence might in fact be warranted.

Nura knew that she was not the only one. The wife of the local member of the *onchol*, a waifish woman with bright eyes who spoke so fast she almost tripped over her words, told Nura that every night her husband had visits from women, who emerged from the shadows with split lips, bruised cheeks and blackened eyes, beseeching him for advice. What Nura did not know was what would happen when her oldest son, and her protector, had undertaken his journey and was thousands of kilometres away in Kashmir. Thinking of her sister's murder thirteen years ago, she knew only too well just how violent men could be.

PART THREE

Fragile Winter

Chapter Nine

Aches and Pains

Mist hung low over the island. The sun was neglectful, fleetingly occupied elsewhere, and there were days when the clouds were spread so thick across the sky that it would not show its face at all. On other days the sky was cloudless and the land was burnished in that fragile light of winter, a startled brightness it was unable to sustain for very long. The nights lingered now, and unlike the summer when the choking heat and humidity made sleep elusive, almost everyone in the village was huddled down in slumber by midnight, sleeping late into the morning and reluctant to venture out when their breath would hang thick in the air.

The cold that arrived with winter caused everyone to become more aware of their bodies. These were not the superficial but untreatable afflictions of the heat or damp, the itches, the rashes, the insect bites, the fungal creep. These complaints were deeper: aching muscles and bones, stiffening joints, hacking coughs, shuddering chills.

Bodies and their ailments are a particular Bengali obsession. Each morning is often heralded by a frank examination of the matter in hand, what new troubles have presented themselves or grateful acknowledgement of the retreat of existing complaints.

Few things could bring more delight than a sharing of intimate maladies, the laboured exploration and critique of the thus-far-sampled cures and the gleeful proffering up of suggested alternatives. Diet is a significant focus: too much rice or not enough, cooling foods as opposed to warming ones, more fruits or fewer, no onions or garlic, more turmeric and less salt for too much acidity, green chilli and mustard oil to boost a flagging nervous system, or a combination of all of these and more to tackle the dreaded all-encompassing complaint – that of full body pain.

On the island, at least, bodies were also things that people did not understand. Most had at best a rudimentary comprehension of biology, leaving a gaping fissure between their clumsily acquired knowledge and the complicated afflictions that often befell them. Even the doctors they saw gave garbled medical diagnoses, when they bothered to explain themselves to their patients at all, of brainstroke or of 'tenshun'. Those working at the rundown government hospital on the island were as likely to recommend the oldest of cures, that of prayer, as they were able to prescribe a suitable course of treatment that their patients could afford. Many asked their patients during their initial examinations whether they had been prudent enough to seek out some other kind of remedy first.

It was thus that three curative systems worked alongside one another, their paths overlapping and intersecting like three runaway coins. There was Western medicine, found in the first instance at the unqualified and unregulated doctors' studios in town, where things such as painkillers and antibiotics were dispensed after a cursory examination. For more serious cases there was the local hospital, an overcrowded, desperate place that most avoided whenever they could, preferring to take their chances at home. Sometimes such interventions could not be evaded, although when in dire need, people would always attempt to travel to a better-equipped facility in the city if possible.

Then there was traditional medicine: homeopathy, Ayurveda, naturopathy, herbology, yoga, Unani, Siddha. In almost every town there would be a small shop owned by a practitioner skilled in one or more of these disciplines, seated at a wooden counter, on top of which sat heavy, well-thumbed ledgers, scales, a pestle and mortar, and behind which stood walls of glass jars of powders and dried herbs and pills. In the bigger clinics of the cities, patients would wait in serene reception areas, replete with rattling air-conditioning units and piped music, before being shown into sterile private examination rooms.

Finally, there was another kind of healing. There were many people in the village with enough devotion to Islam and interest in the supernatural to try their hand at *gunbidda*. It was a unique practice that relied on the forgotten arts – on words, on recitations, on the collection and brewing of wild plants, on the placement of protective talismans in certain locations, on items that bore the essence of their owner, and on occasional sacrifice. It dealt with things that the other kinds of healing could not, by simply recognising them in the first place. *Gunbidda* understood the power of an evil glance, a muttered curse, a harboured grievance, a supernatural presence, taking into account the need for balance in the potent forces that governed life around them.

Whilst many people had some familiarity with the practices, they would not have called themselves *gunnin*, the name given to those who were highly skilled. The *gunnin* worked from established 'chambers' on a full-time basis, and this ancient mode of healing had become their sole undertaking. To find them one had to leave the village and cross the island, down jagged brick paths and bumpy back roads, arriving in houses on the outskirts of other villages, where in the crowded rooms one waited patiently for a turn with the healer. The *gunnin* were always Muslim, normally male, but were sought out by all.

On this occasion Maryam had relied on Western medicine to help with her agonising back pain. Hot flares shot up and down her spine, as though her bones themselves were objecting to the slightest movement. Although as a rule she avoided modern medicine, a restless night in which the pain had continually wrenched her from sleep had forced her reluctantly to take two of the crumbling white pills that Tabina had helped her to procure from a local doctor. She had barely been able to afford them, the problems with her ration card still ongoing, and had to surreptitiously remove a crumpled R50 note from the small emergency supply that she kept sewn into her winter blanket, without uttering a word to anyone.

Although still uncomfortable, she was now at least able to stand up without crying out. She hobbled outside, shrinking from the bright morning sun. She relinquished her stick and, with a hand against the cold, cracked mud wall behind her, lowered herself down cautiously onto the top step and leaned back. She sighed with the release, enjoying the soft warmth of the sun on her face, knowing that in a little while she would rouse herself once again and haltingly make her way down the steps in search of a steaming cup of *cha*.

'Still hurting, is it?'

She opened her eyes to see Tabina standing at the bottom of the steps, an empty canvas bag hanging loosely from her shoulder as she fished around in the top of her bright-yellow sari for her tobacco tin.

'I took two of the pills that doctor gave me,' Maryam replied, shuffling taller, making every effort to straighten her spine. 'It's much better now,' she lied breezily.

The last thing she wanted from her daughter-in-law was pity.

Tabina shifted, kicking a piece of straw from the mud step below and glancing at it with disdain, before sitting down herself. Though she was not slight, Tabina was short and compact; and although battered, her body moved with the powerful assuredness with which her mind worked. Head cocked, staring up quizzically at Maryam, she resembled a scavenger awaiting the scraps.

'You know they say Jafar is dying,' Tabina said, clasping the wedge of tobacco and *paan* and agilely hooking it into the cavity at the back of her gums.

'Who?'

'Oh, come on – Jafar, the father of Hasan, who is married to my niece. My sister Priti's daughter.'

Maryam nodded slowly, little interested in her daughter-in-law's family, but always fascinated with a story of demise. 'Oh, yes. What's happened?'

'I spent half the night there. I'm even more tired than you look this morning, I expect. They wanted to conduct the *kotom* ritual before he passed. All thirty of us women clustered around him in a circle, moving the counters backwards and forwards onto his body and then off again whilst saying the prayers. Eleven placed onto the body, eleven taken off, start again – all the while praying for his salvation. He's wasting away now . . . he eats and eats, but only gets thinner. Not even that old, and with two tractors and seven *bigha* of land still to his name. However, I know he's not going to die.'

Something tugged at Maryam's curiosity; she fought it, but could not help but ask, 'How?'

'His nose is straight, pointing clean out into the world, just like that! That's not how someone who is about to die looks. When they're truly going, everything crumples, softens. The nose in particular always bends to one side.'

Though she certainly believed in such signs and understandings of the world, finding them far more palatable than modern scientific explanations, Maryam was not as willing to accept them when delivered by this particular messenger. Tabina could sense her antipathy.

'I know about these things! Three times I have been cut open. And do you not remember the woman with the blade inside her?'

Maryam inclined her head reluctantly. There had been a woman a few years ago who had suffered a horrific yet inexplicable infection after surgery in the local hospital. More familiar with the operating table than most, Tabina had said straight away that they must have left something inside her when they had sewn her back together. When a small blade was removed from her abdomen days later, she had been proven right.

'And just think! That man, supposedly a respected doctor!'

With that, Tabina stood up and, without a backwards glance, she loped off across the clearing towards the road, eyes already searching for an auto towards the town. Maryam thought that she must be on the scent of some new opportunity; Tabina never missed a trick.

Months before, when teachers at the local school had incorrectly administered vaccinations to the children, causing widespread sickness and in one tragic case death, that evening they found themselves, predictably, besieged. The school was surrounded by a mob of angry parents, and sparks of violence began to appear at the ragged edges of the crowd. Although not directly involved – her youngest boy now eighteen and at a different school altogether – Tabina had snuck in, effortlessly sporting the guise of a concerned parent. She knew the building well, its dark spaces. She had smuggled several of the teachers out of the back, away from the crowd, and her husband had then driven them to safety in his rickshaw to the small town on the other side of the bridge. The teachers had paid her R200 apiece for their escape.

Maryam stayed on her step, waiting until she could be sure that Tabina was out of sight and unable to witness her efforts to stand up. This was the definition of old age, she thought: moments of discomfort followed by moments of respite, until the will to submit oneself to that caustic pendulum swing was finally extinguished.

A new year had begun. Maryam had seen the dawns of many years, not that she was ever aware of those precise moments, the subtle shifts as one number slipped away to be replaced by another. She could not read, or even recognise numbers or decipher certain crucial words, as the women in the generation that came after her were mostly able to. Calendars were impenetrable, dates irrelevant. She measured time in events, both local and further removed: a particularly hot summer, a good harvest, a beloved coconut palm felled in a violent storm, a birth, the moment they had heard the news that Bangladesh had defeated East Pakistan in a bloody war of liberation.

Though she did not know precisely how old she was, Maryam would tell anyone who asked her that she must be over seventy now, for she had seen Independence, *shadinota* – the word indistinguishable from 'freedom' in Bangla. She had been a girl admittedly, not yet married, and too young to fully comprehend the magnitude of the pen strokes that had, far away across the sea, made into law the glorious moment of emancipation whilst also facilitating a tragedy of unimaginable proportions. The violence had not reached her father's village, but they had heard reports of what was going on in Kolkata, and Delhi and Lahore. As terrified Hindus streamed across the new border and into the city, a similar fear and desperation drove many Muslims out and down towards the islands, looking for places to live where the business of surviving was enough of a distraction from the business of killing those who believed in a different God.

Maryam shook her head, the twists of grey streaked through a mane that was once a lustrous black. There was comfort in her way of rehearsing and embodying the past, in which generalised rules were shed in favour of deeply personal reflections. She was never left to wonder what she had been doing at a specific time, because all she could remember were the moments that were already particular to her. There were no arbitrary recollections; she was her history and it gave her contentment. As her daughters-in-laws knew only too well, it also made her a formidable opponent.

She had worked hard during the monsoon and autumn to repair the walls of her house in preparation for these colder months. In winter the houses were called upon to provide other services to their inhabitants, coaxed to trap the warmth from the fire and from sleeping bodies, and to prevent the threads of bitter air sneaking their way in through the cracks. The relationships with the buildings in which they dwelled could be fraught, though Maryam's was one of an old, respectful familiarity. She knew it had been standing since before Indira Gandhi had been murdered.

It had taken until the following morning for the news of the assassination to reach them in the village, and Maryam could remember the household gathered together in the courtyard, her mother-in-law weeping, the urgent discussions of her husband, his father, their brothers, undercut by the fear that all minorities share when someone else on the bottom rung is targeted. If Sikhs, why not Muslims? She recalled slipping away from these restless, circular conversations, placing a palm to steady herself against the small structure that she now used again to support herself as she carefully stood up.

As she made her way gingerly down the steps, her hand grasping her gnarled stick, her grandson Haider toddled past, watched from the other side of the clearing by his mother, Mira. He was a child whose body always seemed to trouble him, requiring frequent visits to various doctors that the family struggled to afford, and Maryam worried that, at two years old, he was far too young to be plagued by such ailments. She suspected it was due to the manner of his birth, a Caesarean operation carried out in the local hospital, his mother's body unable to release either of her children naturally. In Maryam's eyes, these modern, different ways of doing things could not be trusted – just like Tabina's tumour on her ovary, which Maryam was sure must be due to the contraceptive pills that her daughter-in-law boldly professed she was taking, to anyone who asked her.

Maryam had all of her births at home. She could no longer recall whether she had been anxious or in pain, though she imagined she had experienced both. There was little room for such sentiments in those days, when for women like her, babies were delivered amidst female family members, not in the reassuring presence of doctors or the comfort of strangers. They squatted on earthen floors in familiar houses, soothed only with water warmed over open fires and the knowledge that so many women had done this before them.

The pain she still felt was for the babies that she had lost, those who had lived for only two or three months. There had been so many that, fifty years later, she was no longer sure if it was four, or five, or six. When their small bodies were buried in the graveyard at the edge of the village, she had swept them away in her mind, intent only on the offspring who had survived. Back then, when the island was cut off, with no roads or phones, and an inadequate, tumbledown hospital, the death of a child was something commonplace: one in every four or five was unlikely to make it beyond infancy.

The loss of children was something that she and her daughter-in-law Bashira had in common. Though anyone would have described the two of them as both unusually strong and determined women, Maryam knew that was precisely what had made them so susceptible to attack – they both had enemies. When a woman was pregnant, she was vulnerable, her mind straying to focus on something other than her own survival. Such carelessness left a gap for the malevolent forces that clustered around those bearing a child, causing the body to stutter and fail in its most intuitive, though dangerous of tasks. Like all the most precious things in life, children were the object of unwanted attention.

Nura was another who knew to be careful about a glance from the evil eye. In the foggy January mornings she began to feel once again as though an unwelcome gaze might be trained upon her family. The night before, as Maryam had tossed and turned uncomfortably on the floor, Nura had also been in pain, having just had a tooth removed at the dentist's in town. It had been causing her agony, the discomfort soaring from a low and unrelenting hum to a sharp, blinding twinge that caused her to gasp and clutch her hands to her face. After its removal, appraising her reflection in the smudged and dirty hand-mirror offered to her, Nura had joked that her teeth still looked okay at the front and that no one could see the back anyway. Her tongue kept seeking out the absence, drawn involuntarily to the tender spot, the probing and unthinking inquisitiveness of human nature. The dentist said there was little point filling the gap, and Nura knew that her husband would not have paid for it, had she asked him.

Though the sun was out, it was still early enough that the air was brisk. Despite the cold, her daughter Radhia stood in only a small pair of faded yellow knickers. She protested loudly about being stripped and doused by a bucket of frigid grey water from the pond, seeking with a shriek to slide from her mother's grasp and dash back across the clearing into the house, to throw herself underneath the cot bed – a gap that only she was small enough to squeeze into. Nura dried her daughter's goosefleshy skin roughly with an old sari, ignoring her whimpers, before opening a small bottle filled with amber-coloured oil that she began to rub vigorously over the little body. Her strokes were firm, bringing warmth to the pigeon-toed legs and protruding tummy, which spoke unmistakably of childish protestation.

The air was infused with the tart smell of mustard oil, the pungent liquid used almost daily in every Bengali household to fry, sear and simmer. The practice of covering the body in oil during winter was an old one, the unmistakable heat and vim of the mustard intended to ward off the chills that could worm their way in and settle upon the chest. But this particular bottle was different. It had been blessed by a *maulana* in the village who practised *gunbidda*, in order to combat the relentless pains that Radhia was suffering from in her stomach.

Radhia had always been a fussy eater. From the moments of her *mukhe bhaat*, the ceremonial first grains of rice and milk that were tentatively placed into the mouths of infants to introduce them to solid food, she had rejected this staple, which comprised at least two, if not three meals a day for most in the village. She stubbornly resisted her mother's encouragement to try other kinds of simple, sturdy food that could be made cheaply with a little flour or grain, some water and a fire, instead demanding sweets and snacks from the tea shops along the road. Radhia liked fish, though only the choicest pieces, and would also eat certain vegetables prepared in the ways that she enjoyed them: *beguns* crisply fried into creamy purple discs, a dry potato curry made by her mother. And, of course, she would always devour meat, an expense the family would enjoy at most every Sunday.

Such inconvenient predilections were luxuries that a poor girl could not afford. There had been mutterings from Nura's neighbours, Mahir's family, that Radhia's discomfort might be due to her unconventional diet. But Nura harboured the suspicion that something in the girl's circumstances was different. She suspected that her daughter might be under some kind of attack, and the *maulana* that she had consulted in the village had confirmed her fears.

The man Nura had sought out was old. He was known primarily for giving all of his land away so that the *boro masjid* could be expanded, a decision that he came to rue when he was left with three daughters to marry off and no money to pay for their dowries. It was one that he would be rewarded for in the afterlife, it was assumed, if not whilst on earth. Nura had found him behind the mosque near his rundown home, spreading handfuls of leaves over the ground to dry in the sun so that they could be used as fuel for the cooking fire. This was how his life was now, scratching a living from the once-generous land that had, as the village had grown, become exhausted.

He had begun, as they always do, by asking her what her purpose was; like all who practised *gunbidda*, he believed in the distinction between good and bad magic. Good work was that done for the benefit of everyone: to resolve relationship problems, heal ailments or bring about positive changes in life. This kind of magic was permitted by the Quran, and a small fee would normally be taken by the person responsible for preparing it.

He also knew that there were those who practised bad magic. This would be to the detriment of another: to destroy a marriage or end a relationship, to cause someone to become unwell, or to wish them some other kind of misfortune. It was strictly prohibited by the Quran, and a much larger fee was required by those who were cruel or foolish enough to undertake it. And it was against such practices that the third kind of magic – that of protection – was necessary: to defend against the evil eye, to provide a buttress against ghosts or spirits, or to exorcise when there was something even more malignant present and, in the most extreme cases, to help expel it. The stronger the evil, the stronger the magic required to counter it.

These healing arts needed not only participants, willing or otherwise, but objects. Bottles of oil or water over which Quranic verses would be whispered and puffs of air, blessed by murmured incantations, blown, transforming them into vials of potent *phuker tel* or *phuker jol* to be sipped, rubbed on the body, fastened against windows and doors to ward off evil, or sprinkled on the imagined boundaries around one's home. And *tabiz* amulets – the tarnished metal bullets on coarse black strings that were visible around the necks or upper arms of most people in the village – in which scrolls of paper containing carefully traced verses of the Quran nestled tightly like snails curled within their shells. Sometimes, less frequently, other kinds of objects were called for. It was a particularly violent kind of magic that might require a scrap of clothing, some strands of hair or the blood of an animal.

Nura wrapped the bottle of mustard oil carefully within the sari and tucked it back under her mattress; one had to treat these objects with the reverence they deserved. She felt relieved, as though she had a renewed sense of purpose, a strength derived from taking the steps necessary to protect her family. She knew that she had not been the only one to consult the *maulana* recently about such a cure. When she went to see him he had seemed uneasy, almost wary, although there was also a sense of resigned expectation that people such as her would always come.

Kalima had also consulted this *maulana* in the past. They had grown up alongside one another, his land behind the *boro masjid* not too far from the boundaries of her own. She had visited all kinds of healers, as happy to see a doctor as she was to visit a homeopath or a *gunnin*. She loved the discussion and dissection of bodies, being quick to offer up her own ailments for consideration or to candidly appraise someone else's. She always wore a protection amulet around her neck, currently sporting one that had been given to her by a particularly powerful *gunnin*, who lived along the banks of the Hooghly river, drawing its strength from the mother Ganga herself.

Her own body had just about recovered from her trip to Madhya Pradesh, the long hours on the train and the experience of a different and unfamiliar household taking their toll on her old bones. It had been wonderful to see her friends, to eat their delicious food, to speak the Hindi that tripped from her tongue in the way that childhood languages could, no matter how long they had lain dusty and dormant.

They had even given her a new sari, her old friends presenting it to her with a sombre reverence that had prompted her to feel both proud and somehow slightly ashamed.

But travelling there and back had been unusually tiresome. She could not shake the feeling that someone might try and steal her luggage, so much so that for the entirety of the journey home to Kolkata she had barely slept, jolting awake any moment something shifted as the dilapidated carriages rocked and swayed along the curving, cutting tracks. She had been able to reserve a seat on the aisle, as she preferred, though even this relative luxury had not made the train ride any easier. Rest was elusive, and she realised with a grim self-awareness that some of the weary anxiousness of old age was beginning to creep in. As one who loathed such weakness in others, she struggled to countenance it in herself.

Kalima suffered through the winter. In truth she rarely minded the heat, or the damp, finding little need for the small relief to be obtained from switching on the rickety fan. Having grown up here, she was better acclimatised than most to the particularities of the seasons on the island, the subtle changes in the air as the weeks passed in their comforting, inevitable cycles. But she found that the winters were becoming harder, and she suspected this was due to some external change as opposed to her own shortcomings. She discovered that no matter how hard she tried, she could not get warm, unable to build enough heat through the slog of chores to keep herself comfortable. As the frigid nights swept over the village, she contented herself with the glow of recent achievements and forthcoming celebrations: her son Asad was finally getting married.

In spite of her advancing years, and the absence of a husband and patriarch to oversee proceedings as was customary, Kalima had procured her youngest son a good match entirely by herself and she was thrilled about it. Unlike the Lohanis, who she heard had still not had success with their troublesome daughter, she had not needed to fall back on the services of a *ghatak*, thus avoiding the extra cost and having to submit herself and her son to the scrutiny of a stranger. Although her weakened body had only just regained its former strength, Kalima's face had relaxed into an expression of joy and relief for the happy days since the agreement had been brokered. At last she had been presented with the hallowed opportunity to choose her son a wife, as opposed to having a girl simply thrust upon her.

'Finally,' she had said, loud enough for those around her to hear, 'someone to help me with all of the cooking and the housework. Oh, *ma*, I'm so tired! And too old to be doing all of this myself.' It was someone, she thought to herself, whom she had selected, someone with whom she might even enjoy a friendship.

Her daughter-in-law, Roshini, had heard this repeated so many times on various shouted phone calls, to the neighbours who stopped by to offer their congratulations, that in the days that followed the news she wore her own smile; one of a terse and knowing expectation. She wondered if a successful marriage and a new daughter-in-law would be the balm that could heal the relationship between her and Kalima, who after all these years still nursed a grudge towards her and Riyaz. If there were afflictions of the body, and afflictions of a supernatural nature, then Roshini understood that there were also afflictions of the heart.

Chapter Ten

Night Walks

Aliya allowed her hands to linger near the warmth of the cooking pot. She didn't mind the winter, and a long day of preparations for the festivities that evening had kept her constantly in motion. But the nights were hard when she had no money to buy a warmer jumper, or a thicker quilt, making do with the threadbare blankets and clothing she had owned for as long as she could remember. There was something playing on her mind – something she had heard – and in the quiet of the late afternoon it prompted her to recall stories of similar occurrences.

She had been aware of the girl's disappearance. Although the family lived in the village's northern fringes, where sporadic settlements bled almost unseen into the stillness of the surrounding fields and jungle, she had heard the story nonetheless. News travelled fast in a place such as this, particularly when it involved a scandal.

The family was poor, even by the standards of the village. The father was a day-labourer, sometimes finding work on a building site, at other times driving a rickshaw van, snatching up whatever piecemeal jobs would come his way. The girl's mother had long ago taken up the embroidery work that so many women did, in an attempt to wrest a few extra rupees. She was skilled in the art of making do: mending torn clothes and fashioning new ones from scraps; weaving baskets from the dried grasses she collected from the swaying fields that sloped to the right of their homestead; seeking out the cheapest vendors in the bazaar, those whose rice was littered with small stones. Though only in her early forties, thirty years of marriage, eight children and the steady constrictions of poverty had carved her face into a mask of blunt determination.

The missing girl was almost the same age as Aliya's daughter. Like Amal, she was one of a handful who, at seventeen, still went to school regularly and were not yet married. She was a shy girl, reserved and unassumingly pious in her dress and demeanour. When not poring over her books or attending the Sunday madrasa meetings with her mother, she was most likely to be found taking care of her five younger siblings, all boys – a rapid fire of blessings after the initial disappointment of three daughters. The girl wore a frankness that reflected her mother's, as though when speaking to someone she was conducting an intimate, unflinching appraisal of her interlocutor. All of this, Aliya thought, made what happened the more surprising.

The incident had happened around a year and a half ago. Her family had woken in the morning to find the girl gone, the corner where she normally slept deserted, a crumpled blanket the only indication that she had been there at all. As the boys scampered around the compound in front of the house, her parents reached for the puzzled excuses of those in denial.

Perhaps she had simply gone to the pump.

She could be at the tea stall.

Perhaps she had gone to school early.

Or was visiting the home of a friend in the village.

Maybe.

After the boys had at last grudgingly washed and dressed themselves, scattering down and beyond the path in the direction of school, the girl's mother took the phone from the high-up cluttered shelf on which it was always kept. She falteringly dialled both of her eldest daughters in quick succession. After a pause in which she sat fighting the panic in her chest, listening to the dull trill of the ringtone, they answered, their familiar voices giving a momentary comfort, which was swiftly torn away by the confirmation of what her stomach had already told her: their younger sister was not with them and neither one had heard from her.

When the girl had not materialised by midday, the tide of fear that she had until that point managed to subdue began to overwhelm her mother. They had spoken to the school and the girl was not there, or with any of the few friends she had that they knew of. Her mother moved fast, stumbling through the village, rushing down paths boggy from the monsoon, scouring the fields and plunging into the jungle, which was more verdant and less penetrable than usual after the long, sultry months of continuous rain. Her breath was ragged, her voice grew hoarse from shouts that went unanswered.

They called the police, who took their details and description of their daughter and advised them that, in their experience, she would reappear soon and that at this stage there was little else for them to do but wait. They had asked what kind of a girl she was, and her mother realised with a painful jolt that she was now, for the first time, unsure how to answer their question.

By the afternoon the girl's mother turned to other means. Her husband had been dismissive; he was a quiet though particular man, who regarded people who dabbled in the supernatural with disdain. She had fallen on her knees to beg him. Partially persuaded and out of other ideas, he had driven her on the back of a borrowed scooter down the cracked and jolting red-brick paths to the chamber of a renowned *gunnin*, the most powerful on the island. Once there, they waited, listening to the ailments and dilemmas that were troubling those ahead of them, before the mother was beckoned forward. The *gunnin* listened to her patiently, occasionally tugging the thick brown cloak he wore over his bright white *kurta pyjamas* further across his shoulders. When she had finished her account of the disappearance, wavering with emotion, he busied himself with his preparations. Thumbing through heavy books, scratching out verses from the Quran with a freshly sharpened pencil, blessing a bottle of water that needed to be sprinkled around their home, and whispering incantations over tight screws of paper to be fixed at its corners with twine – these were the charms to bring her back.

After a sleepless vigil in which she had sat on the mud steps in front of their house, her lips moving in frantic prayer, at dawn the girl's mother had seen someone approaching in the mist. Her daughter appeared, her face passive, eerily detached, almost as though she were in a trance, a remove that a hard slap across the face failed to draw her back from. When she began to speak, she had no recollection of anything that had happened, unable to say where she had been and growing increasingly horrified at the realisation of what had transpired without her knowledge. Hours later as the girl finally slept, her parents understood that a *jinn* must have been responsible and decided that greater vigilance was needed. She was withdrawn from school, and now spent each day under the watchful eyes of her mother, until they could be replaced with those of a husband.

This was so often how the stories went. A strange disappearance, an illness for which there was no logical reason or cure, a catastrophic misfortune without explanation, the stirrings of a deep, internal unease manifesting itself in odd, sometimes violent behaviour: these were all known to be the workings of the *jinni*. The *jinni* were an unseen presence familiar to almost everyone in the village, save for the occasional outsider who passed through, blunderingly unaware; or perhaps a new bride from a different, far-away part of the state where such familiars were not entertained.

Everyone had a story – an encounter, a tale of something strange that had happened to them, or a neighbour, or a family member. Have you ever walked down a path, suddenly sensing that someone is behind you, only to turn around and discover that no one is there? This was a way of asking about the *jinni*.

The women all knew that the *jinni* were a part of Islam, whether some of the *jamaatis* with their supposedly modern beliefs wanted to acknowledge it or not. They are created by Allah from a smokeless fire, just as *insan* or humans are made from the earth and the angels are created from light. Though living in parallel to humankind, their lives are far longer and more extraordinary. The *jinni* are capable of remarkable speed and possess the power to undertake great feats of strength or bravery. Yet in many ways they are strikingly similar to those they live alongside. Like their human counterparts, they are born, they grow up, they marry, procreate, raise children and eventually they die. And like their human counterparts, after death all of the *jinni* are also called to judgement.

Though the *jinni* are invisible to humans, they are able to observe us. They are known to come out at night, making their way down the dusty earthen paths that curl through the village, winding silver streams in the moonlight as they steal towards the deserted *masjids*, where they offer their prayers in the darkness. The *jinni*, too, worship Allah, or at least the good ones do. Just like humans, they can be divided into the good and the bad.

The *jinni* are also able to catch humans, and to possess them. In the village, people took measures to try and prevent this misfortune. Almost everyone wore a protection amulet of some kind, or followed the kinds of prohibitive actions that are so intuitive as to be barely noticeable: knotting long hair so that nothing could sneak in and weave itself between the strands; taking care when leaving the house after dark, making sure to give a wide berth to the desolate and abandoned places where such forces were known to dwell. These were things discussed with a forced playfulness, but they were considered a deeply serious matter. Not unlike marriage, Aliya thought.

What had happened to the girl was strange, though not surprising – there were many other stories of those who had vanished and then returned. Everyone knew about the boy who had disappeared from a neighbouring settlement on the island. He had been gone for a year, and returned suddenly with little fanfare, quite perplexed by the fuss and apparently able to speak six languages. It was normal to forget about the *jinni* until they made themselves known, in the same way that those who waded waist-deep to catch the prawn seed from the quick-flowing estuaries further south chose to forget about the sharks or crocodiles that patrolled the silty depths, deciding only occasionally to strike.

Aliya had heard that the family was now struggling to find a husband for the girl who had gone missing. Rumours like this hurried from lips, scared off suitors and ruined prospects. This was despite the fact that encounters with *jinni* were not unusual, particularly amongst women. This was worse at those times when their minds and bodies might be vulnerable: at puberty, marriage, pregnancy, childbirth, breastfeeding, times of maternal worry, the perpetual cycles of womanhood from ripening adolescence to the moment when a mother's children were, at last, no longer her responsibility.

Aliya knew that even older women were not spared. Her neighbour, Kalima, considered herself to be an expert on the *jinni*, although on this occasion Aliya granted that she might in fact be right. As well as the obvious things that everyone knew, Kalima was aware of unusual aspects of their lives. It had been she who had first warned Aliya of the *jinni*'s propensity to lurk outside the homes of newborn babies, of their predilection for certain kinds of food, and described their ability to move on the wind. It was Kalima who explained to her one night as she stopped to chat that, just like humans, *jinni* were punished by Allah for committing a sin.

Kalima had regaled Aliya only the other day with a disquieting experience that she had had on waking in the middle of the night with a desperate need to relieve herself. Slinking into the thick jungle behind her homestead and squatting over the dry winter leaves, she began to release a hot stream of *hishi*, when a sudden almighty crash alerted her to the fact that she had crouched above a place belonging to a *jinn*. Horrified, she had quickly begun to pray and ran home through the darkness, whipped by unseen branches, not stopping until she was back on the cot bed beside her granddaughter, where she had lain awake all the rest of the night, clutching the *tabiz* around her neck and reciting verses from the Quran.

Aliya, too, had endured her fair share of experiences with the *jinni*, though she disliked the way in which other ailments were thought to be the work of these supernatural beings. Many of the *gunnin* whom she had consulted, when seeking answers about her husband's affliction, suggested that the *jinni* might be responsible for his condition, even though she knew better than anyone that his was an illness entirely of human making. Her own daughter-in-law had thought herself caught by a *jinn*, shortly after she had married and moved into their home, although Aliya's pragmatic approach to the problem had quickly put a stop to that nonsense.

And this was what was troubling Aliya now as she stirred the rich gravy of the meat curry that had been simmering for most of the afternoon. She had heard whispers about the new arrival to their village, the one who would be marrying Kalima's son, Asad, tomorrow, and she did not know whether or not to believe them.

Standing and brushing her hands roughly over her sari, Aliya bent and firmly gripped the handles of the large cauldron. Casting a fleeting glance at her husband, who lay unmoving on the cot, she edged slowly from her kitchen out into the dusk, balancing some of the weight of the heavy pot between her calves as she shuffled across the clearing. With a grunt of effort, she heaved it onto the makeshift stove that had been constructed for the occasion, just as Riyaz arrived to steady the juddering steel and help her to position it over the hissing flames below, muttering under his breath, 'Aliya-*di* . . . why are you not calling for help? I would have come! It smells delicious, of course.'

With a smile he was gone, flitting through the shadows to help an elderly guest into a waiting chair, encouraging a group huddled together deep in conversation to edge nearer to the cooking fires to enjoy their warmth. He snatched up his daughter, Shahara, as she dashed past, throwing her over his shoulder and spinning her round to delighted yelps, his easy charm allowing him to slip effortlessly into the roles of host and doting father.

Aliya cast her eyes around the clearing. Faces swam in and out of focus in the flicker of lamplights, cooking fires and the blaze of the emergency lanterns. Dusk had only just fallen, but it was already cold, and the guests' breath danced and hovered in the air. Though the winter days were fairly mild, the nights were harsh, dramatic in their arrival, the clearness of the night sky failing to trap the limited warmth that the sun bestowed during the day. Looking up, she could see that the stars were coming out, still pale imitations of the brilliant orbs they would soon become.

Kalima had asked Aliya to take charge of the cooking, both from necessity and from a reluctant kindness. At her age, Kalima simply could not manage alone to provide food for all of the extended family members and guests who would travel to the village for the wedding party. She needed help, and Aliya was a skilled cook who would be grateful for the money that Kalima would pay her. Aliya had been happy to oblige; the extra work would give her enough both for this month and maybe the next, perhaps even permitting her to begin to repay the secret debts that tormented her. Not that Kalima, famed for her love of collecting gossip, knew anything about that.

They had gone together into the town to buy the food, Aliya's practised frugality and Kalima's inescapable meanness ensuring that they posed a formidable duo for the unsuspecting vendors. Returning home on the back of a wooden cart attached to a spluttering motorcycle, their shopping bags bulging as they bounced unsteadily upon their laps, the women could not help but giggle at the memory of the exasperated *sobji* seller, who repeatedly, and nervously, brushed his moustache as, again and again, they undercut his prices, eventually giving them the onions and handfuls of gleaming red *lonka* for free, simply to be rid of the two impossible women.

Aliya oversaw the saucepans serenely, stirring the huge cauldron of rice to ensure that the tender grains did not stick and catch upon the bottom. Next to this was the giant pot of meat curry that she had spent the day preparing, and as she occasionally lifted the lid to warm her frigid hands on the steam that sped into the sky, the smell of the rich, spicy gravy drew even the most ascetic of the guests unwittingly into the fire's domain.

Kalima was a few metres away, focused on her own preparation of the *kheer*, the unctuous milk-and-rice pudding that was essential for the ceremonies carried out the night before a wedding. Aliya could see that her neighbour was wound tight with excitement and agitation, speaking almost continuously as she stirred, answering questions, sharing anecdotes and giving orders.

'The girl's village is just a little way from here, only five or ten minutes in an auto – so convenient! Can you imagine being so close to your family? Well, of course I was lucky, eventually coming back here to my father's home. Hey! Stop running so close to the fire, Iffat-*ma* – if it sparks, your *kurta* may catch on fire . . .'

Seated on woven mats, the ground stiffening with the cold beneath them, a group of women were chatting with the subdued ease of the elderly, whilst making perfectly spherical *roti* with the gentle repetition and unfocused precision that can only be acquired through years of practice. Close by, in front of her outdoor stove, the groom's sister-in-law, Roshini, rested on her heels, in charge of maintaining the fickle flames over which the breads would soon be cooked. She was apart from the older women, not included in their discussions, despite their half-hearted efforts at drawing her in. Bathed in the amber bloom of the fire, Roshini shone, her pale face warmed by the light, her high forehead softened by a lock of dark hair that she had allowed to escape from beneath the *dupatta* draped across her shoulders. She had permitted herself to relax into a half-smile, abandoning the cool veneer that she normally wore for a softer expression. She glanced up frequently, seeking out the cavorting shapes of her children dashing around the clearing with the others, smiling at her husband as he indulged them, reminding her why she loved him – and what Riyaz was like when he was good.

It occurred to Roshini that she and Riyaz had been drawn closer by their shared undertaking of the public roles they were performing during these days of celebration. He was a natural on such occasions, chatting easily with his cousins and sisters, adopting the mantle of the dutiful son and older brother, even though it was one that in daily life he no longer undertook. Roshini was the epitome of the well-meaning daughter-in-law, sweeping, boiling water, stoking fires, offering her help without being asked, encouraging her mother-in-law to rest, for did she not do everything around here? Kalima was so flustered that she was unable even to detect the glint of sarcasm that lay beneath Roshini's words. For the first time in many years Roshini felt calm, as though she were able once again to feel the earth solid and dependable beneath her feet, a sensation that someone better versed in such things might have referred to as confidence. She knew, after all, that soon there would be another object for her mother-in-law's attentions.

Roshini was too shuttered to have become entangled with the *jinni*. Although Kalima would often speak of them, Roshini merely listened and never offered up tales or experiences of her own. That she kept parts of herself aloof was another thing that her mother-in-law hated. Even had she become a member of their family under different, less troubled circumstances, Roshini would never have been one to spill her secrets. She guarded her own thoughts. This was just one of many reasons why Kalima would never have chosen her.

Roshini's reflections were interrupted by Said, who ran into her, his small arms clutching her shoulders and his face buried tight into her chest. The children would soon be exhausted, she thought, having spent most of the afternoon sprinting around screaming, intoxicated by the sheer numbers of people, many of whom they knew and all of whom they felt entirely comfortable with. Releasing her son back into the night as he skittered off with a giggle to catch up with his older sisters, Roshini could see that a chair had been placed in the centre of the clearing, around which people had begun to gather; it was time for the *gaye holud* ceremony to begin.

Asad had been strangely absent for most of the evening, but he appeared now from inside the main house. He was led to the chair by friends and eager family members, the blanket he had wrapped around his shoulders snatched away as he was pushed forcefully down onto the chair. He shivered in his vest and a *dhoti*, his thick flesh puckered by the night air. A phone was produced from someone's pocket, the torch turned on and the light shone onto the groom-in-waiting, who squinted into the brightness and tried to shield his face with his arm.

His sisters made their way to the centre of the circle, each holding a small bowl in which the *holud* had been mashed into a thick golden paste. Delicately they began to smear this onto his skin, their brother gasping and trying not to flinch as the cool poultice was spread over his body. As they did so, they recalled the ancestors across the subcontinent who had sat similarly before their nuptials, their skin also plastered with a mixture intended to brighten it and, in doing so, render them even more beautiful. Taking place across religious, geographic, class and caste lines, such celebrations in cities were often grand affairs in sterile hotel banquet halls or ornamental palace gardens, although in essence they were no different from what was happening now in the dirt clearing, surrounded by the violent silhouettes of coconut palms.

It was not long before others in the crowd began to join in, shrieking as they hid their faces from the gloopy fingers of others, whilst trying in turn to smear the paste onto the face of somebody else. Someone started to play music from their phone, the tinny thrum of the beat and the mischievous calls of the singer mingling with claps and laughter and the stamping of feet.

Kalima, with the other older members of the party, stood back from the throng, their faces drifting into indulgent smiles. The food preparation now done, she was free to move around the clearing, bristling with the excitement and combative expectation of a host who is sure something is going to go wrong. Briefly she came close to those gathered around her son, pulling gently at Aliya's elbow and drawing her away from the crowd.

'It is almost time. Will you sit with him for the *kheer* ceremony?' she asked, her gaze wandering left and right as she tried to identify the best location for the next stage of the evening.

'Of course. You want to begin now?'

Kalima looked at her son, seeking shelter crouched behind the chair, resisting the onslaught with playful shouts, his skin and the white of his vest stained a vibrant yellow.

'I think he has suffered enough.'

Aliya inclined her head to one side, turned and strode purpose-fully into the huddle, clearing a path towards Asad.

'Enough now. Enough! Come, let us feed him and then we can all eat.'

Placing a hand lightly on his shoulder, she guided Asad towards the house, suggesting that he wipe the excess paste from his skin and change his vest before he would once again become the centre of attention for the excited crowd.

When he emerged from the inner room, Aliya steered Asad to the place on the verandah where Kalima had at last decided that he would sit, and placed the woollen blanket gently over his shoulders, allowing him to tug it over his head so that it was concealed, much as a woman might. Aliya sat down behind him, this boy she had known since his birth, from the time when she herself was little more than a girl recently arrived in the village. She relaxed in his familiarity, but felt little warmth. In her opinion, Asad behaved more like a spoilt child than a man. She frequently overheard him being rude and spiteful to Kalima, in a way that she knew her sons would never dare to speak to her. She would not be sad to see Asad married and have someone else to look after him.

Aliya picked up the plate that Kalima had set down on the floor, holding it forward between her palms. A crisp R100 note had already been placed on top suggestively, urging and embarrassing others into donating a similar amount. Kalima would never miss an opportunity to extract money, even from family and friends.

In front of Asad was set a large silver platter, laden with portions of the meal to come: a steaming mound of rice, some soft *roti*, a generous ladle of meat curry, a large scoop of Aliya's home-made mango *chatni* and a battered tin dish of the *kheer* into which a spoon had already been submerged. The guests had begun to line up, waiting their turn to feed the groom a mouthful of food and wish him good luck for his impending marriage, before placing a note or a few coins onto the plate. Though it lacked the raucousness of the *holud* ceremony that has just taken place, the solemnity of some of the guests was undercut by the impish amusement of others. People were deliberately over-generous with their servings, an uncle chuckling as he stuffed a large scoop of curry into Asad's mouth, the gravy dribbling thickly down his chin, prompting calls for more water. Before long, the line of peti-tioners had dwindled and it was time for everyone to eat.

Aliya rose, making her way down the steps back to the clearing and taking her place behind the large cauldrons. The flames beneath them had softened, but the fires guarded their potency, the embers smouldering white-hot. The silver ladle in her hands flashed as it dipped in and out of the pans in front of her, those queuing urging her to give a little more and commending her on the food, even though they hadn't tasted it yet. With the last guest finally served, the air was filled with the peaceful and satisfied muttering of those eating a long-anticipated meal. The clearing was littered with figures huddled together over steaming plates of food, lanterns and soft moonlight casting silver shadows. There was magic moving through the night air too, the glimmer of unfulfilled promises.

Kalima appeared at Aliya's side, taking her hand firmly and plac-ing a bundle of notes into her palm.

'Take some food now, and some to your family too.'

Aliya nodded.

Kalima turned to meet her eyes, one eyebrow raised, as much a question as a statement.

'Tomorrow?'

Aliya smiled, inclined her head. *'Hai, didi* – yes, sister.'

And with that she withdrew, stopping to ladle some of the curry into a battered metal pot that she had set aside in preparation, weaving her way out of the clearing, bearing the food home to her waiting family.

Chapter Eleven

Partings

It was the day of Asad's wedding when *Nani* Ashima died. Her side of the village had been quiet, with so many absent to observe the marriage festivities of Kalima's youngest and most demanding son. Very few had heard the cries when the dead woman's daughter-in-law had stirred from her lunchtime doze, firmly rubbed her eyes and replaced her glasses, before glancing over to her mother-in-law's cot bed to see her motionless, her gaze fixed blankly on the cracks of the mud ceiling. Kalima – enjoying a few moments of peace before the jubilant, though demanding wedding party would return, bringing with them the new bride – had run the short distance through the undergrowth to her neighbour's homestead, towards the keening sound. She had stopped in the clearing at the foot of the steps that led up to the house, hesitating at the sight of the woman, her back heaving with sobs on the floor beside the body. Kalima turned her face away, torn between her sadness at the old woman's passing and her fear of the omen that a death on this supposedly auspicious day might represent.

The morning had passed as one might expect, in the hours before a wedding: a mixture of excitement, boredom and nervous anticipation. Men sat around the clearing chatting to one another, or stood off at a distance shouting into the budget phones cupped in their palms. They were smartly attired, some in traditional Islamic dress specially adorned with red-and-white *keffiyeh* around their shoulders, others in carefully pressed mismatched shirts and suit trousers. Never particularly pious, Riyaz was sporting cream chinos and a green, yellow and pink striped shirt, his thick hair and trimmed moustache rendering him the image of a charismatic eighties daytime soap star.

Roshini, already dressed in a sparkling turquoise *salwar kameez*, sat amongst the tight cluster of women on the verandah, wryly observing their preening and primping. Face powder many shades lighter than their skin was abundant, as well as shimmering eye-shadow, heavy kohl, thick mascara and bright-pink and blood-red lipstick, which turned mouths into violent slashes that parted only occasionally into tense smiles. Mirrors were prised unwillingly from clammy hands, reflections splintering and dancing as bodies jostled for space. Gaudy jewels were carefully removed from cardboard boxes, unwrapped from crumpled tissue paper, redolent with the scent of past occasions. Earrings, bangles, necklaces and hair-pieces flashed as they were positioned and repositioned appropriately. Flowers were woven into hair with firm, uncompromising strokes. Bright crystal-encrusted saris were draped, pleated, tucked and pinned, whilst sparkling *lenghas* were slid over close-fitting leggings and twirled in their Catherine wheels of colour.

Children were everywhere. Older boys darted around the clearing, trailed by little ones who were only able to totter, and by the disapproving calls of their parents to watch that they didn't get themselves dirty. Girls nervously patted smart new hairstyles that had been carefully coated in a sheen of hairspray. They wiggled stickily polished nails and admired each other's new outfits and garishly applied make-up. In her purple eyeshadow and sparkling hairband, Roshini's daughter Shahara looked both more beautiful and more vulnerable than ever before.

The sky was pewter. The air was almost sticky, unusual for the time of year, and it felt as though it might rain. The unexpected warmth and the work of preparation caused drops of sweat to blossom on the backs of powdered necks and slip surreptitiously down into the hidden clefts of sari blouses, mingling with the generous splashes of cheap scent. The heat drew out the rancid smell of the chickens and the ducks pecking around the clearing, and gave an unwelcome reminder of the physical needs of forty extra people with no proper bathroom facilities. Roshini grimaced. There was only the single long-drop toilet shared between Kalima's and Aliya's households, which was at the best of times not pleasant, and her mother-in-law, for one, was happier to go in the jungle.

In spite of the mugginess, Kalima was cold and had layered an old mothballed navy jumper under her faded blue sari. She moved purposefully, checking on her guests, offering more tea, overseeing the final preparations. Roshini knew that her mother-in-law had barely slept and had refused all offers of food that morning. In keeping with custom, she would be remaining behind today. The mothers of the bride and groom were never allowed to participate in the celebrations of their offspring, being left at home or concealed within an interior room to contemplate what they had gained, or perhaps what they had lost. Instead it would be Roshini, along with Asad's sisters, who would venture forth to prepare the new bride and escort her back.

The barring of mothers was a cultural custom, one knitted from stories and ways of belonging to the lands around them, as opposed to any religious obligation. The belief was that the rupture of a precious child's marriage was too much for mothers to withstand, causing them either unwittingly or with malicious intent to manifest the evil eye against their progeny, cursing their prospective union. Some said the practice could be traced to their favourite goddess Durga, who, on the day of her son Kartik's wedding, had been caught by him scoffing food in secret. When he had asked her what she was doing, Durga had responded mournfully that perhaps her new daughter-in-law would not let her eat. So horrified was he by this prospect that Kartik had not gone through with his marriage, remaining unattached for life. If one as powerful as *Ma* Durga could not control herself on such occasions, it would be better for mortal mothers to be kept out of sight.

There had been a delay. Someone had gone to collect the flowers ordered from the bazaar, the blooms that nimble fingers had delicately fashioned into beautiful floral veils. Tendrils of fragrant jasmine, white roses and twists of scarlet carnations would be hung to partially conceal the faces of the bride and groom. They had been expected back by twelve, when they would depart for the girl's home, but what had happened? Where were they? It was now inching closer to one o'clock, and people were beginning to grow restless, muttering loudly that many of them faced long journeys home by public transport and were required to be at work first thing the following morning.

At last the flowers arrived and the party set off. The crowds of visiting relatives, carefully selected neighbours and uninvited, though determined, participants milled about the roadside, before eagerly cramming themselves into packed autorickshaws, which groaned under the weight of fifteen or twenty occupants. The few coveted places in a battered maroon saloon car, hired by Kalima for the occasion and adorned with hundreds of carefully taped-on pink roses, prompted a flurry of sharp reprimands, hissing aunties and children's disappointed tears.

By the time the groom materialised, the back-seat negotiations had resulted in passengers being wedged in at least three-deep. Asad was dressed entirely in gold, twinkling brocade *kurta pyjamas* and gilded slippers, with toes turned up in a curlicue flourish. He removed his elaborate wedding turban with its makeshift veil of scrappy tinsel before squeezing himself into the front passenger seat onto the imam's lap, and the procession departed, unhurriedly making the five-minute journey down the road. The vehicles then stopped, and the passengers alighted, rearranging stiffly woven prayer caps and glittering costume jewellery before palming the creases in their attire that the sweat and confinement had begun to make. Once reassembled, they proceeded slowly by foot down the sun-baked mud paths, winding their way through gently whispering paddy fields past clutches of mud houses towards the girl's village.

Roshini could tell when they were getting close. Along the path up ahead she could begin to discern the figures who had gathered to watch, anxious to catch a glimpse of the groom's arrival, and the glare of a large blue tarpaulin spread over the ground. Before long she could see the low dais set up beneath a canvas canopy, upon which the groom, his most significant male relatives and the imam would be seated for the meal. Everyone else would sit on the ground, the dismal scratch of the tarpaulin offering little comfort against the packed earth.

Already she could hear the comments of Asad's relatives from

Kolkata, delivered at a volume just loud enough to be uncomfortable for those who overheard, about how modest the surroundings were, that the tent bore no decorations, how simple it all was! She flushed with anger. One of them, only that morning, had moaned in a stage whisper that she had taken her first-ever bath in a pond. Roshini dreaded to think what they would say when they realised that no religious wedding ceremony would be taking place today before the celebratory meal, as was customary.

The crowd began to stream under the awning, seeking out the most comfortable places on the floor, gently nudging and jostling one another in their attempts to avoid a stubborn tree root, or to nestle a generous behind comfortably into an accommodating crevice. The bride's family would not be joining them, the women being sequestered for the most part indoors, the men solely responsible for the serving of food to their guests.

Roshini knew how things would go; there would be paper plates on which piles of sodden *puris* were placed, silver buckets full of *daal*, dishes of some kind of winter *sobji* – pumpkin or beans perhaps – cauldrons of rice and a meat curry, though not beef, for it would be too expensive to provide for so many people. There would be *sharbat* to drink, and when this ran out, water: from the pump if they were lucky, or boiled from the pond if they were not. There would be no music, no real atmosphere, just the sounds of eating, followed by the perfunctory calls for a little more *daal* perhaps, another piece of chicken – less gravy this time – or some more *puris*: were there any hot ones? After the meal, many would leave immediately. Others would sit around for a while, picking their teeth and complaining about how bad the food was. They would all be full, though none of them would be satisfied. That was the cruel reality of weddings here;

they were not for enjoyment, except for those who took pleasure in passing judgement.

On this occasion Roshini would not partake in these predictable proceedings. Along with Said, too small to be left with his father, Asad's sisters and a couple of other close female relatives, she was led by a member of the hosting family to the bride. They were directed to an inner room of the cramped dwelling, where a few women sat conversing in hushed voices, one of whom was set apart in the corner, a sari drawn determinedly across her face. That was her, Roshini thought as they crowded in, stooping under the low ceilings. She quickly sat down beside her future sister-in-law. This was in part due to burning curiosity, and in part due to the protective instincts she had already begun to nurture for this unknown potential ally. She knew that Asad's sisters could be cruel; even now she sometimes fell prey to their barbed comments and contemptuous looks. Their malice was nothing compared to one of their distant relatives, Raksha-*di*, who was notable for her languid rolls of flesh and the sharpness of her tongue.

The women chatted happily amongst themselves, ignoring the weeping figure in the corner, and before too long a large platter of food was brought inside and set down in the middle of the floor. Roshini savoured each mouthful, enjoying the chance to eat something that she had not had to prepare for once, and with only one child to trouble her as she did so. Asad's youngest sister lay stretched out on her side like a reclining film star in order to accommodate her heavily pregnant belly, eating daintily and complaining that there was no salad to accompany the meal, as that was all she really wanted. Her face was impassive, gentle even, but disdain dripped thickly from her voice, like honey.

The mood swung between one of tenderness and unmistakable cruelty.

'She won't eat,' sighed Raksha-*di*, rolling her eyes theatrically and signalling the bride with a jut of her chins.

Asad's younger sister muttered something under her breath that Roshini didn't catch, but the others exploded into snorts of laughter, and reproachful shouts of '*Chi! Chi!*'

There were recollections of other weddings, other days such as this when these women had sat anticipating their own futures; the easy sharing of confidences that such special occasions seemed able to conjure amongst those who otherwise held each other in little regard. Roshini did not offer her own story; hers was not one for a day like this. Instead she fell into a relaxed discussion with the bride's older sister, another exhausted mother relieved to be free from domestic burdens, even for a couple of hours. Whilst they were talking, she leaned over Roshini and passed her sniffling sister a crisp navy floral sari from a small pile of possessions to be packed and taken away with her, instructing her firmly to wipe away her tears, for there wasn't much time. And she was right. Soon there was a knock at the door; lunch had finished and it was almost time to leave.

Raksha-*di* ran a magenta nail over the corners of her mouth, wiping away the remains of any grease. She then rose, slowly, swaying across the room and gesturing at the others to move the tray from the centre of the circle so that she could be seated directly in front of the girl.

'Oil,' she said, left palm open, eyes still trained on the quarry in front of her.

There was a brutality to the silence that preceded her ministrations, as without a word Raksha-*di* began to rub the oil briskly into the bride's scalp. She brushed her hair vigorously, thrusting the girl's head backwards and forwards as she did so, treating her just like a doll, helpless to the circumstances that had befallen her. The bride's tears of discomfort flowed uncontrollably as her hair was wrenched back and tied tightly with a red ribbon, long and generous extensions were firmly clipped in, and the whole lot was then wound and secured in a glossy bun at the nape of her neck.

'Dry your face,' Raksha-*di* said, as she cast a dubious glance through the old and encrusted make-up products that the girl's family had assembled.

She handed the bride a small compact mirror, and a foundation paste a similarly strange shade of pale to that with which she had painted her own skin, her face grey and spectre-like. After this a lipstick, a modest shade compared to the garish colours that others wore – something suitable for a bride, and for a virgin. A new sari was produced from a cloth bag, along with a matching blouse, a *dupatta* and, unusually, a bra, as though a final reminder to the girl that her body was no longer to be her concern alone. She put these things on with the greatest modesty that she could muster, fumbling beneath her existing clothes in an attempt to avoid showing too much flesh to the roomful of women, should she somehow be considered immodest. Next was an *abaya*, a pretty one, Roshini thought, the colour of night and embroidered all along the edges with pink-and-white flowers; then a scarf, a head covering, a veil of cloth and, finally, one of flowers, the white roses and jasmine hanging in forlorn, drooping lines. There were to be no chances taken.

The groom's family were ushered back outside, to allow the bride a final few minutes with her family. As she emerged from the house, Roshini squinted in the glare; the afternoon was bright, the clouds of the morning burned away. Looking over to the makeshift tent, she could see that most of the guests had now left, and it was only Asad and a handful of the men dawdling in the shade, those responsible for bringing the girl safely back to their village.

There was one ritual left to perform, and with polite though insistent calls of '*bosun, bosun* – sit, sit', the men were reluctantly seated once again, this time in a circle on the tarpaulin. Two of the bride's family members walked unsteadily towards the circle, precariously bearing a giant plate of *kheer* studded with beautiful *mishti*, their parakeet greens and gentle ambers of burnt sugar vivid against the milk beneath. The men leaned back, allowing space for the plate to be placed in the centre. And then the game began.

The men were required to eat the entire contents of the plate set before them. This would be an impossible task for anyone, let alone guests who had just eaten such a heavy meal – a bargain would need to be struck. They would remain seated until they had brokered an agreement with the girl's female relatives, who now encircled them, on the payment required to release them from their obligations. Should anyone attempt to leave before a deal had been agreed, the sharpened safety pins and glinting needles that the women drew from their saris and held deftly between their thumbs and forefingers would be used to punish them.

Initially the men ate quickly and with relish, savouring the heat of the cinnamon and other spices that infused the sweetened milk. The youngest boys were cheered and urged on as they plucked the *mishti* from the top, and revelled in praise so easily earned. But with each spoonful of the gelatinous, cloying pudding, it seemed they were making barely any progress. As the men grew tired and uncomfortable, Roshini watched as Riyaz started the negotiations. His nonchalant suggestion that perhaps they should pay nothing, having been such impeccable guests, was delivered flirtatiously but drew little warmth from any but the youngest girls.

'*Bhai*, give us a thousand rupees and you may go,' the older women retorted.

'Just a thousand! It's not a lot. Give us the money, then you'll be free to leave.'

They quickly descended into the heat of good-humoured arbitrage. As Asad's brother-in-law, the *maulana*, tried to rise from the circle in order to perform the four o'clock *namaz*, he was jabbed forcefully in the shoulder with a needle, a small dot of blood flowering on his white *kurta*, prompting angry cries that he would be prevented from prayer by nobody.

Grudgingly allowing him to leave, the women responded with their own shouts: that they had been deceived, that their family had been promised *paan* for the reception that had never materialised, an assertion met with furious denials by the groom's party.

Eventually, after a quick-fire exchange, a deal was reached and Riyaz, shaking his head in bemused defeat, removed five R100 notes from his cracked leather wallet. Roshini smiled to herself; the women had done well.

Behind her, the sounds of low sobbing prompted her to turn and see that the bride had appeared at the entrance to the house. Roshini walked over, taking one of her arms with a gentle firmness, and nodded to the girl's sister-in-law at her other elbow. As was tradition, this was the woman who would accompany the bride and spend the first nights with her in her new and terrifyingly unfamiliar home. She was family, but by marriage as opposed to by blood – a link to the life the bride was leaving behind, but one that would not draw too much emotion.

They began to walk. The bride's mother, permitted visibility at these last moments, moaned as her daughter was led away, her older sister circling her in a protective embrace as her own sobs escaped. Their cries were no match for the bride, who wailed as she stumbled between the two women holding her arms, her feet suddenly unfamiliar with the ground. Her clothes were in disarray: the veil askew and the *abaya* coming undone in several places – the dignified departure the family had hoped for vanquished.

When they finally arrived at the waiting car, Roshini helped the girl into the back seat beside Asad, who already looked bored. The bride's sister-in-law scooched in next to them as delicately as she could and, with the soft thunk of the door, they were off, driving slowly up the tarmac road in the direction of the village. Roshini stood amongst the last of the wedding party and the excited children from the bride's village, who waved frantically, shouting, '*Abar asbe! Abar asbe!*' as they rushed, squealing, into the middle of the road before retreating once again to the safety of the verge. Roshini kept her eyes on the car until it was lost to the horizon, then let them close, savouring the last of these moments outside the village, unsure when such freedom would come again.

As soon as Roshini and the last of the wedding party returned to the village in the late afternoon, it was clear there was trouble. Children bolted up to them with whispered snatches of news.

'She is dead! She is dead!'

'*Ki bolche?* What are you saying?'

'*Uni!*' A small hand was flung in the direction of the homestead lying on the other side of Aliya's vegetable garden. '*Uni! Nani!*'

'Oh, *ma*! How awful. And on Asad's wedding day.'

'*Ki jhoghra hoche?* Who is fighting?'

As they began to make their way up the path that wove through the rows of green, raised voices drifted towards them on the breeze. The words were unclear, but the tone warned of a confrontation. As Roshini entered the clearing she could see Raksha-*di* standing uncomfortably close to Kalima, who stood facing her, her gaze impassive, arms crossed. She had arranged her features evenly, but Roshini was drawn to her eyes, smouldering like hot coals, a dark and dangerous black.

Raksha-*di* was shouting, 'I'm leaving! Come on, *cholo*!', gesturing to her husband and relatives, all of whom stood grim-faced, also aggrieved, though anxious not to be drawn into the fray.

'You've been crafty! That's just what we should have expected from you. Such sneaky behaviour. We have all travelled here from all over, and not even a proper wedding to attend!'

Roshini realised that Kalima's secret had, inevitably, been uncovered. She, of course, had known all along. When the match was agreed between the two families and the legal, civil union was perfunctorily officiated, they had then discussed the religious wedding. The *nikah* would normally be a large event, taking place after last night's *gaye holud* but before today's wedding feast, with ceremonial readings of the Quran, the exchange of vows between the couple and blessings from the imam. But this is not how things had happened. Both families were keen for a small, more sober affair, Kalima ever tight-fisted and the bride's family reluctant for reasons that would only later become clear. As such, they had conducted the *nikah* ceremony quietly beforehand.

This in itself would have caused a few ripples, but it was Kalima's failure to inform her guests that had so infuriated them. They had arrived at the bride's house earlier that day, expecting the pomp and romance of a religious ceremony, but had instead been given just a meal. Having sacrificed time and expense to attend the celebrations, the visitors were now feeling stung by the deceit. Kalima knew they would be unhappy, which is why she had kept it a secret in the first place, understanding full well that were she to warn them in advance, many would not bother to come.

Anger bristled amongst the crowd. As some tried to placate Raksha-*di*, urging her to sit and try to calm down, others took turns to raise their own grievances with their host. Even Kalima's daughters stood watching, shaking their heads, displaying in public their own distaste with the way their mother had chosen to proceed. Roshini wondered whether Kalima's eldest daughter, Rupa, had yet forgiven Kalima for missing the birth of her son – the boy with the strange blue eyes who was clutched against her shoulder.

Slipping across the clearing towards her hut, Roshini busied herself with her own children, all three dancing along the knife edge of over-excitement and exhaustion. As she gently removed their best clothes and carefully folded them into neat piles, she could not help but be impressed by her mother-in-law. Kalima had resolutely stood her ground.

As the light seeped from the sky and a chill descended onto the clearing, the mood was subdued. The discomfort of confrontation, and the death of the elderly woman next door, had dampened any celebratory feelings that might have been summoned by the excitement of a new union. Instead those who were staying were deflated; stripped of their wedding finery and back in their everyday clothes, they sat around speaking softly, anxious to eat and then get to bed. The bride sat on the verandah, still tugging her *hijab* over her face, unwilling yet to relinquish her modesty.

Partings

The following day would normally be the *bou bhat* celebration, the ceremonial first meal of the bride in her new home, but this would be delayed by a day. Instead of welcoming their new arrival, tomorrow the villagers would mourn one they had just lost.

Chapter Twelve

To Speak of the Dead

Rani froze. She sat with her back against the pale cracked wall, in front of the long bamboo sewing frame upon which an emerald-green sari lay stretched, unfinished. An exercise book was open across her knees, the unfilled lines on the flimsy, slightly crumpled pages gently chastising her, when the first cry rang out. It was not long before the sounds of anguish drifted across the pond, laments coiling over the water where the morning mist still idled. These were the sounds of mourning, where heartfelt and manufactured anguish rubbed alongside one another. It was the role of the women of the village to surround the bereaved family, assuaging their grief by joining them in their cries.

Of course she had known the woman who had passed away the day before. *Nani* Ashima was an ancient and familiar figure, whose great age was almost unimaginable for one as young as Rani. As children, she and her siblings had made up snickering stories about her, ascribing to the old woman all of the ghoulish and phantasmagorical qualities given to those who are the most unlike ourselves, and earned a tight slap when they were overheard by their mother. In recent years *Nani* Ashima had rarely been seen, her ailing body confining her to her bed. But Rani knew there had been questions, rumours about the way the old woman was looked after, even suggestions of neglect.

She smoothed the dark blue of her *salwar* under the exercise book and straightened her *dupatta*. Her uniform was a little damp; she had forgotten to remove it from the line strung across the courtyard last night, and now the tiniest flecks of dew settled into the worn material. When her mother came to get her this morning she had already been awake, calculating that if she was ready for school – her uniform neat and her thick, unruly hair pulled back into a stern ponytail – it was less likely that Bashira would demand her help. She was right, although the shouting that had ensued between her mother and her sister, Rubina, to whom the obligation had fallen instead, had driven Rani out into the courtyard, in search of silence.

On her way to school, Rani decided to visit the house of mourning. She was young enough still to be fascinated by death, a distant and therefore intriguing prospect. It also undoubtedly bore the lure of taboo. Though it was often the women's job to prepare the bodies of the departed and to cry for them, the rules of Islam meant that they were strictly prevented from attending the funerary rights or the burial, forbidden even from setting foot into graveyards, their fickle female bodies apparently too vulnerable to the powerful sway of the dead. Rani was not sure that she had seen a dead body before, or at least if she had, she could not remember it. Nonetheless she had heard it described, and one death in particular stalked her thoughts – the image returning to her time and again, of a small body beneath the wheels of a bus.

It was not his fault. That was all her mother had insisted they must repeat to him, after it had happened. Her brother had trained as a bus driver. Faraq had got his licence and then a job, driving a bus for an NGO on the mainland. They wanted someone who understood the inconsistencies of the roads: their sharp corners, their sudden tapering into nothing. It was an early morning not long after he had started, the light was dim, the fog still woven in amongst the trees, the sun just a glimmer in the branches. He had been coming round a corner when the girl had run out into the road. There was no way he could have stopped; she had been killed instantly. The police had investigated, but could find no reasonable grounds to prosecute him. The girl's devastated family did not accept their conclusion, filing a civil suit against Faraq that was still limping through the court system after all these years. He refused to drive again.

This was the tragic accident that had changed her brother for ever. These days Faraq barely spoke, and there was a hunted look in his eyes that made you feel cold when you met his gaze. Rani knew, from the whispered conversations she had overheard between him and his wife Mira late at night, that he still saw the girl, unable to shake the flash of her startled face from his mind. The plan had been to set up the internet shop alongside the tea stall, giving him the chance to run a small business that could ease him back into the world of the living. But it stood shuttered most of the time, the bulky computer rarely turned on because of the frequent power cuts, the beaten-up photocopier sitting in the corner under a thick powdering of dust. Instead her brother would normally be found playing cards on the concrete stoop out front, losing himself amongst the cigarette smoke, the laughter of his fellow players and the kings and queens and hearts.

Rani skirted around the edge of the large pond, up through Aliya's gardens and slowly approached *Nani* Ashima's house. She slipped her *dupatta* over her head, taking her cue from the women standing in the courtyard. The body lay in the centre, set up on a flimsy wooden platform and covered with a black shroud or *chador* festooned with glinting golden stars and the Islamic sliver of a crescent moon. Coffins held no place in the quick and frugal burials on the islands, at which the deceased were simply wrapped in cloth before being placed in the earth. Rani's eyes could not help but trace the contours of the fabric draped over the dead woman's body, marking out the gentle undulations of the frail form beneath.

The women surrounded the body in small clusters, weeping and consoling one another in hushed exchanges, with wails and haunting cries occasionally puncturing the low murmur of conversation. Some sat on the floor in the shade of the open kitchen's bamboo roof, sobbing more freely and crying out, 'Oh, *nani*! *Nani*!'

They tumbled quickly over words that soared on gasped breaths into tattered, wrenching ululations. Rani knew that these were the cried-out memories of the dead woman from those left behind.

'Oh, *nani*! You loved me. You played with me after school, and now I will never hear your voice again! Oh, *nani*!'

Among those seated was Aliya, her face composed, though streaked with tears. Her green-grey eyes stared distractedly into the distance, one arm wrapped comfortingly around her daughter, Amal, who sobbed violently. Rani watched Aliya rise, gently entwining her daughter with another similarly bereft mourner, and move calmly through the crowd towards the body. She accepted condolences with weary composure, gesturing behind her to her daughter and saying only, 'She is young', as if to explain the effect the loss had wrought on her. Of course Rani thought about the stories of what had happened to Aliya's husband Kabir, and overheard many in the crowd speculate as to whether he was even aware of his mother's passing.

The old woman should have been buried by now. Wherever possible, the funeral rites were conducted on the same day as death occurred, the body given to the earth quickly as a sign of the utmost respect. Any kind of embalming or artificial preservation was *haram*, and there were not the facilities to do so anyway. Rani knew that the family was waiting, that *Nani* Ashima's embattled daughter Mumtaz was travelling back from Delhi, making her way across the country in a desperate bid to see her mother one final time.

A couple of men approached the homestead, where they waited near the entrance to the courtyard, anxious to keep their distance from this markedly female space of mourning. They had received a phone call informing them that Mumtaz was at Canning, soon to begin her journey out of town and along the single road that led towards the shifting islands. The crowd began to disperse, agreeing to return that afternoon, shortly before the call to prayer would ring out across the land.

When Rani got back from school later that day, there was word that Mumtaz had arrived. As the *namaz* cut through the still of the afternoon, she slipped away from the tea shop down the dirt track that ran back to her homestead. There she picked her way over squelching mud alongside the murky pond, finding the curved bough of a thick palm tree that she could lean against in order to observe what was going on from a distance. Rani watched as the swell of women who had gathered once more in the courtyard parted, to allow the male relatives to approach and claim the body. Carefully the men hoisted it onto a bamboo pall, which they lifted onto their shoulders, carrying it haltingly along the cracked earth towards the main road. As they moved away, many of the women cried out one last time, 'oh, *nani*!', turning to embrace one another. As women, this was where their final farewells were said.

The procession formed a slow, gradually expanding phalanx, as other male mourners spilled from their homes to join in. They moved silently down the tarmac road, turning right onto the brick path that led up past the pond, towards the mosque. As they reached the *boro masjid*, the body was set down on a raised platform outside the building where the women's madrasa meeting was usually held, the men filing past, splashing water in quick ablutions before taking their places inside.

'Sssss!' Rani turned round to see her mother, Bashira, looking at her sternly and gesturing to a place further behind the trees where, although the view was partly obscured, there would be no risk of anyone seeing her. Reluctantly Rani retreated, and Bashira moved over to join her, leaning her broad shoulders against a gnarled protruding bough. She fished a rusted tin box from the pleats of her sari and adeptly made herself another package of *paan* to wedge into her already-reddened mouth.

'The condition that woman was left in was appalling,' Bashira said, her face thunderous with distaste. 'No one helped her, no one gave her money, and now they jump on planes from Mumbai and Delhi to be here? You know, I heard a story about how she was treated. One day she was lying there on the cot when she asked them for a cup of tea, just a simple cup of tea. And you know what they said? "Tea isn't going to happen!" They left her there on that bed, in her own filth, and now they cry? Pathetic!'

Rani did not know how to answer her mother, so she kept her eyes fixed on the other side of the pond and said nothing.

Soon the men of the village filed back out of the mosque and formed a long, single line in front of the body. Here the imam stood before them, like a conductor in front of his waiting orchestra, and led a further, final funerary prayer, in which the living sought pardon from Allah on behalf of the dead. Rani watched as the men moved in supplication, their pale-clad forms lowering and rising together but slightly out of time, like little waves splashing and breaking on rocks along a shore.

Nura, too, had watched them bring out the body. She had been standing on the path as the men passed, her limbs recoiling unconsciously as she stepped back. She pulled her sari over her head and dropped her gaze to the floor, before curiosity tugged her eyes back up again. The men walked with a quiet determination, their faces elegant masks of mourning. They made no sound, and it was only the wails of the women left behind in the courtyard that could be heard, their fraying cries lingering in the afternoon air.

Nura was not as familiar with the dead woman as those who had been born or grown up in the village, although having spent two decades of married life here, she was of course acquainted with her. But Nura was an unusual woman. She wasn't like Aliya, who had been absorbed into the village as one of their own. Instead she remained on the periphery, her house directly by the roadside an uncomfortable symbol like a packed bag, a marker of her transient intentions.

A few other women from deeper inside the village materialised on the path alongside her; they too were drawn by the departure of one of their own, and by the rare chance to watch an unfamiliar occurrence – something never to be taken for granted in a place like this, where the days bled aimlessly into one another. Nura raised a thick forearm to shield her eyes from a fleeing sun, unusually intense for a day at winter's ebb, and kept her gaze trained on the bleached lines of figures walking up the black road. She thought she saw a man glance back towards her and flick his head dismissively, as though in admonishment, but she did not care.

She squinted as the men disappeared behind the trees, bearing the body to the stand that had been set up in front of the *masjid*.

'You know, the dead will only stay thirty minutes in the ground,' said Nura.

The other women waited for more. Seconds passed.

'Afterwards, Allah will awaken them in the afterlife, then judgement will happen.'

One of the women assented with an incline of her head, murmuring, '*Thik bolche* – you are right.'

'And what judgement will happen!' exclaimed another, older, wiser maybe, chuckling as she turned to begin making her way slowly through the fields towards home.

Unaware of her restless audience, Nura continued, 'My son showed me a clip – it was on his phone – that revealed all the different kinds of punishments that could happen after death to those who have sinned.'

A younger woman cut in, 'But, sister, are you not committing a sin just by watching something like that? Surely anything that depicts the face of God is itself *haram*, as Allah is without form, he is immaterial . . .'

Undeterred, Nura continued, 'It was absolutely terrifying! My daughter was so scared.'

Radhia had been so afraid that she burst into uncontrollable sobs that only abated when at last they agreed to her demands that they hide the phone under a pillow. Once she had calmed down, even in sleep she had clung to her mother all night. Months later, the mere mention of the video was enough to induce nightmares.

'That person who was playing Allah in the clip, that was a sin, no?' a third woman said, drawing her sari end closer around her face, as though speaking about such things could itself somehow be defiling. If God were immaterial, how could a mere mortal represent Him? Was it not a sin even to attempt such a feat?

Nura considered this, then changed tack. 'Allah came to earth once in the form of the Prophet, peace be upon him, and thus his face was God's face, was it not?'

'We do not know Allah in this way,' the first woman interjected again, incredulity written across her brow.

'We know something of God,' Nura responded. 'Humans are made from earth, the *jinni* from fire, and Allah from light.'

'Light – that is the angels' sister,' the woman replied, but Nura had already turned and begun to walk away, placing one deliberate step in front of the other.

Nura wasn't sure how long she had been both unnerved and fascinated by the world beyond this one. It was an obsession that had come to animate her days, shaping her actions and her thoughts, providing a steely kind of comfort when she felt listless and alone. It gave her a brutal certainty in what was to come. In words that she had picked up from her sons and the Sunday madrasa meetings, she now considered her whole life to be like an exam, in which a series of tests must be completed under the watchful eye of those tasked with passing judgement.

She wanted to discuss the afterlife with anyone who was willing to listen. Her oldest sons, both more religious than their father and still revelling in a childish fascination with the macabre, were keen interlocutors. They would spend the hushed hours of the evening before their father arrived home chatting with her about the horrors of the punishments that awaited. They excitedly described the single hair strung across a raging fire, which those who had been good would be able to walk effortlessly the length of, whilst those who had sinned would be plunged into the fire's anguished depths for eternity. They told her of the scales of judgement on which good and bad deeds would be weighed, and depicted the brutality with which the dead would be made to pay for their sins.

A few days after *Nani* Ashima's burial and Nura's brief exchange on the path, she sat with a woman from the far fringes of the village, who supported herself by travelling from house to house selling jewellery to anyone who, through piety, poverty or family obligation, was not able to visit the bazaar. This woman herself was deeply pious, and in truth would have preferred to remain sequestered at home, in keeping with what she believed was right for a woman. But her husband had died, and she had little choice but to go out and earn a living. She sat cross-legged on Nura's verandah in her bright-blue *abaya*, a matching headscarf wound tightly around her head.

Spread along the verandah and across her lap were the plastic sleeves that contained her wares, enticing see-through envelopes stuffed with gold hoop earrings of all sizes, stacks of bangles in a rainbow of colours, heavy necklaces, crystal hair pieces shaped into birds or flowers, glinting nose studs, *bindis* and tightly packed cases of lipsticks standing sentry in expectant lines. Beside her, Nura pored over them like a crow picking over carrion, a diamond-eyed scavenger who took as much pleasure in trying on the sparkly trinkets as she did in their conversations about faith. They were client and customer rather than friends, but nonetheless enjoyed these infrequent afternoons together.

They had been talking about fate. Nura was enthralled by the idea that one's fate was written fifty years before birth, the certainty of death authored long before it happened. As she squeezed a row of carmine bangles over a dark fleshy wrist, Nura listened as her companion described the giant banyan tree that stood in paradise, thick with branches, their limbs heavy with leaves upon which the details of everyone's life were written. When someone died, angels waited patiently beneath the tree to collect the leaves as they fluttered to the ground, examining their contents to ensure that they belonged to the right person before going to retrieve the soul of the recently departed.

Nura had always wondered whether her sister's fate had been fixed, and often considered, perhaps against her better judgement, whether if she had not been married to her husband, things might have been different, or whether her life would still have been cut short. Her sister had always been remarkably beautiful. The third of five daughters, and the glorious midpoint, she was her father's favourite child. The two of them often worked in the fields together, father alongside cherished daughter, and had joined forces to campaign on behalf of the Revolutionary Socialist Party. She had loved work, the satisfaction of achievement, and had been unable to shake this yearning when she married.

A needle, some thread and a fold of cloth. This was all that her sister had asked of her husband, time and again, aware that anything like the political canvassing she had done before her marriage would be out of the question. Although she begged him to allow her to work, he repeatedly refused her requests. She refused to give in. She spoke to her family, who advised her to persevere, but carefully. And although no one knew exactly what had happened on that day thirteen years ago, the family believed she must have issued a threat – that she would leave him perhaps and take their daughter back to her father's village.

What they did know was that her husband had picked up a broom and had beaten her to death. He had then tied a sari around her neck and hoisted her body from a low beam in their house, clumsily trying to make it appear like a suicide, her lifeless toes barely brushing the floor. The family and the police knew that he was lying, and it was not long before they had evidence enough. Her husband was arrested, tried and sentenced to life in prison, but after serving only twelve years he was out on bail. Not too long ago Nura had seen him, passing by on the road towards the town.

Nura looked out towards the roadside as Kalima and her family gathered, preparing to send off the new bride as she returned to her father's village. This was not the sign of a fracturing union – all that was yet to come – but was instead the normal custom whereby the first overwhelming few days of marriage for a girl were softened by the promise of a week back at home. The bride's sister-in-law would of course go with her, her duty to oversee the initial transition now done, as would her new husband, although Asad would stay just a night, two at most. The girl would pass those remaining days in a blissful reprieve, as though none of it had ever happened, as if it had been some temporary mirage, before she was brought to the village once again, for reality to bite.

The bride looked elegant in a new sari of mossy green with splashes of white and terracotta along its starched borders. She wore gold jewellery: looping earrings shimmering about her neck, golden bracelets guarding her wrists, tiny chains extending from them to encircle each finger, glinting as her hands moved. She had given up trying to cover her face, and everyone could now see that she was a simple, plain-looking girl, her abrupt mouth and hooded eyes no match for the strange, ethereal beauty of her new sister-in-law, Roshini. The bride placed her small brown suitcase delicately on the edge of the road in order to adjust her *abaya* to better cover her clothing. At sixteen, she was young enough that the proscriptions of womanly modesty were still somehow beguiling in their unfamiliar restraint, and yet to grow cumbersome.

Asad preened and strutted in the dust, wielding the good humour that had been so noticeably absent during the days of the wedding celebrations themselves. He was in rare high spirits, speaking rapidly and too loudly as he joshed and flirted with the large group of women who had gathered to see them off. He wore a new yellow shirt and a pair of recently washed blue jeans, only his scuffed and dusty sandals betraying the fact that he was not from the city. He had gelled his hair, and was so heavily drenched in cologne that it could be smelled from the steps where Nura sat watching. With one hand he threw out gestures to the crowd, eyes widening in dramatised shock as people laughed, whilst with the other he clutched several white boxes to his side, each bearing the teal-green ribbon and bold typeface of a well-known *mishti* shop in the bazaar.

Kalima would also be accompanying them on this visit, and she too held a stack of boxes, hers clasped like a book of prayer in front of her, tight between her palms. It was clear to anyone that she was exhausted. She looked drawn, her shoulders sagged and the jut of her clavicle was clearly visible. Even the thick kohl she had drawn around her eyes could not hide the pouches underneath them. Her demeanour was one of a wilted flower, deprived of water for too long, its petals turning in colour and falling dejectedly towards the ground.

She had felt for days now as though she might be unwell. There were no definitive or striking symptoms, just a cluster of uneasy feelings, a general and pervasive sense that something wasn't quite right. In moments of repose she would remind herself to feel satisfied, for after all she had managed to marry off this boy, perhaps the most difficult of all of her six children. What the distant relatives didn't know, and what she chose not to share, was that it was a small wedding precisely to reflect her youngest son's stunted achievements and minimal aspirations. She loved him – she was his mother – but she knew in her heart that were his father still alive, he would have been ashamed of Asad.

Her relatives could say what they liked about the scaled-back celebration, but it had, at least, taken place. In fact it had been Asad who had requested a simple wedding, without the pomp and revelry that usually accompanied these occasions. The upset had been unfortunate, certainly, but didn't worry her too much; it would take more than the spittle-flecked protestations of an irrelevant family member to unsettle Kalima.

The bride's father had agreed graciously to a simpler wedding, perhaps aware that his own prize was so diminutive. Kalima couldn't work out whether the girl was stupid or still in shock. When she spoke to her, she was slow to respond and giggled at any suggestions that she might want to start assuming some of the domestic responsibilities. Her father had begged for a little more time before the wedding, so that he was able to get together the dowry. But he was yet to hand over the larger dowry gifts, and Kalima had decided she would raise the matter in person, when her black eyes could be trained upon his face.

Aliya also looked tired. She was there to wave off the group, as well as keep an eye out for her two oldest, absent children, who were returning to mourn their grandmother. The speed with which everything had happened meant they had been unable to be present on the day she was laid to rest, but they had managed to make the arrangements to come home shortly afterwards – her son from the nearby town of Diamond Harbour, her daughter from the village in which she now lived, over an hour away.

Letting the chatter drift over her, Aliya tried to shake off the memory of explaining to Kabir that his mother had died. He had slept through the noise of the sobs coming from the other side of their vegetable garden, and so he had not known anything was wrong. She had been forced to rouse him to deliver the news, and to watch the different emotions move across his face. It had been years since he had cried.

She looked up the road and saw a van approaching, its wooden cart mostly empty, with space for the group leaving the village. She waved it down, hoping her children might be on it, but was disappointed to see they were not.

'Why are we taking these gifts, when we are yet to receive anything?' muttered Kalima as she hopped up onto the wooden frame. Pulling her sari around her shoulders as though to banish an imaginary chill, she shouted at the others to hurry. The vehicle made its way out of the village towards the girl's home and the southern edge of the island, where civilisation curled back, leaving what was ahead in nature's grasp.

Maryam had not seen the wedding party go. She had visited Aliya's house earlier, hobbling her way around the large pond, passing the mosque, passing *Nani* Ashima's homestead and heading through the tumbling gardens to her neighbour's home. Maryam liked Aliya. The skill with which she cultivated her land both impressed her and produced a tug of nostalgia, a reminder of how beautiful the village had once been, before it became worn out and overcrowded.

Maryam wanted some of Aliya's *shaak* leaves, and although she had taken her place in the courtyard of the dead woman's house days before, she wanted again to pay her respects to the family after their loss of *Nani* Ashima. These were also both handy excuses to visit and ferret out some news about the wedding. Her blunt questioning was the kind that only the very young or the very old could get away with. How were the celebrations? What was given in the dowry? How generous or, more intriguingly, parsimonious had the families been?

Her errand completed, she now sat enjoying the cool shade of Tabina's concrete verandah. It was unlikely she would see another wedding soon, she thought, as she used a pearly mollusc shell to relieve a basket of potatoes of their skins, the rough sound like that of a cat's tongue cleaning its fur. In spite of the family's efforts over the preceding months, no match had materialised for Rubina – the shame of her past clung to her, no matter how hard they tried to expunge it. Maryam had resigned herself to this state of affairs long ago. If she were honest, she had gradually severed the emotional ties to her wayward granddaughter, the more destructive her behaviour had become. Rubina was a lost cause. Maryam's concern now was for Rani, who, by custom, would be unable to marry until her older sister had been successfully paired off. The girl was almost fifteen; there was little time left.

Unbeknownst to Bashira, who would be furious at the discovery, Maryam had begun a search of her own. Furtively she had started to ask about distant relatives who lived too far away to be privy to the gossip about Rubina. She was sure there was a cousin in Baruipur, a polluted funk of a town where the edges of the yawning city of Kolkata finally petered out. Then again, whether they could expect anyone else to shoulder the responsibility of a girl like Rubina was another matter entirely.

Maryam batted away the flies that danced around the bowl of chicken by her side. The poultry-cuts woman had been by that morning, walking from village to village selling the offcuts of carcasses, the skin, the feet, the heads, the innards and the slivers of discarded flesh. This was not desirable meat – that was far too expensive – but it was *halal* and, having lived through leaner times, Maryam knew how they could use it to make a tasty meal, wringing out every last bit of flavour from the scraps. Normally they would not prepare something like this in the evening, instead making do with some *muri* or *roti*, or reheating the food left over from lunch. But Tabina and her husband had been out all day and the cooler weather meant that they were happy to eat later on this day of commemoration.

It was the day of Fatima, the day on which to celebrate the Prophet's youngest daughter. Although people might have believed there were few stories of women in the Quran, and while they were often nameless, mothers, daughters, sisters and wives *were* there. The Prophet himself, peace be upon him, was often said to have preferred the company of women to that of men; there was his first wife, Khadija, a smart businesswoman and a formidable presence; and his favoured daughter, Fatima, whose husband he did not permit to take a second wife, in what many identified as a blatant act of indulgence from a loving and protective father.

Maryam revelled in Fatima's story, particularly in recounting it to squirming grandchildren years before, beginning each time in identical fashion: Now! You have heard of Fatima? When she died, her soul became the subject of a bitter dispute between Allah and Shaytan. Allah wanted to take her soul straight to paradise, skipping over the necessity of judgement day. He had good reason – she had led an unblemished life, never sinning, never missing a single *namaz*, and being a good and dutiful daughter in every possible way. But Shaytan said no, why should she receive special treatment? How was he supposed to know that Fatima had lived a life just as Allah had described? Her soul would be judged, as every soul was, and that would decide whether she went to paradise or to hell. As Shaytan approached her body, there was a violent, almighty *crack!*

And with this, Maryam would smash her stick against the earth, causing her audience to jump.

A miracle had happened. Fatima's soul had moved, splitting the ground in two, opening up a two-metre chasm around her body. Shaytan paused, unable to reach her, and reluctantly relented, leaving her to Allah, who gently collected her soul and bore it straight to paradise. Now, around the world, her open palm was worn around necks, painted on doorways and inked onto skin, as a symbol of power and being without sin. Maryam smiled to herself as she dropped the last potato back into the basket. No wonder Fatima had been the Prophet's favourite child.

PART FOUR
Biting Spring, Feverish Summer

Chapter Thirteen

Caught

Her name is Nusrat and she is possessed by a *jinn*. These were two of the three things that Sara had managed to ascertain about the new arrival, the girl that Kalima's Asad had married a month before. She also knew that Nusrat had gone. When making her way home from the primary school the day before, Sara had overheard gossip from the crowd that regularly loitered at the barber's stall, lolling around in the hot shade of the tin roof as they waited their turn for a shave. The rumour was that the girl had returned to her father's village, presumably in the hope that she could quickly be cured of her affliction, before she had to come back once again.

Sara's husband was at home. This was welcome – it had been weeks since they had seen him – but his presence was like a magnet that restricted her orbits, tugging her closer into his path. As a result, she had not yet had a chance to find out anything further about Kalima's much-anticipated daughter-in-law who, it seemed, was another disappointment. She would get the details once Khan had gone again in a few days' time, back to the city, back to the life of work and excitement and eating from food stalls and walking through the embrace of congested streets – the life that she deeply envied.

His heavy breathing and occasional starts could be heard from the bedroom as she sat in the indoor kitchen, slicing vegetables, washing lentils until they released their cloudy plumes into the water, pounding ginger, chilli and garlic into a thick paste as her eyes began to spill. Domestic chores were almost unfamiliar, now that she had Parveen to do them, their small family in truth requiring only a modest amount of servitude. But Khan, although for the most part softly spoken, was exacting, and Sara did not trust her daughter-in-law to prepare things just as he liked them: the intimate alchemy of tastes and temperatures he favoured, which, in the twenty-five years they had been together, she had learned by heart.

What she knew of being a good Muslim wife came from lived experience. Her mother-in-law had guided her as she would any wife of her son, shaping her as she herself had once been sculpted and making the subtle changes that meant Sara's work would always bear her imprint. She had also given Sara pamphlets and books about Islam, designed to educate a convert, whose browning gossamer pages radiated a stiff embarrassment as they described in detail personal etiquette for Muslim women. There were other, even more intimate things that Sara's mother-in-law had whispered to her that were not contained in these pages. That a man and woman were required to undergo a cleansing similar to that undertaken in advance of prayer, both before and after they lay together, was something that Sara could still not fully comprehend, though she was unsure whether that particular requirement belonged to Islam or to her fastidious husband.

As time passed, practising her faith had become simpler as well as harder. Even now she struggled to pull herself from bed at four thirty in the morning and to wash away the warmth of sleep before her prayers, although that did not make her so different from many others in the village. She grappled uneasily with fasting during Ramzan, but so did many around her; and in her defence, her job outside the village came with restrictions and demands that were unlike those of other women's lives. She accepted covering her head on occasion, almost instinctively now reaching for the end of her sari when the call of the *azaan* broke apart her thoughts, although – unlike other women – she was not preoccupied with an afterlife. Sara believed that when you died, you died, and that was that. This was one of many reasons why she was dissatisfied with her life on this earth, believing as she did that it would be her only one.

This morning she was late. With a glance outside across the shaded pond, Sara could tell that the sun was already steaming into the sky, piercing the thick cover of the trees and casting golden spotlights onto the grey water. *Saraswati pujo* had taken place a week ago – the honouring of the goddess of knowledge announcing the arrival of spring – and the days were becoming warmer and brighter. She knew she was going to be late for work at the school in a nearby hamlet, at least a twenty-minute walk away down the paths that snaked through the swaying fields running behind the village. The children would just have to wait.

She wondered what Khan's family would have done, had she become possessed after they had married. Sara was one of the few in the village who did not believe in the *jinni*, convinced that there was enough evil in the world without invoking the supernatural. In her experience, humans were more than capable of spreading misery themselves; it was other people's jealousy that one had to be wary of, she would warn her daughter Nadia, not the shape-shifting *jinni*. Against such human malignancy she wore a *tabiz* protection amulet looped around her neck, and although she did not make Nadia or her grandson wear one, after his accident last year she was keener than ever that a large, dark kohl circle be drawn onto Aryan's forehead every morning to ward off the evil eye.

These marks were common on children, one of the many superstitious beliefs that guarded their safety. Dark circles were drawn on their foreheads or cheeks to deflect *kharap drishti*, a malevolent gaze; and *kajal* would be pencilled thickly around their eyes to protect against everything from sunlight to pure evil. Heads were shorn in infancy and early childhood to encourage hair to grow back thicker and more lustrous; and names should be chosen only after birth, and by the paternal grandfather, in order to bring luck. Many would not dare to compliment their children or those of others, worried that such open praise might jinx them. Sara may not have believed in the *jinni*, but she was enough of a *desher meye*, a country girl, to adhere to these other practices without question.

As she sliced the gnarled, spiky husks of the bitter gourds on the sharp blade of the *bonti* she considered whether she could ask her husband again about leaving the village. She could not read him at the moment, unsure if the mention of a grievance that was growing like a crack between them would irrevocably spoil his few days at home.

They had always talked about leaving one day. Khan's work in Kolkata was a solid, tangible reason for them to quit the village, even if only for part of the year, retaining this home for holidays and weekends whilst maybe renting somewhere in the city. But as the years had passed, the prospect of any escape seemed to dwindle and fade. Each time Sara raised the question, frustratingly he once again demurred.

They would talk about it another time. And what about the house? Did she remember the challenges they had faced from those in his extended family? Would they be able to sell off some of their land, that which they would no longer be able to keep an eye on, for a sum it was worth? And what about their son? How could they afford another home in the city? Would Sara be able to find a job there? Their path was littered with questions, to which she did not possess the answers.

As the only surviving male of his family, Khan had obligations to maintain and honour the graves of his parents and his brother. His sister who lived in the village was another reason to stay, her position as the former *onchol pradhan* of the area bestowing her with a still-smouldering political potency. Although the party she used to represent had now fallen out of favour, replaced by one led by the woman they all called *Didi*, or sister, her old connections nonetheless granted their family the kind of low-level prestige that would vanish in the throng of Kolkata. Who did they know there anyway, in the city? Who could they call? There was also an election coming, and this made everything more complicated, as a significant part of everyone's daily life, and Sara's husband's work, was temporarily focused on ensuring a fair vote for all across a state of more than ninety million people. This was nothing compared to a general election like the one that had occurred two summers before and had involved more than 1.3 billion.

There was a noise from the other room; Khan was stirring. Sara filled a small pan with water from a bucket and set it to boil over the gas stove for *cha*. She watched as the tiny bubbles began to form along the bottom. She allowed the steam to gather on her cheeks until the heat grew too much to bear, and then she pulled her head back, bringing a cool palm to wipe away the water. There were other things that tied her to the village, although never spoken about. Ties that she would cut, if only she knew how.

Kalima was enduring an uncomfortable reminder of the impossibility of privacy in this place. Though she had tried her best to keep the situation with Nusrat quiet, it wasn't long before the women appeared at her doorstep, wanting to buy an egg, or to see how she was feeling after the wedding, or to meet the new bride, only to be told what of course they already knew – she had gone.

When forced to explain, Kalima stripped the story of everything but the bare facts, holding back the tangled details lest they be spun into an elaborate web of supposition and half-truths. The girl had been acting strangely and they had assumed it was the stress of the wedding, and of her new circumstances, which of course it might have been; who could say with such things? But then there had been an episode, and it was clear that she was unwell, so they had called for the imam of the *boro masjid* right away. He had come to see her, conducted as thorough an examination as he could and confirmed their suspicions that a *jinn* was dwelling inside her. Wanting what was best for her, Asad's family had taken Nusrat back to the comfort of her home where her father, suitably mortified, had assured them they would see Nusrat cured so that she might return as soon as possible. Now all there was for Kalima to do was to muzzle her imperious nature and wait.

She knew all about the *jinni*. After all, their history was entwined with her family's – some of the oldest and original inhabitants of their village. The pages of her past were filled with ancestors who had cultivated close and intimate relationships with the *jinni*. There had been a great-grandmother in particular who always left out food for them on special occasions, each time finding it gone in the morning and sometimes receiving an offering of special *jinner khabar*, or *jinn*'s food, in return. She had once even been given a block of gold as a gift by a *jinn* who was particularly fond of her. But these relationships didn't happen any longer. Instead the *jinni* had begun to attack the people of the village.

No one could be sure why this was the case, and whether it was the villagers or the *jinni* who had changed. Some suggested that perhaps the *jinni* had grown unhappy with their increasing exclusion from the lives of humans, and with the shunning of the old ways of which they were so much a part. Kalima wondered if the attacks were a way of punishing them, of reminding them that the *jinni* were still there.

It was true that the girl's predicament was not that uncommon. After all, Kalima's eldest daughter Rupa – softly spoken, thoughtful and resolutely sensible – had a similar experience after her own marriage years before. Kalima had somehow forgotten her daughter's encounters until recently, the shock buried under the passing of the years, the memories of the beautiful children Rupa had given birth to and the stable marriage she had managed to cultivate.

Weeks before, during the afternoon hush between the wedding celebrations, the siblings had sat sprawled across the verandah of their mother's home talking to one another, enjoying the unhurried conversation and comfortable silences that came from the company of one's kin. They had somehow been drawn to the topic of the *jinni*, with Riyaz complaining of the echoing pain in his stomach after eating so much of the *kheer* at the wedding feast, which prompted Rupa's husband to discuss how he had recently endured a similar stomach complaint. Leaving nothing to chance, he had sought consultations with a *gunnin* in his healing room, with a homeopath in a dusty shop front and with a doctor in a well-regarded hospital in Kolkata. On each occasion he had, unsurprisingly, been diagnosed differently and provided with a remedy unique to that profession. One of the three had worked, and he was now much better.

'A *jinn* must have been striking you!' Riyaz joked, mocking the wavering intonations of an elderly medicine man.

After a pause, Rupa said softly, 'I have known a *jinn*.'

Calmly she related her own story, which had begun when she was first married almost sixteen years ago. In the shadowy uncertainties of those first months as a wife, in an unfamiliar home surrounded by strangers and with new and intimidating obligations, Rupa realised that she was unable to feel love for her husband, although he was a good man, a *maulana*, in a comfortable financial situation. Struggling to understand why this could be, she had gradually become aware of a presence – something almost there, but also not, so that when she turned round quickly in order to startle it into being, she found herself alone. Slowly she understood that a *jinn* was following her, dwelling at the edges of her awareness, preventing her from feeling the affection and tenderness every wife should possess.

'What fear I felt . . . It was a giant black thing,' Rupa said, standing up and placing her right arm over her left shoulder with an outspread palm, indicating the malevolent presence hovering behind her, just out of sight.

There was a pause. Her younger sister asked her when the *jinn* had disappeared.

'Oh, it hasn't gone,' she replied. 'But now it stays over there – much, much further away from me.' She pointed behind her, gesturing past the edge of the family land, into the jungle beyond.

'And now you are able to love your husband?' Riyaz asked, his face torn between amusement and concern.

Rupa looked away with a small smile and said nothing.

Aliya too had overheard this conversation, as she had sat quietly on the verandah helping Kalima pack away things from the wedding, stacking metal tumblers into dented towers, folding chewed-up pieces of cloth that had served their purpose as blankets. Now, in the stillness of mid-afternoon, as she moved slowly up and down the darkened furrows of her garden, tending to her crops in preparation for their imminent harvest, she wondered whether she should have mentioned something to Kalima before the wedding. Her cautious ear pressed always now to the ground, she had picked up on the subtle susurrations surrounding the girl in the run-up to the event. She sighed. Kalima would not have listened to her anyway.

The speed with which Nusrat had become caught had not been surprising, for after all it was not long after someone had been caught by a *jinn* that the signs would begin to show. The afflicted would be plagued by strange behaviour: body aches, stomach complaints, night terrors, speaking backwards or in tongues, having fits, a body wasting away inexplicably. Once a possession was suspected on the island, it would need to be confirmed by someone such as a *maulana* or a *gunnin*.

Elsewhere in India *dargahs*, the tombs of revered Sufi saints, might be visited, where the very proximity to someone so holy would draw the *jinn* thrashing to the surface. The victim would scream and cry out, slashing at their limbs with razor blades or rusted nails or bits of broken glass they had hidden away, even smashing their head into the cool marble of the tombs until they drew blood. *Gunbidda* would be given, and this would often be enough. For stronger, more malevolent *jinni*, several attempts of more complicated kinds of healing might be needed. And very occasionally, there was simply nothing to be done.

Aliya's daughter-in-law Munira had once claimed to have been caught by a *jinn*, but her quick response had snapped the girl from her stupor soon enough. It had not been long after she had come to live with them, when Munira had suddenly begun to complain of feeling unwell. The morning had passed uneventfully. Both women were working at the bamboo sewing frame, their concentration trained on the swirling patterns etched in white chalk on the gauzy fabric. Aware of a sudden cessation in activity, Aliya had looked up to see her companion frozen, the needle in her hand stopped in mid-air, the thread a taut line between her fingertips and the fabric. Slowly, dreamily, Munira had asked if she could go and lie down, as she did not feel well. By nightfall she was listless, and over the following days she weakened, now confined to her bed. Eventually all she was able to say was that there was a *jinn* inside her.

By chance, the girl's parents arrived for a planned visit in the days after, along with some other relatives of Aliya who had been unable to make the wedding. Once they had settled themselves, gratefully accepting a glass of home-made *nimbu pani*, they had looked around for their daughter. Aliya outlined the situation for them, emphasising with a humble weariness that she could not possibly have the girl remain with her in such circumstances; she was barely surviving as it was. No, they would have to take her home and look after her until she was better. She also told them that she had just sent a message to the imam, asking his sage advice on what to do. Aliya knew that the Tablighi Jamaat were trying to weed out superstition, in the way they had begun to make the women feel uncomfortable about so many things.

But she also knew that the imam was a good man who, despite his personal reservations, was indulgent of the beliefs of others.

The imam arrived with two other *maulanas* from the village. He asked whether he could examine the girl. The men conferred briefly, before he confirmed to the anxious relatives that yes, they thought it was a *jinn*, but there was a sure-fire way to check. They would need a length of cloth, some pieces of *holud* and a bucket of water, all of which Aliya's youngest boys scampered off to fetch. What they would do, the imam explained, was try to make the *jinn* speak. They would place the pieces of *holud* in each of the girl's nostrils and then wrap the cloth over her head. They would then pour water slowly over her, making it almost impossible to breathe, let alone speak. However, if there was a *jinn* in there, such a powerful being would have no problem in answering.

The imam's plan was delivered in his usual soft-spoken voice, though at a volume just loud enough for Aliya's daughter-in-law to hear. Munira flung herself upright in bed, proclaiming, 'No, I am fine, I am fine! I am feeling so much better!' and almost ran from the cot to the cooking fire, where she began to stir the pot her mother-in-law had left unattended. The imam smiled at Aliya and, knowing her financial predicament, accepted just a glass of *nimbu pani* for his troubles. Just like that, the matter was fixed.

As she splashed dirty water onto the bright-green leaves, Aliya struggled to keep the smile from playing at the corners of her mouth. It was good to be reminded of such things once again: how everything, no matter how troublesome, will pass.

Her present concerns were more substantive than her neighbour's. Although the money Kalima had paid her for the wedding had kept the wolf from the door, Aliya knew that her reprieve was temporary.

Her gardens might help, and in these initial weeks of spring she would harvest the last of her winter vegetables, keeping a close eye on the fortunes of the first of the summer crop. A lot of this her family would eat, some she would sell and some she would preserve, as syrupy and spiced *chatnis* to be eaten in leaner times when the markets and the gardens were bare.

But future demands hovered. Her daughter Amal's schooling would soon finish, there would be plans to make, and her three younger boys were still years away from discarding their books and uniforms and earning their keep. She had begun to request more complicated embroidery designs from the sari broker, forgoing sleep in exchange for ten or twenty rupees more a piece. This was how she had faced the pervasive unease since their fortunes had curdled, matching multiplying worries with concrete actions. At times it was as though her efforts amounted to little more than filling a cracked vessel, water dribbling hopelessly away each time a little more was poured in.

The events that had shattered Aliya's happiness had begun many years before. There had been a need for a primary school – that much she could accept. This was fifteen years ago, when the only option was for children to travel up the potholed earthen road to a school in the town. Some people in the village, those in local politics, had decided that they should build a school in the village. Furthermore they had identified a tract of land belonging to her husband's family as the perfect spot. It was right by the road, just across the washed-out athletics field from where the high school already stood, adjacent to the plot owned by Nura's husband's family. But the land was not for sale, and Kabir had politely told them no. That was when the visits began.

Over the course of the following months their home was frequented on an almost weekly basis, some visits being prearranged and others unannounced. Party members, neighbours, friends, all came and sat for long and animated discussions with her husband, for Kabir was too gentle and good-natured to turn them away, belonging as he did to an old family that had always benefited from large tracts of land and the financial security and temporal largesse that brought. Aliya would sit in silence or make tea whilst listening. The meetings had been polite enough at the start, amiable entreaties. But each time Kabir had refused them, growing both more stubborn and exasperated with every request. The pressure mounted, but still he resisted; what he was being offered was far too small a sum and, besides, he did not want to sell his land. Aliya agreed with him. Surely people would accept their decision after a while.

But two and then three years passed, and people began to get impatient. Words turned to actions. It was an imperceptible shift, beginning first with the turning of backs. Then neighbours started to refuse to lend Kabir the tools he required to farm the land; the easy exchanges that had always been a part of village life suddenly dissolved. Others refused to help him farm this small plot that had always provided some much-needed work for the poorest, and he was not a farmer, but a tailor after all. In the bazaar, people would not sell him the items he needed for agricultural labour, claiming that they had run out or had never stocked this particular item in the first place. When he travelled further afield, to buy from the shops where they did not know him, his new tools were then vandalised, his crops destroyed overnight, and he began to dread what devastation might greet him in the mornings.

He had gone to the police, who had at first appeared sympathetic.

They had listened as Kabir explained the story: how the gradual requests had turned into something far more threatening and sinister. They had documented everything, and they promised to look into it and get back to him. Only they did not call him, or visit the village as they had agreed. He tried again, but they would not take his calls; or when they did, they said only that they were still looking into things. It became clear that, like so many in public office, the police had eaten the bribes of others and would do nothing.

The land became Kabir's fixation, this gentle man, whose tailor shop in the bazaar was eventually forced to close after he lost so many customers, and the ones he still had became dissatisfied with the work of the distracted, brittle individual they no longer recognised. All the while Aliya had stood by him, tending to the fields and their six children, urging him not to give in, confident that they could weather the storm.

But the day came when he had enough. Isolated and broken, Kabir agreed to sell the land for far less than had originally been offered – a pittance compared to what it was worth. On the day the sale was finalised, he collapsed. Aliya had rushed him to the local hospital, leaving her eldest daughter in charge of her five younger siblings. She had no other choice.

It was some kind of paralysis, they said, not physical but mental. All of their money went to the doctors and healers: what could Aliya do but desperately try to find a cure? They had seen several doctors on the island, growing increasingly frustrated with their explanations that they did not know what had happened to him. They had seen several *gunnin*. She had followed their methods and then gone back to them when their cures failed to work. She had tried again, only still nothing happened. They had gone to Kolkata, where they had consulted an expert, who told her that in his opinion her husband was unlikely ever to recover. She had heard that before.

Aliya had sold off their possessions piece by piece. First another parcel of land. Then their animals. Then what was left of the tailoring business, which she had tried, and failed, to keep going. Then vegetables from the gardens that she had planted. Then her hours, the back-breaking hours, that she spent in front of the sewing frame embroidering saris to be sold for twenty times what she would be paid, worn by people and in places that she would never see. She had spent almost R10,000 trying to find a cure to bring back her husband. When things were untenable, she had taken on debts from loan sharks that she struggled to repay. Although her eldest daughter's in-laws had been understanding, half a *lakh* was still needed as dowry. Aliya had managed to keep her in school until the age of eighteen, just like her younger daughter Amal, and of that Aliya was proud.

Now Kabir lay confined to the cot bed most of the time. He rose each day only for around an hour, normally in the late afternoon as the sun lowered and the call to prayer rang out across the village. Sometimes he would go to the mosque and pray, sometimes he would not. He would then eat before returning to the bed, where he would sleep, or stare at the ceiling, unresponsive. Sometimes there were flickers of the man he had once been. He would sit bolt upright and say something entirely lucid, about how one of their children needed to work harder at school, or that she should consider planting a particular vegetable in the garden, or that he hoped the wedding next door would go smoothly. Most of the time he was absent. It was like living with the dead.

Satisfied that all was well in the garden, Aliya stood up now and stretched. Along with her imminent harvest, other events were gaining momentum – soon there would be an election. Such occurrences were arguably the most important things to happen in the life of the village, in which events linked with the outside world strayed into their messy and self-contained midst. Already along the benches of the tea shop the chatter had turned to politics. Would Mamata be able to maintain her comfortable advantage? Possibly even increase her majority? The island was an old stronghold for the Revolutionary Socialist Party, but over recent years its control had begun to wane, as more and more people were swayed by *Didi*'s charms. Aliya liked the charismatic female leader, her plain white saris, her blunt determination.

Turning her back to the road, she walked slowly back up through her garden, towards the embroidery work that awaited her. Unusually for spring, the sky was the colour of bruised knuckles, and on the horizon heavy clouds had begun to gather, promising rain.

Chapter Fourteen

A Boy Killed by Thunder

The weather had been strange, even for those accustomed to uncertainty and flux. These were supposed to be the sweeter months, the winter banished for another year and the long season of inescapable heat and relentless humidity of the monsoon not yet begun. Storms had blown across the island, tracking up from the Bay of Bengal and reminding everyone of their exposure to the moods of nature, just in case they had become too complacent. It had rained for almost a day without stopping, pausing only briefly as though to draw breath, before gleefully releasing further torrents. The roads were flooded. Thunder bellowed across the fields and jungle, casting angry ripples in the ponds and causing the island to feel untethered, as though it no longer had the protection of the mainland and could drift unexpectedly into the ocean. Or an abyss.

Roshini liked the rain. It made her feel peaceful, allaying her usual restlessness, but even she conceded that it was too early for the *kaal-boishaakhi*, the storms of April and early May that were not anticipated for another month at least. Tempers were already running high at their home, and the unsettling weather only served to further set her mother-in-law on edge. Roshini held a reluctant respect for the way in which Kalima understood their landscape, its generosity as familiar to her as its occasional selfishness and inconsistency. She would tell anyone who listened that in recent years things had begun to change. For Kalima, the land was no different from an old acquaintance who had unnervingly started to act quite unlike herself.

The summers seemed to burn more fervently, their fiery hunger eating greedily into the spring so that its glorious reign now only lasted for a handful of weeks. The rains had been devastating for several years, far exceeding expectations, and last year submerging so much of the island that life had become almost unbearable. The winters had always been cold, but now there was also a choking fog or smog that seemed to congeal in the air. Then in times such as this, when the weather should be mild, pleasant and sunny, furious rain clouds dominated the sky and the rain fell incessantly.

Everyone was fretful about the girl Nusrat, with Kalima growing more and more agitated with each day that she remained absent and unaccounted for. Over the weeks of her absence, Asad had sunk into a bitter sulk, unjustly blaming his mother for their predicament, as though she could somehow be held responsible and should have predicted that an old woman's heart would stop beating on his wedding day; as though she should have known that his bride would become possessed by a *jinn*. Riyaz, too, detached though still sensitive to the fluctuations of his family's fortunes, had swung into one of his dark moods. They had both thought that the presence of this new wife and daughter might have softened Kalima's disposition towards them, when instead she had hardened in the girl's absence. It was all about money, as it so often was. It was also about the past.

Although she may have hoped that her love-marriage might one day be forgiven, the resistance with which Roshini was initially taken into Kalima's household had failed to abate over time. Years passed, relations soured, children were born, tensions rose. Things had come to a head one monsoon night three years before, when the clouds hung low and the sky was black and starless. In the light of a kerosene lantern, Kalima had laid out her case: she could not tolerate all eight of them living under one roof; Asad and his youngest sister were still at home, as well as the new burden of Iffat, who had been unceremoniously left in the care of her grandmother. Kalima would loan Riyaz some money to build a small house on the other side of the clearing, giving them space and privacy for their burgeoning family, and he and Roshini had agreed.

It had not taken Kalima long to begin to ask for repayments, or for rent – whatever they preferred to call it. As Riyaz was technically no longer a member of her household, she also asked him to start paying her some money towards the upkeep of the bicycle, given that he used it to cycle to and from work. At first he had been dismayed at her suggestions, then furious, flinging out threats that if she continued to demand money from her own son in such a fashion, then he would cut off all relations with her, that he and his family would pack up and leave the village entirely. Kalima had responded with a single word: 'Jao' – go.

They had not gone. Where could they go? Their son Said was born soon afterwards and an unhappy truce was agreed, with only occasional flashes of discord when Kalima dragged out the threat of repayment. Both Riyaz and Roshini had hoped that Nusrat's arrival might improve things, Kalima at last having the satisfaction of choosing a bride for her son and acquiring someone to help her with the pressing demands of a home and a growing grandchild. Behind her fierceness, they could both see that a new frailty had crept into her features, and sometimes at night, once their children were sleeping, Riyaz quietly admonished the way in which Asad treated their ageing mother. Nusrat was right to be wary of marriage to a man such as that.

Roshini had carefully watched the girl's deterioration over the days after her brief sojourn in her father's village. Of course Nusrat had been quiet at first, that was to be expected. They had all assumed that a week away would enable her to settle herself, allow her mother and her sister-in-law to better prepare her. But on her return, Nusrat was somehow more afraid and even more uncertain. Not long after that, her alarming behaviour started.

She had begun rocking, whispering verses of the Quran in what sounded like fragmented conversations with herself. She tore at her clothes, but in a way that never revealed her flesh. She pulled out clumps of her hair. She had screamed, fitted, thrown herself to the floor and beaten her arms and legs on the ground with sickening thumps. This had broken her bangles, the symbol of marriage worn by all Bengali women – the red of coral, the white of the conch shell – fragile things, just like a marriage. They lay in glinting shards across the ground. A wife's bangles should only be broken when her husband was dead.

It had not taken long for things to unravel. With a bit of digging, Kalima had quickly learned of Nusrat's previous encounters with the *jinni*. The rundown secondary school that Nusrat had attended was known to hold such malignancies. Shortly after the school was built, the land on which it sat was rumoured to have become *noshto*, or rotten. Nusrat was one of three girls to have been caught by the *jinni* at the same time, and had been treated by a *gunnin* near her father's village. The girls recovered and resumed their schooling shortly afterwards. But Kalima had not been given this information prior to the marriage agreement; she who had so prided herself on her research had been satisfied that she had not needed the services of a *ghatak* to make the requisite checks.

The imam had come after dusk to see the girl, the darkness granting the beleaguered family a little privacy. Roshini knew there was also some respite for her mother-in-law in her conviction that the *jinn* itself was good. The girl had been careful to keep herself covered and had screamed Islamic verses and prayers, all signs that what was inside her was as pious and observant as Kalima believed her new daughter-in-law to be. At other times when caught by *jinni*, women tore their clothes off, swearing, spitting curses, unimaginable vulgarity spewing from their mouths. Roshini knew that Kalima believed there were good and bad *jinni*, just as there were good and bad humans, and that the good were attracted to the good, and the bad to the bad.

Roshini was playing with Said, who was lying on his tummy at her side, transfixed by pushing a broken toy car with only three wheels in looping circles along the floor. She wondered whether there was anything that could be said to the girl that might help her. Nusrat was sixteen, old enough, Roshini thought; after all, she had been two years younger than Nusrat when she had first arrived in the village. And as the burning light of their illicit, youthful union had dimmed, she had faced a marital reckoning of her own: the creeping realisation that this was her life – cooking and sweeping, feeding children, tending a mother-in-law and obeying a husband, this was all that stretched out before her.

At least Riyaz had work at the moment. He had found a labouring job nearby, working on the construction of a new madrasa school up towards a town on the mainland. It was fifteen days' work a month, but it was paid weekly and it was something. When he was occupied he was in a far better humour, less resentful of the family that bound him to the village. Unlike his mother and his younger siblings, Riyaz had been born in Kolkata, leaving when the family returned to the island when he was still a boy. He had lived there again since, and still felt the pull of the city somewhere deep within him, the yearning call that spoke of a different life out there, somewhere.

Roshini could feel the bruise on her shoulder where he had struck her from behind: it was not the sharp pain she was sometimes left with, but a dull ache that presented itself when she moved in a certain way, momentarily forgetting the imprint of his anger on her body. In the past he had beaten her so badly there had been blood, from where her teeth had cut into her cheek, small crescents that stung for days, or where her skin had split from the force of a fist against the bone underneath.

She had never reported it. Roshini knew that some women spoke to the local *onchol* member, the person with arguably the most political power in the village; or sought out the imam, another benign male presence who was willing to offer firm, though calmly delivered, admonishment to the man concerned. A handful even went to the police when something particularly bad happened and discussed filing a case – not that the police would ever do anything about it. Her parents knew. They had always known and would remind her, not infrequently, that she could come home and they would do their utmost to look after her and her children. She was their youngest after all, and a life of violence was not what they wanted for her. But would she be able to take her children? Roshini could never see Kalima allowing that.

Rani watched her nephew Haider toddle along the verandah, advancing a few paces only to glance round and start back in her direction. He would then turn again and forge bravely onwards, making his way in this stop–start fashion towards the steps to peer out into the blanket of rain. The gloam of the afternoon was occasionally splintered by a blaze of lightning on the horizon, followed by a grumble of thunder that shook the earth. Rani worried about Haider in this weather, his small body always sensitive to the fluctuations of their hostile climate. In the cloying, pervasive humidity of the monsoon months his skin rebelled, erupting into rashes that caused him to fuss continuously.

The year before he had looked like a different child. In one of the bouts of sickness that had plagued him ever since he had been pulled, silent and blue, into the world, Haider was suddenly unable to eat. Refusing food was not altogether uncommon for this clingy and anxious little boy, though as the days elapsed the family had shifted from unconcerned to slightly irritated, to panicked. They tried everything, but were unable to cajole or trick him into consuming a single bite, his body growing weaker by the day. For seven days and seven nights all Haider was able to do was cry.

Increasingly concerned, his parents Faraq and Mira had sought the help of two different doctors, both of whom had told them there was nothing medically wrong with him and therefore little they could do to help. Finally, at Bashira's request, they had visited a *gunnin*. This powerful stranger had felt the presence of a *jinn* and looped a protective amulet around the boy's neck, one that he still wore now tucked beneath his T-shirt, and had given them some *phuker tel*, blessed oil imbued with a defensive potency to be smeared over his exhausted body. The following morning Haider had managed a few sodden grains of rice from the breakfast pot of *panta bhat*, at lunchtime a couple of pieces of potato that his mother fed him with tearful relief, and by the evening she was tearing off strips of warm *roti* and placing them into his mouth.

The *jinn* had snared the boy through food, they said. Tabina's daughter-in-law had herself been afflicted a little while before and had unthinkingly followed the instructions of the *gunnin*, bathing in the brackish pond water to wash away the *jinn* from her body. Once it had slid from her slender, slippery form back into the water, she had failed to warn the rest of the Lohani family about what might be lurking in the pond, beneath the surface. The *jinni* were known to love the water, to loiter around the banks and conceal themselves amid the reeds and the gnarled roots of thirsty trees, ready to catch those who strayed into their territory. When Mira washed some vegetables the following morning, crouched in the cool grey mud at the edge of the same pond, the *jinn* must have slid back with her, wrapping itself around the food that she then cooked and fed to her vulnerable, innocent son.

Something similar had happened to Rani's *cha-cha*, her mother Bashira's brother. He too had become possessed after eating *noshto khabar*, rotten or defiling food that, unbeknownst to him, also contained a wicked *jinn*. He had become *pagol*, crazy, so unhinged that he was unable to work, unable even to care for himself. They were never sure exactly what had caused it, although a *gunnin* the family consulted had seen a vision of tiny red flowers, which he concluded must have been sprinkled into the food somehow, opening the door for Rani's uncle to become caught. He had suffered for weeks and although he recovered eventually, he still complained that his digestive system was not quite right. Rani had overheard Tabina say that she would not be too surprised if someone had tried to poison him instead, given how insufferable he was, prompting her mother and her aunt to have one of their infrequent but incendiary rows.

Rani sighed and stretched out her legs to ease the muscles in her calves, which ached from two days cooped up inside while the rain beat down. She wouldn't tell anyone, but she still ran sometimes, sneaking away from the tea shop or from the house during the hot abeyance of the early afternoon, when she knew no one else would be around. And then she would sprint down the paths and through the deserted fields and disgruntled crops, only stopping once her breathing grew fast and jagged in her chest. Inactivity left her despondent, this nervous girl whose limbs were never still.

She had reached the uncomfortable age when she was painfully aware of how others perceived her. How would people describe her? Rani felt embarrassed by her physical appearance, her height and gait ungainly somehow, her hair so thick and with a slight curl that it was almost wild, resonant of the snaking coils of the goddess Kali. Rubina teased her relentlessly about the dark hair that had begun to grow along her top lip, which Sara had also noticed and offered to help with, provided that Bashira agreed. At the moment it was not worth even mentioning Sara's name in front of her mother.

Rani did know that everyone believed she was good at keeping secrets. She had never revealed anything that wasn't hers to tell, instead carrying around the heavy, hidden truths of her family with a resigned determination. She failed to confide in even her closest friend, Nadia, despite the persistent requests for family secrets of the kind that teenage friendships are forged on. It made others wary of Rani, building an impenetrable wall around this ungraceful girl who wore her goodness and her insecurity too close to the surface. As she sat watching her nephew, she wondered whether her siblings would ever reveal their secrets to others; whether her sister would ever find someone to marry her; and whether her brother would one day tell his son that he had killed a little girl.

She did not think that Faraq and Mira would have any more children, her sister-in-law's body no longer being able to withstand the strain. Her pregnancy with Haider had been fraught, as had his birth, and the doctors had advised her not to try again. Rani liked Mira a lot, often feeling closer to her than any of her blood-relatives. Mira was serene, practical, but with a hidden, mischievous sense of humour, a buried gem that, as the quietest in her rowdy family, was frequently overlooked.

As Haider sat mesmerised, drawing a line across the dirt with a drop of rain that had strayed onto the verandah, Rani's thoughts were broken by the shrill chirrups of a phone. She squinted across the courtyard through the curtain of rain to see Mira stand up in the outdoor kitchen and reach for the phone, which she had tucked in an accommodating nook whilst she sliced the vegetables for lunch. Rani could just about hear over the storm as Mira answered with a word, '*Ma?*'

And then Rani saw her fall to the ground.

That night it was Bashira who was seated under the bamboo roof of the outdoor kitchen, stirring a pot by the glow of the lamp. Her daughter-in-law had gone back to her father's village on the mainland, twenty minutes away, although probably longer, given the state the roads were in. The rain had stopped at last sometime that afternoon, but the ravaged ground was swampy, with large puddles gathering along the roadsides and where the land lay flat, creating shimmering pools that stretched across the tarmac. They planned to bury the boy that night, though Bashira could not imagine how the earth would submit, so bloated and sopped that it seemed unlikely a neat hole could be dug. It might be possible as the body was so small, or perhaps they would wait until tomorrow.

She focused again on the pan simmering over the fire, checking the progress of the curry before turning her attention to picking stones from the rice. Her role in these circumstances was to cook, to help the family provide food for the mourners who would soon descend upon their household, the countless relatives who would travel to pay their respects but would nonetheless create an obligation to look after them. Tabina had also offered to spend the evening cooking, no doubt roping in her daughter-in-law for the majority share.

Bashira had watched, dismayed, as both her husband and her son struggled to comfort Mira earlier on, tentative and unsure, as though her indescribable pain at losing her brother might be somehow defiling. It was known by all of the women that the Tablighi Jamaat had questioned their familiar ways of mourning, and that many of the men now found any overt expressions of grief distasteful. After all, they would say, was it not part of God's plan? And weren't they all, sooner or later, to be called to judgement? Many of the women could not understand this, and had no impulse to change their ways.

The boy had been killed by thunder. He had gone into the fields with his father during the storm to help him round up their cows that had been stranded outside since the day before, soaked through and skittish, too valuable to be left to fend for themselves. Their timing had been poor, the wind picking up just as they left the shelter of their huts, the flashes and bellows that cut through the unnatural darkness coming ever closer. And the boy had been struck down. They did not understand how the sound claimed its victim, only that with a deafening roar he was gone, half his body black, the other untouched, as though he were merely sleeping. His father had stumbled home, the corpse of his son in his arms.

In the days that followed, Mira would return to the village, her face dimmed by the loss of her younger brother. She and Faraq would at least console each other in their sadness, both holding close their own losses.

Death was no stranger here and, in most cases, it was just another regular occurrence, to be expected in a place on the margins where life was served up raw. Though undoubtedly distressing, the passing of the old or infirm allowed for the most part only a few days of mourning, before the brusque pace of life resumed. There was always rice to sieve, water to boil, a floor to be swept. And there was often relief, both for those trapped in broken bodies with neither the medications nor the resources to heal them, and for the women (because they were always women) who were responsible for the cleaning and care of the sick or infirm. Even the loss of children was, though devastating, nothing particularly out of the ordinary; of a thousand children born, thirty-five would not survive.

Bashira understood loss intimately, especially what it was like to lose a child. Her body had been like her mother-in-law Maryam's, subject to the nervous quivers of pregnancy, unable to carry all of her children into the world in one piece. She had lost eight babies, some in the early weeks of pregnancy, others later, and a couple just moments after birth. With each one it was as though she had grown both harder and softer, a toughening of her exterior and a hopeless disintegration inside. Although she knew it was not accepted by her faith, and a belief she would likely be condemned for, Bashira took comfort in the idea of reincarnation. She sometimes wondered whether the little ghosts of her children were now grown-up, animating new bodies, leading fulfilling lives somewhere else.

She growled as her foot went numb and shifted her legs, a few firm strikes of an open palm on her roughened sole encouraging her sluggish blood to flow again. Sitting on the floor by the open fire was not easy for a body as unwieldy as hers, a body that had endured an undeniably hard existence.

Bashira had been abandoned as a little girl. Twenty-one days after she had been born, her father had divorced her mother. When her mother quickly remarried, Bashira was left behind with her grandparents, as was customary. As soon as she could toddle a few steps, she was put to work on the land and she rarely attended school. There was no choice but to marry her off at thirteen to a poor family in order to ease their own financial woes. Her grandfather died two years after her marriage, her grandmother not long after that, and from then on Bashira was an orphan. Unlike Kalima's daughter, who came back to the village now and again to visit

Iffat after she had remarried, her mother had nothing further to do with Bashira.

Though it had only ever known hardship, Bashira's body had nonetheless expanded. By the time she was married she was taller than almost everyone, the monotonous years of child-bearing adding bulk to her already-broad frame. Maryam was also tall, and struggled to conceal her anger at her inability to use her height to look down upon Bashira, the new addition to their family. The early clashes between them had been quite something to witness, a tiger and a wolf drawing a snarling, snapping circle around each other.

Bashira's stature gave her power. She could visit the bazaar unaccompanied, day or night, without the usual concerns for her safety. Unlike most women, she knew that she could even use her body to intimidate others. It also granted her freedom, and in the past she had made the journey to Delhi alone to visit her daughter. Of course, as a woman, she had to be careful, but she was not plagued to the same extent by the fear of being raped and thrown off a moving train, as happens in India at least once a year. She loved that long, grinding cut across the country, a whole day – more in fact – spent aboard a rusty and overcrowded carriage: unfamiliar people to talk to, the excitement of the city with its busy streets and enticing smells, a place where no one knew her family.

Her physical attributes also created problems. Her towering height cast a dark shadow, her voice was a low rumble, her mouth was always crimson with *paan* and people were frightened of her. Most other women were too afraid or repulsed to entertain a friendship with a woman of her size and, she would admit, her coarse disposition. A body like hers, many thought, should not really belong to a woman. Which begged the question: what kind of a woman was she? Bashira knew of the rumours about her, not that anyone would have been bold or stupid enough to repeat them to her face. She knew of the suggestions about how she made her money, the questions about how she spent those long, torrid hours in the bazaar. But she didn't care; let them think what they like.

Chapter Fifteen

Tensions Rising

It had happened a month before. April, early one morning, there was a commotion in the road. The shouting came from near Tabina's house, and a man's voice punctured the reticent dawn with bellowed threats. Sara's voice was heard, begging him not to, followed by a yelp of pain.

No one wanted to discuss what was said, though many had heard it.

He would tell everyone.

He could identify the intricacies of the moles and scars on her body.

He would prove it, if they asked him to.

The following day, Sara had gone.

Tabina should have known there would be trouble. As she sat on her verandah, seeking shade in the rising throb of the late-morning summer heat whilst easing the last of the broad beans from their furred husks, her thoughts were distracted. Sara had first approached her so long ago now that she struggled to remember when it had all begun.

After the last of her operations, her memory had become unreliable and she had on occasion found herself in the jostle of the bazaar unable even to recall the cost of the kilo of rice she was haggling over. What she knew was that Sara had offered her a not-immaterial amount of money for the use of her room for an occasional hour or two at dawn, and for her silence. Tabina had assented, asking few questions.

She was happy to rise early and vacate the cluttered room, wrapping herself in a shawl and sitting at the other end of the verandah, allowing her body to unknit itself from sleep. An early start meant that her husband could make a few long journeys to Canning and back again in the cool of the morning, taking passengers who commuted to the city, where they would cram themselves into the rusted carriages of the lumbering local train to be borne north. They had never spoken about what Sara was doing, or why she was meeting in secret a man who was not her husband, although of course Tabina knew. But what others did in their personal lives was none of her business.

What she did not need, however, was trouble, which was what made what had happened so unwelcome. In the days after the incident she had called Sara several times, on each occasion the ringtone eventually being cut off by the curt pre-recorded voice inviting her to leave a message. Tabina did not want to leave a message. She had overheard Sara's daughter Nadia explaining loudly to Rani that her mother had gone to take care of a sick brother in Kolkata, which, given what they knew of her family on the island, could only be a lie.

A week or so after the altercation, Sara reappeared. She arrived during the mid-morning hush when the village was quiet, climbing as elegantly as she could manage out of a rickshaw with a small bag.

Though she had undoubtedly timed her arrival to draw as little attention as possible, Tabina caught sight of her from her customary position at the tea shop. From the other side of the road, she could see the sterile green of the sling that now cradled Sara's left arm, but was unable to catch the expression on her face, her eyes hidden behind large sunglasses.

Since then Sara had largely kept out of sight, although her name remained on everyone's lips. Who was the man? How long had the affair been going on? Did Khan know and, if so, what was he going to do about it?

Tabina avoided these discussions, keen to minimise any role she might have had in the sordid affair in which everyone was interested. And her attention was soon occupied elsewhere. As the summer heat rose, anticipation hummed and all thoughts turned to politics. The election was almost here.

Voting fervour had swept across the state with characteristic aplomb. TV channels fixated on flamboyant political characters: former actors, religious firebrands, white-clad spinsters and their bitterly fought electoral contests. Billboards materialised overnight, with towering murals depicting benevolent smiles and hands graciously pressed together. Strings of flags danced between the buildings and along shop fronts, their owners often hedging their bets and displaying those of multiple parties, keen not to deter any potential customers. Bumper-stickers loudly declared not only that drivers loved their India, but also their support for Mamata or Modi, or the RSP or the CPIM. Symbols of the two main parties were everywhere: flowers blossomed, whilst hammers and sickles shone.

In the village grubby newspapers, softened by the caress of many fingers, were examined intently, their details torn apart in animated debates amongst the men in the tea shops, over steaming cups of *cha*. Crackling radios relished the scandals that rocked the ruling TMC party when a grainy video clip was released, appearing to show a high-ranking official accepting a bribe. Yet most people still thought that *Didi*'s grip on power in the state looked unshakable, even likely to be strengthened perhaps, and were unconvinced that the bribe had ever taken place, the amount stipulated being regarded as too small to warrant all the fuss.

Those who had left the island for work in Kolkata, or Mumbai or Delhi, reappeared, leaner, hungrier from the cities, anxious to cast their votes before returning once more to their adopted homes. All were worried that, should they fail to vote, their citizenship might be called into question. These were only rumours of course, but they were so well-worn that they possessed the authority of facts. Loss of statehood was a terrifying prospect for those on the bottom rungs of society, particularly Muslims, who might be accused of slipping across the shifting border with Bangladesh in search of something better. Flowers, spades and sickles sprouted on the earthen walls of houses in the village and, for some, the air was fragrant with the scent of nascent opportunity.

Tabina possessed the mind of a huntress and found the election thrilling. As in most households in the village, she knew that her husband would gather together the family members and instruct them for whom they must cast their vote. She indulged him in this little charade, but as soon as he had left – sloping off to work or to shoot the breeze with the men at the tea and toddy shops – she would issue counter-orders to the family. To begin with, she urged them to vote for whomever they wanted, before expressing her own preferences for a different party from that of her husband. She posed hers as advice, not instruction, and was convinced that it worked, able to tell from the small nods and reticent half-smiles that the family would be voting with her.

This was one of many ways that she had endeared herself to the ruling party. Tabina had approached them long before this particular election, asking whether there was anything she could do to assist, letting them know that her house was always available for use as a temporary refuge, should sparks of electoral violence disrupt the peace of the village. This contest was less significant, however, being only for state representatives. It was during the local battles that politics became especially dirty.

Tabina had heard that in the last local contest the elected member to the *onchol* had been required to spend one and a half *lakhs* of his family's own money to buy enough of the votes in the village to ensure a majority. This was a laborious art, going under the cover of darkness from house to house, offering women a new sari or a palmful of notes. Some asked for both, or more, and there was little choice but to acquiesce. It was a forward-looking investment, an amount that would certainly be recouped through the torrent of bribes that the elected member would soon receive from all corners: police officers, aspirational party members and political supplicants.

During the first two years of Tabina's marriage, when her husband was absent in Delhi, there had been an election. One night, days before the vote itself, the tension of an evening in her mother-in-law's company had been eased by the arrival of an unfamiliar woman. Maryam had welcomed her and a short conversation had taken place, asking about family members, exchanging titbits of village gossip, before the visitor drew from a cloth bag a new sari and placed it on the floor, along with the weighty words of gratitude for their support.

And then she had left. An hour or so later, feeling that enough time had passed, Tabina asked her mother-in-law what exactly had happened. Maryam had turned slowly to look at her, wolfish eyebrow raised, and said simply, '*Gramer niyom* – it's the rule of the village.'

As the beans clattered into the metal bowl now, the husks tossed aside into a growing pile on a scrap of newspaper, Tabina shook her head at her own naïvety. She had been only fifteen when she had married, a somewhat pointless exercise when one considered what had happened next. The ceremony had taken place at 12 p.m. on a Thursday. The following day, after attending the customary Friday *namaz*, her new husband had left for Delhi, where he had remained for the next two years.

First uprooted, then abandoned, Tabina had learned a lot during that time, not least how to navigate her mother-in-law. As the years passed, she came to understand Maryam's earlier losses, the old wounds that made her fiercely, understandably protective of the children who had survived. She learned how to balance their conflicting tempers – when to stand up to Maryam, and when to submit – so that now at last they had reached a comfortable kind of truce. Tabina ran the household, seeing that when women controlled the finances families stayed afloat, often foundering when they did not. She had worked tirelessly to get her family where they were: charming party members, exploiting government schemes, demanding support. Three sons, all educated to Class 12, two with jobs, the last at college. The problem was that she wanted more.

Dawn broke with a fiery kiss. It would be scorching, hotter even than yesterday maybe. And it would be a day not filled with the usual, relentless hum of mundane activities. Instead the scattering of shops along the road were shut, the paths quiet, no queue of impatient though resigned women waiting to use the water pump. An order was in place on the island and elsewhere, intended to curb any clashes between warring party factions, stipulating that there was but one reason for people to leave their houses today: to cast their vote.

The peace stood in contrast to the chaos of the day before when the road was crammed with buses and minivans, bringing with them electoral monitors, members of the central forces whose job it was to oversee proceedings, and anxious voters returning home. Rickshaws close to spilling their riders careered down the road, eager to deposit their numerous patrons onto the searing tarmac before returning for another load. On the crowded rooftops of the buses, groups of men braved the blistering sun. The army officers, from Kerala and Rajasthan – far-away places that, hopefully, ensured their impartiality – loitered on the roadside in their smartly pressed uniforms, their presence itself enough of a suggestion of the rule of law. Excitement coursed through the air, along with its cousin, violence.

The voting would take place at the primary school next to Nura's house. The officials had gathered long before the gates were opened at 7 a.m., checking that the voting machines were working, the entrances and exits secured, and taking every possible precaution to ensure that what transpired would be beyond reproach. Two lines of eager voters began to form outside, snaking in opposite directions, one of women, one of men. The aged and the infirm were brought to the gates on wooden cycle carts, their limp and fragile bodies swathed in loose cloth, waiting to be carried inside by younger relatives. When the gates were finally opened, the officers stood guard on either side, checking names against a crumpled list, barring anyone who did not live in the village from entering.

Kalima arrived early, anxious to avoid the fevered heat of the midday sun. Like so many, she had bathed and put on one of her better saris, relishing the ritual of the occasion and the momentary feeling of being witnessed. She carried with her a tattered umbrella that she shared happily with another woman in the line, craning to see who else had come early to vote. Emerging sometime later with her blue-inked forefinger proudly displayed, she loitered near the gate, speaking in excited Hindi to the officers stationed outside, who indulged her for a few minutes before politely reminding her of the need to hurry along. No one was supposed to go beyond the boundary of their home if they didn't need to.

It was late morning when Sara walked down the road. By then the heat was radiating in soft waves off the tarmac, casting shimmers through the air. She was swathed in a sari of teal-coloured crêpe, as bright as the eye of a peacock feather, adorned with glinting costume jewellery, dark maroon lipstick and the sunglasses that she had not been seen without since her return. Her husband walked beside her, smart in his short-sleeved shirt, ironed beige chinos and groomed moustache, all bearing the mark of one for whom discipline was a way of life. Those waiting could not help but stare at the couple, who appeared to have been lifted from a page of a magazine, as if they did not truly belong in this dusty, out-of-the-way place. Of course they stopped to chat to the army personnel flanking the entrance, their Hindi surprising and delighting the military observers, pleased to have an excuse to speak to the glamorous pair. In the courtyard of the school they parted, each taking their place in the separate queues, one of vibrant saris, the other of white *kurtis*. Whilst Khan exchanged pleasant small talk with those around him, Sara stood in silence.

Not long afterwards, the former *onchol pradhan* arrived. She was

Khan's sister and, though no longer in power, she remained a significant figure in the village. She moved with as much grace as she could
muster along the dry road, constrained by her age and her large and
uncooperative body. Her appearance was one of an abandoned dessert,
her alabaster skin gently melting in a pastel purple sari under a parasol
held high above her head. She glided in her measured way to the front
of the line, beckoned to Sara to join her and they entered to cast their
votes immediately. No one uttered a word of rebuke. Afterwards they
all left together, her sister-in-law taking Khan's left arm, Sara the right,
walking slowly back up the road until they disappeared in the glint of
the wavering air against the horizon, making their way home.

In a swirl of dust the district overseer arrived; there had been allega-
tions of disturbances at some of the polling stations on the island. The
officials moved quickly from the car to the gate into the courtyard,
ignoring the startled looks of those waiting patiently in line. Heavily
fortified cars cruised slowly past, one containing bulky video equipment mounted on its roof like some audio-visual gun turret in order to
document what was taking place, for any alleged impropriety. Tension
peppered the air before deflating – the violence was elsewhere and everybody visibly relaxed. The cars left as quickly as they had arrived, but
a muttering circulated down the lines: the curfew would remain in
place until tomorrow morning, and no one must venture out after dark.

In the flaccidity of the early afternoon the courtyard in front of the
school was almost deserted, save for the shadows cast by the large
banyan tree. The crowds inevitably picked up once it was cooler, and
people hurried to cast their votes before nightfall. The calm belied
what would happen – the Revolutionary Socialist Party's stronghold
had unexpectedly fallen, and Mamata had won.

*

Aliya had sat on her verandah and watched those going to and from the primary school, waiting to cast her own vote in the lavender light of the early evening, shortly before the iron gates would be shuttered, the voting machines disconnected and stored securely and then transported away for the count. Now the village was eerily still and the road deserted, unusual for a summer's night in which the rustle and hiss of the cicadas and other insects would steadily build into a cacophonous roar as the heat began finally to depart. She was desperately behind with her embroidery work – the build-up to the election had been fraught and she had been managing a political drama of her own.

It was almost two weeks since her son Imran had been attacked. The wound on his head had closed over the bone into a jagged and angry scar, one that would undoubtedly leave a permanent mark upon which his hair would never again grow. The boy was still not quite himself, though he had gone through the stage of frenetic jumpiness and then lethargy commonly experienced after an assault, as though initially summoning the energy to flee before sinking into the resigned stupor of prey.

It had happened on the next island down. One afternoon after college he and a couple of friends had caught a boat over, one of those low and overcrowded vessels whose edges barely skimmed the muddy river's surface. Imran had been hanging about in the main town when the group approached him, accusing him of stealing something. That he was innocent should have meant something, although it did not. That he was Muslim should have meant nothing, although it did. They belonged to the RSS, purportedly a benign religious organisation, but in fact a Hindu nationalist paramilitary group, members of which felt with increasing impunity that they had the licence to police what went on in this all-of-a-sudden Hindutva nation. Imran's friends had run away, terrified. Somehow he had made his way home, back through the town, back to the *ghat*, limping, bleeding. By the time Aliya had seen him stumbling up the path towards her, her boy could barely stand.

Aliya's hands had not shaken when she called the journalist. The man had come the following afternoon, bringing with him a camera and a notebook, and he had sat with Imran indoors, out of sight, as he recounted what had happened. The doctors had given him painkillers for the stitches in his scalp, but the wound throbbed and his skin felt as though it had somehow shrunken his head. Watching this man, this stranger, record the intimate details was so uncomfortable for Aliya that she grappled with the urge to stand up and scream. But what choice did she have? The journalist's money could pay for the doctor's fees, any future medical bills, the extra tuition her son might need to make up for the schooling he had missed and even cover some of the family's most pressing debts. She sat on her hands and encouraged her son with gentle nods of her head. It had not taken long for the journalist to track down those responsible; and not long for their families to make them an offer, to keep the story quiet.

Aliya rubbed her aching neck. Visiting the primary school to cast her vote was always bittersweet. In the hush of moonlight, when dreams for the future can be unashamedly uncovered, she and her husband had once talked of their sons building their own houses there, their family swelling and expanding close together in contented bliss. This dream, of course, would now never materialise.

Her sister-in-law Mumtaz had returned to the village once again, this time to cast her vote. Her presence reminded Aliya of the misfortune that had befallen her husband's family, whose foundations had once seemed so secure, their fortunes so prosperous.

Mumtaz had hardened in the city, Aliya thought. She had moved there ten or eleven years ago after being divorced by her husband, choosing to make her own way rather than remain a burden to her family. She had nurtured a belief in the capital, the pulsing heart of the nation in which she was sure there must be something for her to do. She had found a job collecting newspapers for recycling and was earning good money, the wages far higher in the city, although so were the costs of everything else. Little by little she was saving up enough to buy a small piece of land in the village. All she wanted was one day to come back to her place of birth, her *jonmostan*.

The two women had sat up late into the darkness the night before the election. Aliya had been sewing, and although her sister-in-law would not help, she did offer her conversation. Their discussions had turned to the *milat* for *Nani* Ashima, an event that had already begun to pester Aliya's thoughts. It was a tradition, an expected ceremony after someone had passed away in the village, at which the Quran was read by several *maulanas* and a feast was provided for all who attended. It was believed that the recitation could be dedicated to the soul of the departed, aiding them in their passage through the afterlife and improving their standing in the eyes of Allah. There would be money and new clothes required for those reciting, plus the expense of the food for an as-yet-unspecified number, which could feasibly run into the hundreds.

'It will take us time,' Aliya had said, winding crimson thread around a spool.

'*Santi thak, didi* – we will all do our part, sister,' replied Mumtaz, smiling at Aliya, her reassurance revealing that she had sensed her sister-in-law's worry.

Aliya wanted to do all she could for the soul of her mother-in-law.

She was a fervent believer in the afterlife, taking comfort in the fact that the challenges of life were at least fleeting, and that in judgement one reaped what one sowed. Like all of the women, except for Sara, she believed that death was followed by a reawakening in the afterlife, at which point one's life on earth would be subject to judgement. Any sins or wrongdoings counted against a speedy passage to *Jannah*, although the prayers and recitations of those still on earth could help to mitigate these impediments, allowing a soul to travel more quickly to paradise.

There was never a shred of self-pity about Aliya, and many around her marvelled privately at the graceful way she had dealt with adversity. Yet deep within her, she did hope that balance would be restored. Given the injustice she had suffered in her life on earth, the worldly wrongs that she had no ability to redress, she longed – as many of the powerless do – for a divine resolution.

Chapter Sixteen

Waiting for the Moon

They were waiting for the moon. The summer had conceded days before; the steamy, stifling pressure in which air and water grew ever closer together was broken at last by the settling in of the monsoon. The heat had been unbearable, so unrelenting in its persistence that many had wondered in disgruntled mutters what they had done to deserve such unwanted attentions. They did not know that it was part of a wider shift, a pervasive global lurch towards combustion that would be recorded as the hottest six months ever on record. On the island the monsoon had brought relief, but now they were left with the rain and the ravenous ache of hunger.

The end of Ramzan was about to fall. The torturous month of fasting would once again draw to a close, and the strictures of the everyday would be shaken loose for the momentary joy of shared celebration. In repetitive days that bled into one another in their laborious constraints, this occasion was special, the one in the year that everyone looked forward to most. Perhaps it was the heat, but in the village the mood was somehow different this year, less gleefully expectant and more impatient, restless, and the news about the fickle moon had not helped.

There were rumours that it would not appear when expected. They relied on cues from far-away places that they heard about in sermons at the mosque or could recognise on the woven prayer mats or the out-of-date calendars purchased at the Islamic book-*mela*. The word had been relayed from Saudi Arabia that the anticipated sighting of the moon the following evening was likely to be delayed by at least a day, possibly even two. The curve of the world and the curve of the moon had collided, and the sliver of silver would only be glimpsed in Polynesia. For the rest of the global *Ummah* there would be one more day to wait.

By the following afternoon a delay was almost certain. Nura had listened to the sleepy chatter by the water pump that morning, and overheard the complaints of people making their way down the path behind her house to and from the roadside. She had decided that she would allow Radhia to henna her hands regardless, desperate for a way to occupy her increasingly boisterous daughter for another long afternoon in which she herself was woozy from fasting. She knew that the time it would take to coax Radhia into sitting still, and then to keep her hands unencumbered lest she smudge the dye, would make it a lengthy task and one that, given the demands of the day before Eid, she could really do without. Nura was exhausted. The month of fasting had been unexpectedly hard; she had once again become caught by a *jinn*.

It had happened at dusk two months before. She had felt uncomfortable as soon as she had left her house at the call to prayer, making her way in the dull light of the early evening towards the pond. Treading carefully down the muddy bank, Nura had crouched at the edge of the water, its coolness a welcome respite on her hot, sticky skin. As she had begun to wash her hands and feet with practised care, she felt a creeping sensation of unease, as though something or someone was behind her. Only there was no one; she was alone. Walking back up the bank and through the fields towards home, she moved quickly, keen to shake off the stirrings of disquiet within. But when she rolled out her mat and began to pray, she could not rid herself of the feeling that something was inside her, moving around in her blood and constricting the space around her skull.

Her nights soon became a torment of ghoulish nightmares, unbroken fevers and a body racked with pain. She would wake each morning exhausted and deeply shaken, unable or unwilling to articulate what was happening to her.

As she sat now on the step, watching Radhia drag a small wooden stick through the thick, umber paste to trace over the swirling flowers she had outlined on her daughter's palm, Nura ran her own fingertips along her forearm. Small bumps and blisters in curling lines and other strange, deliberate patterns had begun to appear on her body. These welts were proof: there was something there.

She had gone to visit a powerful *gunnin* on the island, explaining to him what had happened. She had revealed her past – how this was not the first time, how she had been caught before, back in Delhi almost twenty years ago. Then it had not been in the dark that the *jinn* had caught her, but when she was asleep, whiling away the lonely hours bolted inside the cramped room that she and her husband rented. There was little else for her to do. It was not too long before she had begun to wake up on the pavement outside the gates to their apartment compound, with no idea or explanation of how she got there.

She had been cured that first time. On this second occasion the *gunnin* prescribed a particularly strong kind of magic. He sent her back to the village and asked her to return with a chicken to be sacrificed, the blood from which he used to scratch out the Quranic verses and numerical codes of the *tabiz* protection amulets to be placed at the four corners of her home. A further piece of paper was to be hung above the door to the cluttered inner room in which she and her husband slept, in an attempt to combat the violent dreams she was suffering.

It had only been days later that there had been an earthquake on the islands, nothing like the tremors that had been felt here all the way from Nepal the year before, but the land pitching violently nonetheless, the houses shaking, the magic unceremoniously undone. Nura knew this meant that the spell would have been broken, and she was once again waiting. She would visit the *gunnin* again after Eid.

Up the path, past Aliya's homestead, at Kalima's home, things were quieter than in previous months after another *gunnin*'s magic had taken effect. Nusrat had returned to the village and was better, if not quite the girl she had been before. She had spent the long and static weeks of Ramzan succumbing to the inevitable pull of domestic chores, learning under the stern guidance of her mother-in-law and Roshini's gentler suggestions how to cook the rice until it was just the way they liked, how to cajole the dust and dirt from the nooks of the earthen floor, how to brew the first cups of morning *cha* a little stronger than those drunk later on in the day. She made many mistakes, but no longer seemed determined to free herself of her surroundings; and when not called upon to help, she would sit placidly out of the way, allowing the lives of the family to wash over and around her.

As hoped for, the troubles with her new daughter-in-law had softened Kalima towards her already-familiar one. There were moments when an exasperated glance would flick between her and Roshini, or a shared smile would tickle the corners of their mouths as they overheard Asad exclaiming in frustration from the inner room at yet another clumsy misstep of his new bride. Kalima would never forgive Roshini for the past and kept her grievances close to her heart, but it was as though at last she had realised that no daughter-in-law would ever be perfect.

Kalima felt old. Her body had been plundered by the events of recent months – the monsoon and the dramatic change in the weather further rattling a depleted figure already worn out from the wedding and the tumultuous revelations that had followed. She had caught a chill, shivering beneath the scratchy wool of the moth-eaten jumper she wore in spite of the humidity, her bossiness and caustic bravado unable to shake the cold that had crept into her bones. She decided that she would do without a new sari for Eid this year, and instead a fleece blanket was all she wanted, something to keep the night's cool fingers away, now that her granddaughter, Iffat, was growing to an age when she no longer wanted to sleep cuddled up to her grandmother.

The fire of Kalima's eyes was, however, undiminished; only those who knew her well would even have detected that she was a little under the weather, as she bustled around the clearing making the final preparations for Eid, chatty and commanding as normal.

'O! O Shahara! O Iffat! O! Come and watch your grandmother! One day you will need to do this.'

She was making *shimai*, the milky, syrupy desert for which she was famous. The smell of perfectly caramelised sugar sliced apart the heavy air of the rain waiting to fall.

The children were desperately excited. Roshini watched as they ran full pelt around the clearing, ignoring their grandmother's calls, screaming and chasing one another and tumbling into the knotted undergrowth before they reappeared, breathless with shrieks of laughter.

In due course she relented, allowing them to look at the outfits that had been so carefully chosen for them, the one gift that she and Riyaz would be able to give them this year. She struggled to keep the tears from her eyes as her daughters admired the tiny pieces of majestic blue and golden-yellow fabric, covered in sequins and stones, full of the as-yet-untasted excitement of putting them on. She was looking forward to the end of Ramzan, the end of fasting and the joy of Eid, longing for the comfortable familiarity of the everyday, when she would once again be left alone with the dark.

Unlike Roshini, Rani had come to dread the fall of darkness. It was the time when distraction ceased, when the family gathered in the lamplight to break their fast, before they returned once again to the inevitable discussions surrounding her older sister. They had still not found a groom for Rubina; another year had been squandered. The monsoon months were those in which weddings were unthinkable, the weather and the inconvenience making travel on the islands and the mainland a foolish prospect. The elders in her family nursed a simmering frustration. Rubina was almost eighteen, and Rani would be sixteen in the spring; they were running out of time.

In spite of the other pressures that buffeted her away from education, Rani had managed to remain in school. There was no extra tuition to help her, and for many frustrating hours she was stranded behind the counter in the tea shop, itching to be elsewhere. But nonetheless she had persevered, allowing her sari-embroidering work to fall away completely in favour of attending class and trying to keep on top of her homework, doing the best she could.

She was also able to spend time with her closest friend Nadia again, her mother no longer forbidding her from setting foot in Sara's home. A fragile truce appeared to have been brokered with the family across the road, her aunt Tabina ever the pragmatist, easing the tension between the warring women. Bashira's anger and Sara's belligerence had both cooled, perhaps in the presence of other more pressing matters to focus upon, or perhaps in the creeping realisation that they were really not so different after all.

Tabina might have said that she was happy, though given what she understood to be the twists and turns of life, she was wary of such an emotion. In the aftermath of the election, she had resolved to try and ingratiate herself further with this newly successful political party – its electoral permanence and widespread popularity seemingly fixed. It was three years until another general election would take place; ample time, she thought, to ensure that she benefited heartily from their victory.

After a year in which her family had not done badly, she was also planning a journey. It had been too long since she had seen her middle son, who lived in Delhi, where he worked in a factory as a poultry-cutter. She missed her boy, and her grandson, whom she had not laid eyes on for more than two years, and she could not wait for the excitement of a trip to the capital and to scoop them both into her arms.

Bashira, too, was plotting to undertake a similar voyage – it was high time she visited that filthy, frantic metropolis. Her daughter had begged her to come, her husband being unable to take enough time off from the sportswear factory for them to make the trip back to the island over Eid. Although the journey would be expensive, Bashira's family fortunes had stabilised, if not advanced. Some of their debts had been repaid, and the tea stall was as busy and popular as ever. It would not be too long before Ali Tariq would be able to drive the rickshaw once again, his additional income desperately welcome.

Sara had spent most of the evenings of Ramzan alone. Her arm had healed, and she no longer needed to wear the sling that announced her secrets loudly to anyone who saw it. Nonetheless she still cradled it gently, with the caged wariness of someone who is reacquainting themselves with a limb. She moved with uncharacteristic caution as she laid out the chipped china plates, the slices of apple, the dates, the sugary cubes of watermelon for the moment when the call from the mosque would relieve them once again of the burden of fasting.

She knew that, after that morning, the details of her affair had slithered around the village, no doubt twisting and morphing into something quite unrecognisable. Her husband had always known, she now believed; the other man was, after all, one of his oldest friends on the island. She knew, too, of the existence of Khan's other life in the city – of women he may have entertained in exactly the same way as she had another man, though she did not know any of the details. They had reached some kind of impasse over the years, the love and the chasm between them both somehow insurmountable, leaving them trapped. As the power cut out and she reached for the emergency lantern, she wondered if it would be tonight that Khan would return home or if he would wait, prolonging his absence until the moon itself was sighted.

Aliya watched from the mud verandah as the final splinters of light dissolved from the sky. She had weathered another storm; her son was better and, aside from an ugly scar, he had been little affected by his attack. Imran had returned to college, quietly resuming his studies. For the first time in many years she had saved enough money from the payout she had negotiated to buy each of her children a small and inexpensive present for Eid, and she basked in the pleasure of treating them. She could feel her eyes stinging as she sought out the thread with her thumb; how many more years could she continue to sew? It was harder during the winter and monsoon months, when the light was low and the shadows stole up on her.

For the women not born on the island, it took a while to become accustomed to the dark. At first they could not help but be overwhelmed by its impenetrable majesty, this looming presence that softened the edges of all they knew, sweeping away the familiar with an ominous hush. But the night soon took on a reassuring quality. The women now frequently failed to notice the onset of evening, so consumed were they in the repetitive cycle of domestic chores and family responsibilities. They had even come to enjoy those hours before nightfall, as the day eased around them, losing its sharp edges, when the fierce gaze of the sun at last began to wane and the world would slowly and defiantly turn black. And for those born here, the untamed night was all they had ever known.

Although it was a test with which she was intimately familiar, the broken nights of fasting had looted Maryam's reserves this year. Waiting all day to eat, only to rise so early that it was still dark when she ate again, left her winded, tiredness settling itself around her in a way that she struggled to shake. Her skin hung loose from her bones, and her face bore the perplexed indignation of a discarded pillowcase suddenly deprived of its stuffing.

The family was not worried about her. There was a flintiness to Maryam; she had seen out storms and monsoons, and Ramzan in the village, many, many times before and would most likely keep on doing so. Though her body suffered, her arrival always being announced by the harsh scrape of her stick, her mind was for the most part still sharp. Only occasionally could they see that the pages had become worn, crumpled together, so that she could no longer always be sure what was real and what she had imagined. In truth, she liked it that way.

The waiting gave time for reflection – the passing of another year. The women thought of their futures and, where they had them, the futures that belonged to their daughters, those magical balloons that seemed to float away untethered from the dust and grit of their reality: Rani avoiding getting married, and Amal going to study not one but two degrees at college, when their families had barely enough money to scrape together in order to feed and clothe them; the hopes that their village might somehow be swept along in that glorious tide they understood as 'development', when they could not even afford to bribe someone from the local *onchol* office to lay some bricks down the path, so that they did not have to wade through ankle-deep mud during the rains.

This month of punishing introspection served to remind the women where their hoped for salvation lay. It was a question they had all considered, one that gnawed at and troubled them: if they were able to read the Quran, would they understand their faith in the same way as men?

Only Kalima was partially able to accomplish this feat, a skill she had been taught at madrasa school as a girl, the Arabic words repeated so many times that they had worn smooth in her memory. Yet she did not understand them, being unable to interpret what was being said for those who might have been curious enough to ask her. This holiest of books – this object that all the women revered, were they lucky enough to possess one – was inaccessible to them, despite the fact that its words and its teachings cast a gossamer net over every part of their lives. Can you imagine, Nura would say to anyone who would listen, that in other countries the rules that bind people are read and understood by everyone? Even women?

Watching the construction of the new girls' and women's madrasa school alongside her vegetable garden, this space designated for female learning and instruction, Aliya grew more certain each day that the answers they were looking for, in order to lead better lives, might soon be revealed. At least this was what she hoped for.

All of the women believed in the power of prayer, along with the power of their dreams. Dreams and visions were understood as being intricately woven into the rich fabric of Islam, fundamental to their religion's origins and the very foundations upon which the faith came into being. It was through strange visions and hearing voices that the Prophet, peace be upon him, was first instructed to begin the Muslim faith. It was in a dream – the famed night of the Miraj, or ascension – that he travelled from Mecca to Jerusalem, led by angels and on the back of a heavenly steed. There he prayed alongside other prophets, before being led through *Jannah* and *Jahannam*, finally coming face-to-face with God.

Years later, Muhammad understood himself to be an interpreter of dreams, an art only able to be practised by those closest to Allah. The Prophet was known to have said that a true dream – one free from both the interference of Shaytan and from the desires and experiences of the dreamer – was a small fragment of prophecy. After the dawn prayers, the stories tell that he would turn to those gathered and ask them whether anyone had dreamed the night before and, if so, of what? Listening carefully, he would then interpret and explain the dreams for those who followed him.

During her most recent operation Tabina had dreamed that she would die on the operating table, a terrifying prospect that had prompted her to cry out to Allah to save her. She had awoken hours later from the grog of the anaesthesia, her abdomen a fist of pain, but alive.

Maryam had dreamed of an accident days before it happened, a dream in which she pleaded with Allah to spare the life of her son. He had survived, and ever since she had ensured that he fulfilled his religious obligations.

Bashira rarely dreamed, and when she did, it was not at night, but during the day when the shop was quiet and she could stare out from behind the counter, losing her thoughts in the sunlight that danced across the road, making treasure from the tiny iridescent stones that dotted its surface. She dreamed of security, of a time when she would no longer be plagued by incessant worry about her daughters.

Although she would not speak of it, her youngest daughter Rani still dreamed of becoming a police officer: the uniform, the purpose, the power of being more than just a girl.

Kalima's dreams were often of the *jinni*. They appeared as shapeshifters, mischievous boys from the madrasa school in the village running down the paths, something unidentifiably out of place on their faces, before they transformed into monstrous apparitions. In her night-time expeditions, all others around her had run away terrified, hiding under their blankets in the hope that the horrifying *jinni* had dissolved back to the world of the unseen. But Kalima had stood firm in their path, too courageous and too pious ever to become caught.

Across the clearing from her slumbering mother-in-law, Roshini watched the play of moonlight on the cracks of the mud ceiling, reserving the night hours as a time to let her mind wander far from the village, keeping her dreaming for the day.

Nura's dreams were prophetic, like those of her family always had been. There was her aunt, who had witnessed all the different kinds of punishment that could be meted out after death, hearing the voice of Allah command her to devote her life to bestowing her newfound knowledge on those around her. There was her father, who spoke often of his recurring dream that his favourite daughter, Nura's sister, was in fact somehow still alive. He watched her bursting into his home, her voice a familiar song that pulled him smiling from his work and told him that she was pregnant, and that it was a boy; and each time he saw her he was so delighted that he slaughtered one of the buffalo.

Sara dreamed of living in an apartment block in Kolkata, the kind that she had seen on television or on her rare forays into the city. She would like to live high up, with a window that she could look out of onto the city below, marvelling at its size and freneticism.

Aliya dreamed only of paradise.

Afterword

Only six of the women are still in the village.

Nura has at last fulfilled her wish of escaping the house beside the road, too close to her meddling in-laws and their sharp ears and even sharper tongues. Her husband has built them a *pukka* house behind his auto-repair shop up at the roundabout towards town, where they now also run a tea stall. Business is thriving, but all is not well with one of their sons. Nura's oldest, and most treasured, lived in Kolkata for several years selling Ayurvedic medicines, but now he has returned home, plagued by incessant headaches. His marriage has broken down and he is unable to work or to build the life his parents desperately wanted for him.

Just like the shadowy histories Maryam cultivated when alive, untethered by the details of dates and times, none of her family are sure exactly when she passed away. They believe it was around a year ago, when the rains had gone and the weather had begun to turn sweeter once again, softening to a beloved autumn. A stroke had recently left her totally paralysed on one side of her body, unable to walk, even with the support of her trusted stick. She is buried in the graveyard that lies at the southern edge of the village, where most days the only sounds are the whispers of the wind through the grass.

Maryam died knowing that her granddaughters were married. A match was eventually found for Rubina, far away from the island and the unhappy rumours that had cluttered her path, threatening to entangle her and render marriage an impossibility. She now lives in a town on the mainland, the dirty, congested place where the Lohanis' distant relatives reside, and which Maryam first suggested might be far enough away for her granddaughter's past to go unnoticed. Rubina confides in her younger sister Rani that she would like to run away, and to marry again.

Tabina played a central part at Rani's wedding, taking on the role of protectress, of bestower – the role that, according to custom, a bride's mother is denied. In the photographs from the day she sits just behind her niece, draped in the swirls of a vibrant red and white sari. Her body is wider now, stouter, and her presence is one of powerful middle age. Her chin is lifted, her eyes meet the camera with a look that forbids entreaty or question. It is only in one of the pictures, perhaps when she believed that the lens was trained elsewhere, that you can see she has allowed herself to break into a half-smile.

Rani is still on the island, but in a different village, not far from home. Though she married for love, with the reluctant consent of her parents, her husband is not a good man. Perhaps the sternness of her aunt's countenance at the wedding spoke of deeper misgivings.

There are stories of infidelity, of scandalous, illicit trysts with family members, of alcohol abuse, of beatings so violent that Rani's face has been made unrecognisable. There are no children yet. Her husband beat her so badly with an iron bar, before kicking her down a flight of stairs, that Rani lost her baby at around three months of pregnancy. Whenever her father and her brother tearfully beg her to return home, she tells them she can't, because she cannot imagine life without him, though she also vows, 'I'll not leave him without taking revenge.' She still dreams of becoming a police officer.

For Bashira, life is bittersweet. Her relief at finding husbands for her daughters is mixed with distress at Rani's predicament, just as good fortune finally happens to have crossed her path. A friendship that she struck up with a police officer long ago has, after careful nurturing, begun to bear fruit at last. Her husband now acts for him as a *dalal*, a middle-man, another of the multitude of informal brokers who guard the creaking corridors of corpulent Indian bureaucracy. People fear the police here, and the family has begun at last to earn back some much-craved respect. They have earned enough to build a *pukka* house of bricks, where five years ago only a crumbling *khacca* dwelling stood.

The Lohanis' change in circumstances has done little to improve their relations with the family across the road. Sara understands intimately the way in which bribes are paid to those in power. Yet she knows that the tea shop barely breaks even, and still has her own questions about where their money comes from. Her own house has grown both in size and incongruity, expanding with her frustrated ambitions for a different life elsewhere. The second storey has been completed, a large paved driveway leads from the road to the front door, and a tall, solid wooden gate now securely bars the entrance. It is hard to know if Sara has at last kept the outside at bay or whether she herself is trapped within.

Kalima has been seen at the *thana*, filing a case with the local police. There are disputes with her sons over her pension, and although her eldest son has returned to the village from the Andaman Islands where he was working, she now lives alone. She has banished her three sons from her home – an exasperated mother shoving her fully fledged chicks from the nest, determined that they will not take her money.

As the weather turns cooler, she is once again preparing for her annual trip to Madhya Pradesh in order to present her paperwork for her deceased husband's pension. Aside from a rotten tooth at the back of her blackened mouth, her body is strong. She has a good *jinn* inside her, she says, one that protects her and looks after her. Her greatest disdain is for Narendra Modi, both for his ineptitude and his divisive politics, which have left many in the village destitute as well as terrified. 'Scoundrel,' she snarls. 'He became king of this kingdom, but could do nothing.'

Nusrat has gone. There are rumours about what happened, the kind spoken only in hushed voices when no one else is listening. Kalima says that soon after being cured of her possession, her new daughter-in-law began a relationship with her cousin and eloped with him. A second wife for Kalima's troublesome youngest son quickly followed Nusrat, although the same thing is said to have happened. Asad is now with his third wife, who has borne him a daughter. There are already murmurs that all is not well.

Roshini and her family have left their shack on the opposite side of Kalima's clearing. It seems that the wounds she, Riyaz and her mother-in-law inflicted on one another were too deep to be forgiven, and a couple of years ago the couple and their three children moved to a new house alongside the school playing field. Riyaz worked on a building site in Mumbai for a while, but he is back in the village now, with no job and no income. Their house does not belong to them, but has been built with Kalima's money, and who knows how long they will be able to stay there before repayments are demanded. Roshini is a shadow of herself, her body is suffering and she does not want to talk.

Afterword

As Aliya's children have grown, the burdens they place upon her have grown, too. Her oldest son now works in Rajasthan, leaving behind his wife Munira and two grandchildren, the first born by Caesarean at a cost to Aliya of R37,000. Her third son has run away for a love-marriage, rejecting his mother's hard-fought plans for him to work in one of Kolkata's best hospitals and leaving behind a trail of debts and an unanswered phone. 'The weight of responsibility is more than the weight of work,' Aliya says, but she does not share the troubles of her family with anyone in the village. She has learned the hard way that weakness will appear to some as opportunity.

Despite Aliya's difficulties, there is hope. Amal is happily married, and both of her sons-in-law do all they can to support her, loaning her money and encouraging her in striving for more. Her second-eldest son – the one attacked by the RSS – now works as a tailor, just as his father once did, and will be married in March 2022. She is building a house on the family's last-remaining strip of land near the school, where she dreams one day of having a tea shop. If she can achieve this, Aliya says, then she will be happy.

These are the glimpses I am left with. They are like fleeting shadows, stirrings in the undergrowth seen from the edges of the path, unable to be fully grasped.

It has been five years since I left the island. For the two years after I returned to England (the final two years of my PhD) the constraints of time, teaching, work and family made a journey back there impossible. After I was awarded my doctorate in December 2018, I discovered that I was pregnant the following month. At the start of 2020, emerging from the deadening fog of early motherhood, I began to make plans for my return, but it was not long before word of a deadly virus started to spread. By the end of March travel had become impossible, and in that same month India banned the entry of foreign visitors. As I write, in November 2021, this prohibition is at last in the nascent stages of being lifted.

From afar, the news from India, and from the island, is concerning.

In the past three years the Sundarbans have been devastated by four tropical cyclones. On each occasion, surging tides have overwhelmed the insufficient embankments, flooding the most exposed of the islands with sea water that poisons the soil and makes future farming almost impossible. Lashing rain and monstrous winds have demolished homes, ripped apart settlements and destroyed crops. During Cyclone Amphan, Kalima lost her beloved coconut palm to a lightning strike and her mango trees were torn down, one of them landing on the roof of the kitchen, flattening the earthen walls and the bamboo roof. She knows she is lucky; other islands have been left uninhabitable, thousands of people have been displaced – many of them permanently – and hundreds have died.

A changing climate is not a looming prospect there, but rather a terrifying daily reality. The land, the rivers, the sea and the sky, those that Kalima loves and knows intimately like family, are changing beyond recognition. In floods this autumn Aliya lost her entire vegetable garden to unceasing rains and stagnant water. The rise in temperature, and of sea levels, means that soon the lowest-lying of the islands will face the threat of permanent submersion. The embankments designed to protect them need urgent repairs and reinforcement, a promised state provision that has not yet materialised. Deforestation – an act of desperation from those for whom there is no other means of income – is slowly stripping away the last natural barriers between people and the cruelty of an unfettered sea.

Afterword

For India's Muslims the past five years have been some of the most frightening and unsettling in memory. From measures intended to strip them of existing Indian nationality, to legislation denying adherents to Islam the same right to Indian citizenship as is enjoyed by other religious minorities, the assault on Muslim Indian identity has cut to the root. Attacks on Muslims continue to go unpunished, and in the Delhi riots of February 2020 there were reports that police and law-makers were complicit in the violence.

Many states have banned marriage as a reason for religious conversion, effectively outlawing inter-faith marriages like Sara's, in what they claim is a response to the threat of 'love-jihad'. Across social media and the national press, Muslim communities have been blamed for intentionally spreading Covid-19, with 'corona jihad' trending on Twitter. Last year an advertisement for jewellery depicting a Muslim man and a Hindu woman in a relationship had to be pulled, after the shops were attacked, and just weeks ago an advert for festive clothing was removed almost instantly for daring to feature a phrase in Urdu. As they wait for what happens next, the atmosphere for Muslims is one of febrile expectation.

In the West Bengal elections of 2021 the women's beloved *Didi* and her Trinamool Congress party held off the BJP advances, strengthening her overall majority in the face of committed campaigning from both the Prime Minister, Narendra Modi, and the Home Minister, Amit Shah, across the state. Muslims continue to remain a significant voting block for her, but it was impassioned women like Tabina who were credited with the overwhelming grass-roots support that ensured her party remained dominant.

For women in India, like so many around the world, the pandemic has been particularly devastating. More often engaged in precarious labour than men, Indian women have been more likely to lose their jobs and take on even greater burdens of unpaid work. They are also commonly the most vulnerable on the front lines of the virus, looking after family in a personal capacity as well as representing more than 80 per cent of nurses and carers. Vaccine rates for women lag more than 6 per cent behind those for men. During strictly enforced lockdowns there were extensive reports of women suffering from restricted access to sanitary products, unwanted pregnancy due to a lack of contraception, and a sharp increase in domestic violence. For girls, the pressure on household finances, disruption to public funding schemes and additional domestic and caring responsibilities have meant that many are now being denied an education.

Although these realities are often heard about in the abstract, they are seeds first nurtured in the lives of ordinary people, like the nine women of the village. I think of the mothers and their daughters, and of their daughters to come, sowing the dreams they shared with me in such stony, hostile ground, tending them when the threat of violence or displacement is never far away. I wonder whether their dreams are the same today, whether they have changed and whether they are any closer to being realised.

My own dream is to be able to return to the village one day soon. When I was still living in India, though not on the island, I would sometimes receive calls from unknown numbers. When I answered, it would not be long before I recognised a familiar voice saying, '*Kaemon acho!*' We would talk a little while, across the fizz of static and the barks of nearby traffic, before the inevitable question: '*Didi, meye . . . kokhon abar asbe?* Sister, daughter . . . when will you come again?'

I hope that one day soon I can answer them.

Acknowledgements

To the nine extraordinary women whose stories shine from these pages, I owe an everlasting debt of gratitude. Not a day passes where I do not think of you, and I cannot wait to return one day soon, as promised, and to show you this book.

Maryam, I miss your smile; Bashira and Tabina, the way you both terrified me and made me laugh whenever we spoke. Rani, *amar choto bon*, I wonder about the woman you have become. Sara, my friend, I miss those easy chats on the sofa. Nura, the storyteller, I long to hear another of your tales. Roshini, I miss the sparkle in your eyes when your children rush past. Kalima, my auntie, I miss your bossy insistence to "*khao meye, khao!*", always making me feel as if I were home. Aliya, I miss your inquiries about the world beyond the village, those that always began "I have a question . . ."

In addition to you individually, thank you to your families, neighbours and everyone in the village who both do and do not appear in these pages, who nonetheless welcomed me into their lives and told me their stories.

To my research assistant KB - without you, fieldwork would have been impossible. Thank you for your calm brilliance, your rickety motorbike, and for being my guide and my companion on this bumpy though amazing journey. To my self-appointed protector Suraj-da, I miss our conversations and our laughter, though definitely not your driving.

I want to thank others in India: Sukla and Syamal Mitra and Soma Mukherjee for your hospitality, direction and your endless kindness. My Bangla teachers and friends, Sahana Bajpaie, Arka Bose, Mithun Dey, Abra-da and the teachers at AIIS in Kolkata – thank you for opening the door to the most beautiful language. Kolpona, Bornali di, Buku and Tuku - thank you for all of your care.

In London, thank you to my incredible supervisors Mukulika Banerjee and Laura Bear at the LSE, who both supported and inspired me in equal measure. Thank you also Mukulika for encouraging me to be brave enough to write beyond academia. In addition, thanks to Lucia Michelutti, Kelly Fagan Robinson, Michael Scott, Nick Long, Deborah James, Magnus Marsden, Annu Jalais, Meghnaa Mehta and Nikita Simpson for all of your help at various points on my anthropological journey.

This book would not have come into being without three amazing women. Thank you to Lyndall Roper, chair of the Bayly Prize judges, and the first person with nothing in the game who strongly encouraged me to do this. To my agent Catherine Clarke, who understood and believed in this project from the very start, thank you for all of your hard work and serene wisdom – I am so lucky to be represented by you. Finally, to my editor at Chatto, Poppy Hampson – it has been a joy to work with you, thank you for being the perfect balance of receptive and instructive – you have made me a better writer.

Acknowledgements

In addition, thank you to Arzu Tahsin and Mandy Greenfield for your edits at different points on this manuscript – it is a more enjoyable read because of your insights. Thank you also to Rhiannon Roy and the whole team at Chatto who have worked to bring this book to life, and to proof reader Ilona Jasiewicz. In addition, thank you to Arati Kumar-Rao for the use of the beautiful photograph on this cover of a woman in the Sundarbans. Unable to use my own images due to privacy concerns, I could not have been more fortunate to have yours.

To all of my wonderful friends who have supported and encouraged me throughout this journey – thank you. In particular, to my earliest readers and best friends Catherine and Hattie – your insights and the loving way in which you delivered them mean more to me than you'll ever know. To Shiva, my writing companion for so many of the days, thank you for your sonorous purrs.

Thank you to my incredible family. My brother Toby, the most amazing poet, thank you for always giving me the courage to tread my own path. To my sister George, thank you for all of your love, laughter and support – you are the best sister I could ask for. To my father Jon, who has read this book in so many different iterations, thank you for your pedantry, resistance to anthropological jargon and the generosity with which you have given your time – a future career as an editor awaits you. To my mother Julia, the best and kindest person I know – thank you for your boundless love, and for giving me both roots and wings.

Lastly, thank you to my wonderful husband Will. You have never doubted me, even when I have continuously doubted myself, and for that I will be forever grateful. Thank you for the love, for making the space in which I could write, and for sharing with me the most important person in our worlds – Jude, you are the light.

Glossary

Abaya – A loose overgarment, similar to a cloak, that covers the entire body

Aloo – potato

Asanti – lack of peace

Azaan – Islamic call to prayer

Begun – aubergine

Bhuja – an Indian snack mix

Bindi – okra

Bonti – a curved vertical blade used by many Bengalis for food preparation

Boro – big

Burqa – an enveloping garment that totally covers the face and body

Cha – tea

Chador – a large piece of cloth that is wrapped around the body and head, leaving the face exposed

Chana – chickpea

Chele – boy

Chi – a colloquial expression used in response to something inappropriate but amusing

Daal – lentils

Dhoti – a type of sarong worn by men

Didi – sister

Dupatta – a shawl

Durga pujo – a Hindu festival celebrating the goddess Durga, very important in West Bengal

Ghat – steps leading to water

Ghatak – a matchmaker

Gunbidda – a healing practice typically associated with a *gunnin*

Gunnin – a kind of Muslim healer frequented by those of all faiths

Hajj – the annual pilgrimage to Mecca undertaken by Muslims

Hijab – a headscarf that covers the head, leaving the face exposed

Holud – turmeric

Jahannam – hell

Jamaati – the loose name for a follower of an Islamic Jamaat, in this case the Tablighi Jamaat

Jannah – heaven

Jinn (plural: *jinni*) – a supernatural being with strong links to Islam

Jonmostan – birthplace

Kacca – a combination of natural materials used to build houses, including earth, straw and cow dung

Kaalboishaakhi – violent thunderstorms that occur from April to June in North Western India

Kheer – a sweet milk-based pudding

Kurta – a long and loose-flowing top

Lonka – chilli

Ma – mother

Masjid – mosque

Maulana – one learned in Islam

Mela – a gathering or fair

Meye – girl

Mishti – sweets

Mishti doi – sweet yoghurt

Mishti jol – a sweetened-water drink

Muezzin – the person who performs the call to prayer from a mosque

Muri – puffed rice

Namaz – prayer

Nani – granny or grandmother

Niqab – a head garment that conceals the face

Nabi – the Prophet

Nadi – river

Onchol – a regional division similar to a district

Paan – a betel nut preparation to be chewed

Panchayat – a village council

Pandal – a temporary marquee

Pani – water

Pani puri – a street food of a crisp fried wheat-bread filled with tamarind water

Panta bhat – rice steeped in water overnight

Pujo – an occasion of worship

Pukka – literally meaning 'ripe' or 'solid' is has become shorthand for permanent, brick-built structures

Purdah – the practice of screening women from men

Ramzan – the month long period of fasting, prayer and reflection also known as Ramadan

Rosogolla – a cottage-cheese sweet soaked in sugar syrup

Roti – a round flatbread eaten across India

Salwar kameez – a loose pair of trousers and flowing top worn by women

Shaak – a green leafy vegetable

Shimai – a dessert of vermicelli noodles, sugar and milk

Sindoor – red powder worn in the central parting of a woman's hair after marriage

Sobji – vegetables

Sondesh – a dairy and sugar-based sweet

Tabiz – a protection amulet

Tablighi Jamaat – an Islamic movement that privileges a return to original forms of the faith

Ummah – the pan-global Muslim community